Ethnic Passages

Literary Immigrants in
Twentieth-Century America

Thomas J. Ferraro

The University of Chicago Press
* Chicago and London *

Thomas J. Ferraro is Andrew W. Mellon Assistant Professor of English
at Duke University.

813
FER
C. 2

The University of Chicago Press, Chicago 60637
The University of Chicago Press, Ltd., London
© 1993 by The University of Chicago
All rights reserved. Published 1993
Printed in the United States of America

02 01 00 99 98 97 96 95 94 93   1 2 3 4 5

ISBN: 0-226-24441-5 (cloth)
       0-226-24442-3 (paper)

Library of Congress Cataloging-in-Publication Data

Ferraro, Thomas J.
    Ethnic passages : literary immigrants in twentieth-century America /
Thomas J. Ferraro.
        p.   cm.
    Includes bibliographical references and index.
    1. American fiction—Minority authors—History and criticism.
    2. Immigrants' writings, American—History and criticism.
    3. American fiction—20th century—History and criticism.
    4. Emigration and immigration in literature.   5. Ethnic groups in
literature.   6. Immigrants in literature.   7. Minorities in
literature.   I. Title.
PS374.I48F47   1993
813'.50992069—dc20   92-24719
                                                             CIP

∞ The paper used in this publication meets the minimum requirements of the
American National Standard for Information Sciences—Permanence of Paper
for Printed Library Materials, ANSI Z39.48-1984.

Ethnic Passages

DISCARDED

*For my parents
and for Beth*

Chi lascia la via vecchia per la nuova,
sa quel che perde e non sa quel che trova.
(Whoever forsakes the old way for the new,
knows what he is losing but not what
he will find.)

Sicilian proverb

Contents

Acknowledgments

I was first drawn to the study of American literature by my teachers at Amherst College, including Jack Cameron, Robert Gross, Leo Marx, Dale Peterson, and the late Elizabeth Bruss; and, more particularly, to the study of literary ethnicity by Mary Gordon, Allen Guttmann, Julius Lester, Barry O'Connell, and David Wills. Laura Wexler knows better than anyone else how I proceeded from Emerson to Yezierska.

This book received its earliest encouragement and critique from my dissertation committee at Yale University—Jean-Christophe Agnew, Richard Brodhead, and R. W. B. Lewis—and its de facto fourth member, Alan Trachtenberg, each of whom ventured with me into the emergent field of ethnic literary studies. Only slightly less formal, although no less extensive, commentaries were provided by Tara Fitzpatrick, Raoul Ibarguen, and Reva Siegel, comrades-in-arms in New Haven, as well as by Jay Blair, Ioana Bertrand, Evelyne Ender, and André Kaenel, *confrères* in Geneva, Switzerland.

Over the years, I have benefited from generous (which is not to say uncritical) exchanges with specialists and practitioners, including Pirio Ahokas, Elizabeth Alexander, Bill Boelhower, Jules Chametzky, Mary Dearborn, Morris Dickstein, Fred Gardaphé, Marcus Klein, Mark Krupnick, Vera Kutzinski, Ishmael Reed, Richard Rodriguez, Joseph Skerrett, Anthony Tamburri, Robert Viscusi, Donald Weber, and Rafia Zafar. Werner Sollors, in particular, made business an education and a pleasure.

Current colleagues, too many to name, gave me the final push. Michael Moses, John Twyning, and Sarah Beckwith shared the drama of first-book production; Cathy Davidson,

Ted Davidson, and Stanley Fish exchanged diverse enthusiasms for diverse North Americas at crucial moments; and
Barbara Herrnstein Smith took the lead in reenacting the
fabled camaraderie of our ancestors. Frank Lentricchia, my
priest for the modern lyric, and Melissa Lentricchia, an aficionada of the multivocal, went beyond the call of friendship
by reading the entire manuscript and holding me to my own
vision. At the end, both insisted that I give this book the title I
had envisioned since graduate school; Frank hit upon the sub-
title that constituted the whole.

Alan Thomas, my editor, took up this manuscript with conviction. He found readers whose responses mattered, urged
me to write a less equivocal and more anticipatory introduction, and gave me those provocations a first author needs to
receive. Ellen Feldman, as copy editor, took care with every
sentence, so that I, tutored and reenergized, once again
did, too.

Out of self-defense, responding to multiple versions of every piece of this manuscript, Beth Eastlick has become a superb
editor. Her radical empathy is everywhere. During the last two
years, Antonio Luigi, our "first-born son," has renewed my
faith.

Adelina Granito Ferraro, my grandmother, provided my
earliest visions of teaching. My four sisters, all younger than
myself, suffered my earliest attempts. I wish finally to thank
my father, who worried about this book from its conception to
delivery, and my mother, who did not.

Chapter 1, "Blood in the Marketplace: The Business of Family in *The Godfather* Narratives," was originally published in *The
Invention of Ethnicity*, ed. Werner Sollors (New York: Oxford
University Press, 1989), 176–207, and is reprinted here with
minor revisions; used by permission. An earlier version of
chapter 2 appeared as " 'Working Ourselves Up' in America,"
South Atlantic Quarterly 89 (Summer 1990): 547–81.

Introduction

I conceived this book as a genre study, an exploration of the ways in which narratives depicting immigration and upward mobility have been undervalued and misread. Ethnic novels have long been considered the poor stepsisters of a benighted realist family: stereotypical in plot and characterization, assimilationist in drive, contestable even as social evidence, and of interest only to group members and historians. But the best of such narratives are powerful acts of the imagination in their own terms as well as exemplifying crucial issues in twentieth-century literary history. Written with an autobiographical backward glance, ethnic novels adopt the paradigm of cultural rebirth—"from alien to American"—then put it to the test of experience. Each draws upon established literary modes—from Howellsian realism to Joycean modernism, from the populist thriller to feminist post-structuralism—to investigate individual and group transformation, and to achieve for that investigation a national readership. These narratives carry us beyond the boundaries of what we traditionally have understood as ethnicity and what we traditionally have appreciated as literature.

The fictional depiction of immigration and mobility in this century has epitomized the unhappy and, in some cases, unintended effects of generic classification. The early twentieth-century term "immigrant novel" gave way after World War II to "ethnic literature," a term now being replaced by "multicultural representation." Academics especially have used the classificatory chain as a means of registering the presence of certain voices while at the same time limiting their resonance and neutralizing their force. Although each replacement term has been intended to bolster the reputation of ethnic writing, the chain of substitution has preserved the original classificatory logic and, with that logic, an understanding of ethnic writing that misconstrues the relation between literariness and ethnicity in fundamental ways. When we rely on these terms, we steer ourselves into a conceptual cul-de-sac.

The first detailed histories of immigrant writing, focused on the representation of Jews in America, appeared in the late 1950s and early 1960s. None other than Leslie Fiedler (in many ways the progenitor of immigrant literary studies) dismissed early Jewish-American fiction in these classic terms: "It is like all the sub-literature which we customarily call 'regional,' writing intended to represent the values and interests of a group which feels itself penalized, even threatened, by the disregard of the larger community."[1] Irving Howe reached the same verdict: "Most of this writing turned out to be of small literary value, the very urgencies behind its composition hardening into narrowness of scene, parochial return, and mere defense. . . . Let us call this body of writing a regional literature."[2] The dismissal of ethnic writing as a version of regionalism dates back to the first decades of this century, was taken for granted during the mid-century heyday of canonical consensus, and is still with us (if behind closed doors) today. When identified as regional, writing by and about immigrants is labeled parochial, transient, and delusive simultaneously: self-congratulation and public relations masquerading, just barely, as literary art.

In "The Hyphenated Writer and American Letters," a 1964 essay exploring multiculturalism in U.S. literature, Daniel Aaron proposed a model of ethnic literary history that illustrates the cultural, aesthetic, and political presuppositions behind the regionalist label. He envisioned in geographic terms the crucial moment of transition when the minority writer "breaks out of his self-determined or enforced segregation into a larger United States, and from there into a universal republic." Aaron analyzed what he called "dehyphenation":

> As a writer he has transcended a mere parochial allegiance and can now operate freely in the republic of the spirit. Without renouncing his ethnic or racial past, he has translated his own and his minority's

> personal experience . . . into the province of the imagination. . . . He no longer peers out from behind the minority barricade. In fact, he is no longer the *conscious* "representative" of a national or racial group—but a writer, a disaffiliate, whose race or religion or ethnic origin are merely so many colors for his writer's palette.[3]

The aspirant to literary election did not necessarily have to forego "ethnic or racial locale," but he had to transcend intrinsically ethnic literary agendas and to universalize his subject matter.

Aaron's account of dehyphenation, an elegant distillation of canonical-era assumptions, forced writers into a Faustian bargain: entrance into the republic of letters in exchange for ethnic consciousness. At the least, Aaron underestimated the degree of cultural self-transformation even the most group-identified writers had undergone; he underestimated as well the degree of cultural persistence (a matter not only of literary material but of informing perspective and intuition) among writers who claim or who have been credited with achieving "disinterestedness."

More troubling was the antithesis between parochial concerns and aesthetic accomplishment: the implication that "ethnic literature" is a contradiction in terms in which, in effect, the adjective cancels out the noun. Do not certain works classify as "ethnic literature" for reasons other than convenient shelving and effective marketing? In such texts, what is most ethnically specific and what is most aesthetically compelling will be found at the same narrative sites, working not in separate registers but in allied, mutually interrogative, and cross-fertilizing ways. Such writing challenges the critic to determine how sociological inquiry and literary inventiveness serve one another; where local understandings face off against national constructions of individuality, family, and community; and which strategies of minority-culture self-representation and majority-culture literary forms undergo reciprocal transformations.

The early 1970s were marked by an intensification of group consciousness in the United States, what sociologists misleadingly termed "the new ethnicity," modeled on the Civil Rights and Black Power movements of the preceding decade. Scholars industriously began reclaiming ethnic literary histories group by group (most often, their own). Founded in 1973, the Society for the Multi-Ethnic Literature of the United States (with its journal *MELUS*) created a forum for comparing the literary traditions of blacks, Indians, Hispanics, immigrant groups from all parts of Europe, and the most recent "new immigrants" (peoples of color from the Carribean, the Middle East, the Indian subcontinent, and the Far East). In subsequent years, MELUS critics made indispensable contributions to bibliography, biography, and republishing. For critical analysis, they relied, by and large, on sociological positivism, stressing the inherent value of each group and its struggle against discrimination.[4]

The best of the immigrant literary studies produced through the early 1980s hypothesized discrete traditions only to emphasize the effort within these traditions to scale the barricades of cultural hermeticism: among them were Dorothy Burton Skårdal's *The Divided Heart*, Allen Guttmann's *The Jewish Writer in America*, Elaine H. Kim's *Asian American Literature*, and the especially insightful *Our Decentralized Literature* by Jules Chametzky.[5] Like the writers they studied, the more provocative critics took the pre-American cultural forces as something other than wholly beneficent and the postmigratory agendas emerging among ethnic offspring as something other than wholly laudable.[6]

Yet even the best of the critics who worked in the shadow of the new ethnicity were reluctant to attend to or even admit to the literariness of the texts they studied. On one hand, they characteristically failed to address the conventionality of ethnic writing, including its dependence on stereotypes (instructive or otherwise); on the other hand, they neglected to pursue the departures ethnic writing made from conventionality, its subversion of convention and its determined creativity. Titles stressing separate hyphenated spheres (*Irish-American Fiction*, *The Italian-American Novel*, *Jewish-American Literature*, *Asian American Literature*, and *Chicano Authors*) suggested that ethnic authors operated in artistic ghettos apart from mainstream letters, both uninfluenced and without influence.[7] Subtitles ("Assimilation and the Crisis of Identity," "A Document of the Interaction of Two Cultures," "Immigrant Experience through Literary Sources") emphasized bicultural citizenship, but often at the cost of dismissing the aesthetic and the creative altogether.

What I found most disturbing about these studies was the recurrent failure of imaginative engagement on the part of individual critics: reluctance to make aesthetic judgments, lack of interest in the deeper ambitions and larger receptions of individual texts, disregard for the still primary task of interpretive (even if polemical) close reading. There was never any doubt that the scholars of the new ethnicity cared about immigrant social history, but still in question was whether the texts warranted a peculiarly literary passion.

In the second half of the 1980s, a series of books, published to varying degrees under the sponsorship of Werner Sollors, appeared that challenged the separatist and "mirror into social history" approaches of the preceding decade: Sollors's own *Beyond Ethnicity* (1986), Mary V. Dearborn's *Pocahontas's Daughters* (1986), William Boelhower's *Through a Glass Darkly* (1987), and an anthology of critical and creative pieces, *The Invention of Ethnicity* (1989), edited and introduced by Sollors.[8] The three book-length studies and most of the essays in *The Invention of Ethnicity* are allied in fundamental ways, although they diverge on the particulars.[9] Each critic pools together the literatures of old-stock Anglo-Saxon families, of the immigrant descended, and of nonimmigrant minorities as representations of "America." Each examines the significant debates within these literatures: national versus group identification, self-determination versus ancestry, Anglo-Saxonism versus its alternatives. Where previous scholars had assumed only literary newness or difference, these critics unveil common, often centuries-old rhetorical and narrative structures, including Puritan typologies, the Pocahontas myth, and Eurocentric mappings. Taken together, the effect of these investigations is to forestall questions of what distinguishes literatures and texts in favor of what facilitates or frustrates their interaction.

Beyond Ethnicity has proved to be the most illuminating and controversial of these works. For me, Sollors's crucial contribution is his insistence that English-language literature written by racial and ethnic minorities is more culturally central than the separatist emphases of the group-by-group approach make it appear. Although the literature has suffered academic ghettoization for most of this century, and although much of this literature is undervalued outside the academy as well as within it, it has been produced for, issued by, and received into the national literary marketplace.[10] By questioning the putative marginality of ethnic literary production, Sollors raises the exhilarating possibility that works of ethnic literature are more than exercises in group documentation and self-analysis. I resist Sollors's call for moving "beyond ethnicity," but I remain convinced that ethnic literature has been and is compelling beyond individual ethnic spheres.

I depart from *Beyond Ethnicity*, first and foremost, by concentrating on the literature of immigration and mobility. This division of labor is justified on practical grounds alone. While African-American literature has a long and voluminous history of advocacy, and while Chicano and Native American studies are at the center of the current academic calendar, immigrant writing, especially European-descended immigrant writing, despite constituting a handsome tradition now a century old, has been little studied. Before a more encompassing history of "dissensus" in American literary history can be written, we must distinguish discrete traditions. The immigrant mobility genre is distinct not only from the traditional canon but also from African-American literature (a tradition of special self-reflexivity), Chicano literature (marked in distinctive ways by the bilingualism and borderlands condition of its makers), and Native American expressive forms (until recently, a "literature" only in non-European terms). At certain boundaries these various ethnic traditions share territory, but the distinctions persisting among them are more than a matter of scholarly turf.[11] The relative inattention to immigrant writing is no mere happenstance, nor is its recovery simply a matter of applying proved techniques of analysis to neglected material.

Critics recently have familiarized us with the risk of discounting white supremacy that arises in *Beyond Ethnicity*.[12] Less well noted is the related danger of failing to credit fully the sine qua non of immigrant writing: that is, immigration and its consequences. In *Beyond Ethnicity*, immigrant writing, like all "ethnic" writing, is understood as a ritual enacting Americanization. Rather than being assessed as efforts to come to terms with the dilemmas of specific groups and of immigration in general (cultures in conflict, cultures in transition), the icons and stories in the repertoire of immigrant writing (the melting pot, exogamous romance, the battle of the generations) are revealed as reproducing national archetypes. Rather than being read as responses to the circumstances of disparate immigrant groups, these archetypes are shown to have originated in the literatures of the Anglo-Protestant forefathers (who fled religious persecution and colonized the continent); they also are shown to structure the literatures of U.S. racial minorities (who were forcibly removed, incorporated, enslaved, and interned). The "problem" lies, then, not so much in what Sollors does as in what he leaves for others to do.[13]

The scholarship of Sollors, Boelhower, and Dearborn has moved us beyond romanticizing literary ethnicity, especially the literary ethnicity of immigrant descendants, by alerting us to the generic Americanness of ethnic self-representation. Paradoxically, one key to recovering immigrant narratives is to push the dialectic of critical investigation they have developed to the next stage. In this book, I use what Sollors and his allies have demonstrated to make discoveries antithetical to theirs.

My procedure has two stages. I first contextualize immigrant writers within social history: How do foreign nationals become American ethnics? How, in fact, do immigrants become writers? I then examine the ends to which they use variations on the up-from-the-ghetto theme: In what ways have recent arrivals deployed the established literary forms of the established culture? What have immigrant writers achieved for themselves and their groups by *variously* participating in national literary and rhetorical traditions? These questions, which articulate the theoretical as well as the methodological underpinnings of this book, clear the way for rereading and hence reevaluating the immigrant mobility genre. They direct me to affirm that these writers were immersed in "mainstream literary discourse" without prejudging such immersion as tantamount to assimilation; they also encourage me to use techniques of close reading without fearing that I shall be colonizing the text against its writer's will or best interest. I see the conventions of the immigrant mobility genre as the means through which writers investigate issues of unrivaled cultural specificity and achieve texts of unprecedented (I mean this literally) imaginative power.

Recently, socialist intellectuals have dismissed the claim of ethnic distinctiveness as a mask for class antagonisms, a classic instance of false consciousness. Irving Howe, Gunnar Myrdal, and Stephen Steinberg accuse the descendants of American immigrants, the middle classes especially, of exercising, in Herbert Gans's frequently quoted words, a merely "symbolic" or "cost-free" ethnicity.[14] I disagree. Ethnicity in the United States is more than a matter of ritual, rhetoric, or dialogue. It is a fact, vexing in the extreme, in which literature is especially implicated and to which it gives special access. Otherness *does* persist, whether one likes it or not—powerfully so among the offspring of immigrants who have attempted Emersonian self-transformation only to experience both the skepticism of the longer-entitled and the return of the culturally repressed.

I have titled this book *Ethnic Passages* because the cultural self-transformation of the literary immigrant is the raison d'être of the genre of immigrant mobility narratives on which I focus. In the singular, "ethnic passage" refers to the movement out of immigrant confines into the larger world of letters. In that sense, "ethnic passage" is what each immigrant or immigrant offspring undergoes in order to become a writer, what each writer then investigates in his or her work, and what each work in turn brings to fruition for its writer. As for the narratives themselves, they may be called, evoking the common term for "a segment of prose," "ethnic passages."

I investigate five immigrant writers, "de-ethnicized intellectuals" (the phrase belongs to Sollors) who turned to narrative in order to reconstruct the cultural changes they or their group had undergone.[15] In making their way into mainstream institutions, these writers schooled themselves in, and gave allegiance to, central forms of twentieth-century American literary creativity at the same time as they learned the risks of generic forms and presuppositions firsthand. Each chose the paradigm of the up-from-the-ghetto narrative, presumably hackneyed and unquestionably mainstream. Each elaborated his or her particular story by appropriating and experimenting with techniques of representation in central circulation: the melodramatic thriller, the realism of William Dean Howells and Theodore Dreiser, Joycean modernism and its variants, or feminist postmodernism. And each inscribed at the very center of his or her narrative one or another prejudicial image— criminal as well as criminally familial Sicilians, neurotic and Oedipally fixated Russian Jews (two sets of these), gregarious barflies of German and Irish extraction, and the inscrutably exotic Chinese—not only recontextualizing these stereotypes but in each instance working to give them mythic stature. Why?

Early on I made a simple deduction: it takes a profound degree of cultural self-distancing for a member of an impoverished immigrant enclave to be in the position to write in English. Most so-called immigrant writers were in fact the children of the migratory proletariat, or raised as if they were: in poor or minimally secure homes where a language other than English, or at least not "proper" English, was spoken; where Old World folkways and transplanted communities commanded allegiance; where there were no books except, perhaps, for sacred texts, and then not everyone at home was able or permitted to read them; and where parental ambitions for their offspring stretched no further than white-collar security. Yet children born into these circumstances did come to write literature in America. This ethnic passage is what unites immigrant writers of all backgrounds.

When individuals from genuinely illiterate or impoverished backgrounds become writers, they pass through or somehow short-circuit far more common and reliable forms of mobility, freely choosing the special kind of marginalization involved in becoming a writer. Typically, they are alienated from family and the friends of their youth; they marry or cohabitate outside the ethnic group; they live not in downtown ghettos but uptown, in ethnic suburbia, or, most likely, in polyethnic bohemias catering to artists and intellectuals. It is, in short, a long walk from Hester Street to Washington Square, and one often goes by way of Riverside Drive.

As writers-in-the-making, they become familiar with middlebrow letters, often with the avant-garde, and, increasingly over this century, with academe. They cannot but take special note of the conventions of representing ethnicity within canonical and popular art, and they frequently undertake the study of "our classic ethnic literature" before deciding whether and what to write. Determined to set the national record straight, they fear that to go public "with what they know" will bring dishonor upon those they have left behind. Coming from the outside, they fear that they do not have what it takes to be a "real writer."

An aspiring writer from an immigrant background feels damned on the one side for having become too American and damned on the other side for not being able to become American enough. "You have deserted us and our old important ways," accuse the writer's kinfolk, who find the desire to become a novelist incredible, literally beyond belief. "Who are you to be writing about us?" demands the community of American letters, protective of its proud heritage back to England and hence suspicious of the legacy and blood knowledge of the newcomer. In all cases, and those of the women paradigmatically, guilt and regret for cultural loss accompany the writer's passage out of the ghetto while defensiveness and an anxiety of insufficient influence accompany the passage into the literary marketplace. The turn to ethnic narrative is an attempt on the part of the writer to negotiate the terms in which the greater freedoms of the United States are to be accepted: on one hand, to dispel the charge by the clan of having undergone an essential and traitorous assimilation; on the other, to dispel the charge by the culture at large of possessing predispositions of mind and heart inappropriate if not antithetical to the developing concerns of a national literature and culture.

In writing of themselves or their people, immigrant offspring incorporate the assimilation paradigm as a framing device in order to measure it against experience. Restaging the struggle for entitlement and self-determination in America provokes them to recognize varieties of cultural persistence they previously had not suspected. Calling into doubt ancestral claims of unbroken continuity, they discover in their alien pasts varieties of cultural transformation already tending toward modernity. Not only in what they see but in how they see it, these ethnic writers portray forms of group determination that turn out to have American precedents and forms of self-determination that originate in one or another premigratory past. In the final analysis, they do more than report cultural continuity; they either make this continuity possible or struggle to break it, through the symbolic act of narrative itself.

In this book, I consider five narratives born of the ethnic writer's double curse: Mario Puzo's *Godfather*, Anzia Yezierska's *Bread Givers*, Henry Roth's *Call It Sleep*, Henry Miller's "Tailor Shop," and Maxine Hong Kingston's *Woman Warrior*. In making these selections, I have had my eye on both individual performances and the constellation they form.

The first three chapters focus on writers of the great migration, descendants of Catholics and Jews from Southern and Eastern Europe. Puzo, Yezierska, and Roth represent a coterie of writers (which also would include writers of Irish Catholic and Scandinavian Protestant extraction) whose reputations continue to suffer, despite if not because of recent efforts to "historicize" and "theorize" ethnic writing. In the final two chapters, I expand my circle of consideration, first with Miller, whose Lutheran German background is closer to the American core culture, and then with Kingston, whose Confucian Chinese background is more distant. I have chosen Miller in part to remind us that in decades past ethnic alienation persisted even among writers of Anglo-Saxon ancestry who identified strongly not only with the literature but also with the philosophy of high modernism. At the opposite end of the spectrum, Kingston illustrates the passion with which the new immigrants of color (especially women, especially those of Asian descent) have revived the genre of ethnic passage.[16]

I begin with *The Godfather* because the novel, in its combination of national mythmaking and Italian-American authorship, is to my mind *the* acid test for prejudice in both academic and belletristic evaluation. Yezierska's *Bread Givers* follows *The Godfather* because of an allied problem of evaluation: a test case for immigrant realism, Yezierska's novel is thought to epitomize the aesthetic costs of ethnic self-consciousness and the courtship of a popular audience, yet it focuses, like *The Godfather* though in less explicit terms and from the contrasting perspectives of Russian Judaism and women's experience, on the interdependence of ethnicity and economic mobility.

I place Roth's *Call It Sleep* in the shadow of *Bread Givers*, introducing Abraham Cahan's *Yekl* as well, in order to show how modernism and realism function as complementary sides of a single ethnic literary tradition, alternative strategies (sociological versus psychological, roughly speaking) for examining Russian Jewish immigration. I thereby demonstrate one potential of currently unfashionable tradition-by-tradition studies, that is, contrasting the uses of competing mainstream modes of representation by writers of the same background.

The chapter on Miller's experimental narrative, "The Tailor Shop," forms an alternative diptych (with Roth) focused on the question of the relationship among high modernist craft, ethnic memory, and aesthetic heritage, in which I challenge the still-prevailing identification of literary modernism with ethnic transcendence. I follow my discussion of Miller with a reading of *The Woman Warrior*, because Kingston addresses head-on her own version of the fear of insufficient ancestral influence that at one time paralyzed Miller. I conclude with Kingston because her feminist postmodernism places the novel squarely and powerfully amidst developing national traditions, both of the immigrant novel and of feminist inquiry into filial inheritance, thereby challenging the overvaluation of difference in the reception of contemporary American writers of color.

Each of these texts resists in crucial ways established techniques of critical exegesis. At the beginning of each chapter, I explain how persisting assumptions about ethnicity and literary form fail to account for fundamental trajectories within the given text. In what follows, I work up a revisionist account of each text in order to explore what most concerned these writers, namely the battles over alternative visions of socioeconomic mobility and cultural accommodation through which immigrant parents have remade America and through which their ethnic offspring, as writers, have contested these remakings. What emerges are varying versions, at times allied and at times competing, of the defining American conflict between ethnic heritages and the opportunities of the greater United States.

Of the five narratives, *The Godfather* (1969) has attracted the most formidable scholarly attention, not because scholars respect the text but because it is the best-selling novel in history. Theoreticians of mass culture regard *The Godfather* saga as a critique of mainstream (increasingly multinational) capitalism, embedded in the way the novel romanticizes Southern Italian familialism and disguised by the way it moralizes capitalist violence. The myth of individual success has proved so strong that none of Puzo's critics, neo-Marxist or not, questions whether capitalist aggrandizement and familial solidarity might not be working for rather than against one another.

In "Blood in the Marketplace," I argue that Puzo uses the Southern Italian Mafia to unveil and scrutinize the interpenetration of family and business. *The Godfather* not only explodes the myth of the self-made man but establishes a populist forum for advanced social inquiry. Since its publication, novelists and filmmakers have produced dozens upon dozens of narratives treating underground enterprises as ethnic endeavors and dozens more depicting less illegitimate forms of communal industry: not only among Southern Italians but reaching back to the Irish and the Jews who preceded them and forward to the Asians, Hispanics, and African Americans now replacing them. In the second half of "Blood in the Marketplace," I analyze two of the strongest entries in this crowded genre: Francis Ford Coppola's film, *The Godfather Part II* (1974), which punishes Don Michael for sacrificing family to business, and Richard Condon's novel, *Prizzi's Honor* (1982), which restores Puzo's vision of interconnectedness while making his anti-romanticism more explicit.

When critics characterize *Bread Givers* (1925) as ghetto reportage, they not only discount the middle-class settings of the novel, which are reminiscent of canonical realism, but they also fail to address what happens at these sites, each of which taxes the reader's credibility. Accounting for the narrative drive of *Bread Givers* means asking what kind of Russian Jewish father plays local hero in a neighborhood version of the Scopes monkey trial and turns professional matchmaker only to sell his eldest daughter into marriage. It means asking, too, what kind of Russian Jewish daughter bitterly renounces her brokered marriage and then conspires to ensnare her only unwed sister. In depicting an otherwise rational and admirable denouement, Yezierska presents an image for the burden of the past that is disturbingly Freudian, erotic, and incestuous. She undercuts her protagonist's rapprochement with an angst that is more middle class than a form of Old World kvetching and more Eastern European than a rehearsal of Emersonian regret.

I read *Bread Givers* as an instance of ethnic realism: belated with regard to canonical realist inquiry into the formation of modern mainstream America, yet ahead of its time as an interrogation into the formation of the Russian Jewish middle classes. Yezierska is not so much helplessly candid vis-à-vis her mainstream audience (as has long been claimed) as she is naively ruthless vis-à-vis her Russian Jewish subjects: offensive in the literal sense and, depending on where one stands with regard to liberal feminist departures from Orthodox Judaism, arguably self-hating as well.

It is ironic that the one immigrant novel Aaron and Howe's generation regarded as an indisputable masterpiece, *Call It Sleep* (1934), has receded from sight since the 1960s without so much as a whisper of complaint, despite the burgeoning of ethnic criticism. Our own generation is so wary of the colonizing energies of the canon of "Western Civilization" that it does not know what to make of Roth's incommensurable debt to James Joyce, T. S. Eliot, and Eugene O'Neill, a trinity of writers who define high modernism in its three principal modes. The members of this trinity are not only Northwestern European in origin but continental in philosophy and Catholic in conviction. Yet critics of Roth's own generation and background— including Howe, Fiedler, and Alfred Kazin—swear that the portrait of Yiddish-driven family life and patois-orchestrated city streets in *Call It Sleep* is as saturatedly Eastern European immigrant Jewish as any work produced in America, then or since. If those who testify on behalf of Roth's Jewishness can be trusted, why fear his commitment to O'Neill, Joyce, and Eliot?

In conceiving the novel, Roth assumes that his autobiographical alter ego was the victim in the saga, primarily the victim of the father. He assumed, too, that progeny and progenitor were separated by differences in temperament and self-knowledge as vast as the Atlantic crossing that divided their upbringings, and that the boy, like himself but unlike his fictionalized father, would succeed in sloughing off the burdens of Old World Jewish masculinity. *Call It Sleep* tells less settled tales. In chapter 3, "Oedipus in Brownsville," I consider the strategies Roth uses to uncover Oedipus's actual dynamic among the males of his descent line and why he turns in the end to lyric invention to defuse the tragic cycle of disaffiliation in Eastern European Judaism.

Although Miller was raised in a German-speaking household on the other side of the East River, although he began his career in the 1920s with a proethnic, anticapitalist protest novel, and although he was regarded by those who started writing in the 1930s as being as authentically "other" as any of them, he has been utterly neglected by scholars of ethnic literature. As the "lost generation" of American expatriates returned home, taking up the banner of Depression-era social relevance, Miller relocated to Paris. The assumption that followed hardly needs to be stated: if any interwar formalist of immigrant background had dissipated all but the aleatory traces of ethnic identity, surely that writer was Henry Miller. In the light of this critical consensus, "The Tailor Shop," the fifty-page centerpiece of *Black Spring* (Paris, 1938) that recounts Miller's time working for his father, a custom tailor, calls attention to itself three times over: as a sweatshop saga of the Miller family business, as a dialect story featuring the down-and-out immigrants who hung around Miller Sr. at the garment shop, and as a portrait of an artistic youth stymied by his family's petit-bourgeois servility and his coworkers' intellectual pipe-dreaming.

I read "The Tailor Shop" as an alternative modernist experiment in up-from-the-ghetto narrative. "The Tailor Shop" begins, in effect, where chapter 21 of *Call It Sleep* leaves off, with an extravagant interplay between proletarian ethnic polyphony and prose poetry beyond Freudian modernism. In my account, Miller does not subordinate the homosocial community of chatty old men to Paris-influenced literary ambition but rather develops a text of visceral sonority in order to reproduce that community. He comes to credit his passage into letters to those who once seemed to stand in the path of his artistry, and in so doing he points the way for other writers, diversely alienated and expatriated, to esteem the preliterary communities from which they have come.

In rapidly canonizing *The Woman Warrior* (1976), teachers and critics have attributed to it a marked resistance to interpretation. This exoticization of the text is especially disturbing because it reproduces the stereotype of Chinese inscrutability as a classificatory precept. One provocation to a more accurate contextualization of *The Woman Warrior* has been made by Kingston's vociferous Chinese-American male detractors; they have shown that she misreads Chinese myth history to feminist ends. What has been less clear from the attacks on Kingston is that the targets of her violently revisionary imagination are not only Chinese men but, more harshly, her immediate female ancestors, gatekeepers of a daughter's transition to American modernity.

In *The Woman Warrior*, Kingston confronts the ghosts of female complicity with patriarchy that haunt three received narratives: the apocryphal story of a dishonorable aunt that her mother told her at first menses, evidently to warn her that migration to the United States does not suspend communal sexual norms and codes of female obedience; the myth-narrative of warrior Fa Mu Lan, a woman and eventual mother who went to battle for her people dressed as a man, which Kingston was supposed to comprehend as mere child's play; and the family story of her mother's training as a midwife in Canton, which may be discountable from a feminist perspective as an unambitious extension of women's sphere. In "Changing the Rituals," I interpret Kingston's transgressive reworkings of these inherited narratives as a studied effort in enabling feminist fantasy: the fashioning of a contemporary women's politics with a feminine Chinese ancestry, namely, Kingston's own.

Despite its ubiquity, the up-from-the-immigrant-colony narrative is the least frequently studied of the genres loosely designated "ethnic" because it is the most underestimated. It is the most underestimated because of the long-prevailing suspicion that if ever there were an instance of a genre (as Henry James once said in another context) "at once ready-made and sadly the worse for wear," it is the immigrant success story.[17]

The ambition of this book, at its most basic, is to read five instances of the genre so well on their own terms that one wonders how any of them were ever taken to be mere formula stories.

Although I offer implicit invitations and (more usually) challenges to theory in the course of this book, my own premium is placed on a seductive, disarming attention to the narratives themselves. Animating each of these five case studies has been my desire to discover the ways in which a given instance of immigrant writing is, if indeed it is, great: that is, "great" much in the manner that canonical modern literature is taken to be great but not (how could it be?) precisely in that manner. My instincts about what to look for have been sharpened by "theorizing" in advance, thus the theses I have presented here, but the exact nature of the greatness such texts achieve can be revealed only by carefully contextualizing and closely reading, text by text.

I have been particularly drawn to the kind of nuanced tale that Puzo, for one, is wont to tell: "The poorest Italian is the proudest of persons. He never complains about being barred from an exclusive country club; when he achieves economic success, he never tries to crash an elite social group. He has always known where he was not wanted, and one of the first places where he knew he was not wanted was Italy."[18] In the chapters that follow, I consider storytellers like Puzo, who are chastened by why their people left for the United States, suspicious about what they have done since their arrival, and determined to shape where they are headed in the future.

1

Blood in the Marketplace: The Business of Family in *The Godfather* Narratives

Giorgio introduces me to his friend Piero Paco, hero of the Italo-American breach into American literature. He looks like a massive gangster but turns out to be a plain, nice guy with a lot of folksy stories and no complexes. He doesn't feel guilty about blacks, doesn't care about elevating Italo-American prestige. He's no missionary for wops. No gripes about the Establishment. He just decided in the best American way to write a book that would make half a million bucks because he was tired of being ignored.

"You don't think struggling Italo-Americans should stick together and give each other a push up from the bottom of the pile where they've always been?" I ask him. But he's no struggling half-breed anymore. He's made his pile; he's all-American now.

"I'm not going to push that crap," he says engagingly.

Helen Barolini, *Umbertina* (1979)

In his 1969 blockbuster *The Godfather,* Mario Puzo presented an image of the Mafia that has become commonplace in American popular culture. Since that time, we have taken for granted that the Mafia operates as a consortium of illegitimate businesses, structured along family lines, with a familial patriarch or "godfather" as the chief executive officer of each syndicate.[1] Puzo's version of the Mafia fuses into one icon the realms of family and economy, of Southern Italian ethnicity and big-time American capitalism, of blood and the marketplace. "Blood" refers to the violence of organized crime. "Blood" also refers to the familial clan and its extension through the symbolic system of the *compare*, or "co-godparenthood." In *The Godfather*, the representation of the Mafia fuses ethnic tribalism with the all-American pursuit of wealth and power. Since its publication, we have regarded this business of family in *The Godfather* as a figment of Puzo's opportunistic imagination, which it remains in part. But the business of family in Puzo's Mafia is also a provocative revision of accepted notions of what ethnicity is and how it works—the new ethnic sociology in popular literary form.

During the late 1970s and early 1980s, there was a short outburst of scholarly interest in *The Godfather* and its myriad offspring. A consensus about the meaning of the popularity of this saga emerges from the books and essays of Fredric Jameson, Eric Hobsbawn, John Cawelti, and John Sutherland. The portrayal of the Corleone family collective allows post-Vietnam-era Americans to fantasize about the glory days of "closely knit traditional authority." The portrayal of the power and destructive greed of the Mafia chieftains allows them to vent their rage at "the managerial elite who hold the reins of corporate power and use it for their own benefit."[2] The themes of family and business, in each instance, are disengaged from one another. As Jameson puts it, on the one hand, the ethnic family imagery satisfies "a Utopian longing" for collectivity, while, on the other hand, "the substitution of crime for big business" is the "ideological function" of the narrative.[3] In such standard treatments, Puzo's narrative is regarded as a brilliant (or brilliantly lucky) instance of satisfying two disparate appetites with a single symbol. This perspective, formulated in the late 1970s, seems to have settled the issue of the popularity of the novel.

I want to reopen that issue. We need to return to *The Godfather* because we have too easily dismissed its representation of the Mafia as a two-part fantasy. Of course, *The Godfather* is not reliable as a roman à clef or a historical novel: Puzo's details are fuzzy, mixed up, and much exaggerated.[4] "There was things he stretched," as Huck Finn would put it, and everyone knows it. But critics have been too ready to accept his major sociological premise—that family and business work in tandem—as pure mythology. I would argue that the importance of *The*

Godfather lies not in its creation of a double mythology but in the way that it takes the fusion of kinship and capitalist enterprise seriously. Its cultural significance lies not in the simultaneous appeals of "family" and "business" imagery but rather in the appeal of an actual structural simultaneity, the business of family. If we fail to pause long enough to consider its surface narrative, we underestimate not only the strategies of the novel but the insights and intuitions of its huge audience as well.

Readers have underestimated the business of family because little in traditional theories of the family, ethnicity, and advanced capitalism has prepared them to recognize it. In both scholarly and popular treatments, ethnic culture and extended kinship are interpreted as barriers to successfully negotiating the mobility ladder, particularly its upper rungs. Southern Italian immigrants and their descendants have long been thought to exemplify the principle that the more clannish an ethnic group, the slower its assimilation and economic advancement.[5] Herbert Gans's *Urban Villagers*, Virginia Yans-McLaughlin's *Family and Community*, Thomas Kessner's *Golden Door*, and Thomas Sowell's *Ethnic America* essentially update the social work perspectives of such writers as Phyllis H. Williams and Leonard Covello.[6] In 1944, Covello wrote, "Any social consciousness of Italo-Americans within 'Little Italies' appertains primarily to sharing and adhering to the family tradition as the main motif of their philosophy of life. . . . The retention of this cultural 'basis' is essentially the source of their retarded adjustment."[7] But this long-standing tradition of identifying the Italian family structure as a dysfunctional survival runs aground when it comes to the Mafia.

Historians and sociologists attest to the difficulty of interpreting the Mafia in terms of a linear model of assimilation and upward mobility. All commentators recognize that the Mafia was not simply transported here: it arose from the polyethnic immigrant streets rather than passing from father to son; Prohibition was the major factor in shaping its growth. In *A Family Business*, sociologist Francis A. J. Ianni concedes these points, only to stress the family structure of the syndicates and the origin of this familialism in Southern Italy. The Lupullo

crime organization *"feels* like a kinship-structured group;
familialism founded it and is still its stock in trade. One
senses immediately not only the strength of the bond, but
the inability of members to see any morality or social order
larger than their own." Ianni's research tempts him into abandoning the tradition of placing ethnic phenomena on a linear
continuum running from Old World marginality to New World
centrality.[8] His research supports and his analysis anticipates,
without quite articulating, the cutting edge of ethnic theory.

Scholars in a number of fields are working to change the way
we think about ethnicity, ethnic groups, and ethnic culture. In
identifying the social bases of ethnicity, theorists are shifting
their emphasis from intergenerational transmission to arenas
of conflict in complex societies. They argue that we need to examine ethnic cultures not as Old World survivals (whatever
their roots) but as improvised strategies to deal with the un-
equal distribution of wealth, power, and status. In this light,
ethnic groups include not only socially marginal peoples but
any group that uses symbols of common descent and tradition
to create or to maintain power. From a historian's perspective,
European family structures and traditions do not necessarily
dissolve in the face of capitalism but rather, as they have always done, evolve to meet its changing needs.[9]

Anthropologist Abner Cohen conceives of ethnic groups as
"interest groups" in which ethnic symbols function in lieu of
more formal structures, such as the law. When he speaks of the
symbolic apparatus of ethnicity, he refers to the emphasis on
common history and tradition, endogamy and social boundary maintenance, religion and ritual, and everyday encoded
behavior, including "accent, manner of speech, etiquette, style
of joking, play" and so forth, that is, the rhetoric and codes
of "blood."[10] As Cohen explains, the symbolic apparatus of
ethnicity incites genuine loyalty and emotion, the power and
idiosyncrasy of which cannot be underestimated. But the apparatus also serves utilitarian purposes within society at large,
including those of the economic marketplace. In many of our
most familiar examples, the function of ethnic ritual is primarily defensive, to organize a group on the margins of society,
but the uses of ethnicity can be quite aggressive as well. The

Italian-American Mafia is a case in point. As Ianni and others have demonstrated, it is the ethos of ethnic solidarity that puts the organization into Italian-American organized crime.

In her discussion of *The Godfather*, Rose Basile Green comes the closest of any critic to unpacking what she calls the "socio-economic ethnic image" of the Corleone crime syndicate. Un-like almost everyone else, Green takes seriously Puzo's portrayal of the syndicates—not as historical fact about actual gangsters but as a treatise (however romanticized) "dealing with the contemporary strategy of gaining and securing power." Yet Green's analysis splits into typical parallel paths: crime as a means for social mobility versus the family as a locus of traditional Southern Italian responsibility. Although Green identifies "a subtle line between personal interest and struc-tural power," she, too, fails to make the strongest connection between the private family life ascribed to Don Corleone and the illegitimate enterprise he heads. When Green says that *The Godfather* explores "the contemporary strategy of gaining and securing power," she means the tactics of bribery, intimida-tion, the brokerage of votes, intergang warfare, and so forth that Don Corleone uses to conduct business outside the con-fines of his own organization. But the most noteworthy device for gaining and securing power in Puzo's depiction is internal to the Corleone syndicate: it is not a gun or payola, but, quite simply, that mystified entity, the "Southern Italian family."[11]

In narrating *The Godfather*, Puzo adopts the familiar role of cultural interpreter, mediating between outside readers and a secret ethnic society. Puzo's agenda, implicit yet universally understood, is to explain why Sicilian Americans have made such good criminals. The answer, generally speaking, is their cult of family honor. The Corleones believe, with a kind of feu-dal fervor, in patriarchy, patronage, and protection. *The God-father* is saturated with the imagery of paternity, family, and intimate friendship; with the rhetoric of respect, loyalty, and the code of silence; with references to Sicilian blood and the machismo attributed to it; with the social events—weddings, christenings, funerals, meals, and so forth—that embody the culture of family honor. The business of crime is always inter-laced with the responsibilities of family. In the film, for instance, Clemenza frets over a request from his wife Eve as he presides over the execution of Paulie Gatto: "Don't forget the cannoli!" Don Vito himself is a true believer in the mutual obligations of kinfolk. He seeks both to expand his wealth and power to protect his dependents and to make his protection available to more and more people. He recruits from within his family to keep the business "all in the family" for the family's sake. "It was at this time that the Don got the idea that he ran his world far better than his enemies ran the greater world which continually obstructed his path."[12] At the same time, "not his best friends would have called Don Corleone a saint from heaven"; there is always "some self-interest" in his generosity (215). For everyone recognizes the wisdom of family honor, Corleone's Honor, given the special exigencies of operating in a big way in an outlawed underground economy.

In his analysis of the ethnic group as an interest group, Cohen stresses the growth potential wherever there is a sector of an economy that has not been organized formally:

> Even in the advanced liberal industrial societies there are some structural conditions under which an interest group cannot organize itself on formal lines. Its formal organization may be opposed by the state or by other groups within the state, or may be incompatible with some important principles in the society; or the interests it represents may be newly developed and not yet articulated in terms of a formal organization and accommodated with the formal structure of the society. Under these conditions the group will articulate its organization on informal lines, making use of the kinship, friendship, ritual, ceremonial, and other symbolic activities that are implicit in what is known as style of life.[13]

The ethnic ethos means sticking together, respecting the authority of the group rather than that of outsiders, defending the group's turf, and abiding by tradition. The reasoning comes full circle, for tradition is equated with group solidarity. The family is the core element of the group and its most powerful symbol. Under appropriate conditions, the ethos of ethnicity is by no means anachronistic in late capitalism, no matter how rooted such values might be in the history of particular groups. Wherever ethnicity can facilitate enterprise, ethnicity as a system can be said to be one of the primary motors of capitalism, not its antithesis. Focusing on the old moneyed elite of London, Cohen has argued that ethnicity functions among the privileged as well as among the impoverished, among "core" castes as well as among racial and national minorities. In another case study, historian Peter Dobkin Hall implicates family and tradition in the mercantile practices of Massachusetts elites in the eighteenth and nineteenth centuries.[14] As both Cohen and Hall contend, a precondition for capitalized ethnicity is a legal vacuum. I would add to this a corollary based on the history of the Mafia: the desire to engage in enterprise, not simply in a vacuum (where law and formal arrangements are lacking) but in an economic zone outside the law and opposed to formal arrangements, makes some form of family and ethnic organization a necessity.

The seemingly feudal, deeply internalized ethos of family honor cements individuals together in American crime, structuring syndicates and giving them their aggrandizing momentum. Loyalty and devotion to group honor are the values according to which individuals are motivated, recruited, judged, and policed in the Mafia. These values are especially effective at binding criminals together and at making criminals out of those not otherwise drawn to the outlaw life. These values surfaced in the United States when Prohibition created an enormous unorganized sector of the national economy, legally proscribed but driven by immense appetites and the willingness of legal institutions to play along, especially for a price. Such values are also necessary to hold together the large-scale enterprises not structured or protected by law, which Prohibition created but which survived after it: rackets devoted to gambling, loan-sharking, prostitution, various forms of extortion, and eventually drugs. In legitimate business, a prized executive who sells himself and perhaps a secret or two to another company is written off as an unexpected operating loss. A *capo-regime* who becomes a stool pigeon can bring the whole system down. The ideologies of tradition and group solidarity, principally of the family, are ideal for rationalizing crime syndicates in both senses of the word "rationalize": ideal for organizing them because such ideologies are ideal for justifying their existence and their hold over their members.

Scholars report that actual mafiosi crime syndicates are family based. In *A Family Business,* Ianni analyzes the structure of a major American Mafia clan, the "Lupullo" family, abstracting four general rules of organization: "the merging of social and business functions into one kin-centered enterprise; the assignment of leadership positions on the basis of kinship; the correlation between closeness of kin relationship and the hierarchy of positions; and the requirement of close consanguineal or affinal relationship for inclusion in the core group."[15] Ianni produces several diagrams to illustrate his thesis: a genealogical table of actual and symbolic (godparent-godchild) relations, a flow chart of the subdivisions and their operations within the crime syndicate, and a third table combining the preceding two.[16] The third table diagrams what Ianni calls the "power alliances"—relations of respect and deference—among leaders within the Lupullo crime hierarchy. The pattern of authority within the syndicate mimics the pattern within the patriarchal clan.

In *The Godfather,* Mario Puzo provides a narrative equivalent of the Lupullos' power chart. During the wedding scene, he introduces the Corleones in terms of their dual roles as family members and company executives. Vito Corleone is president and chief executive officer as well as father or godfather to everyone within the organization. Genco Abbandando, *consigliori* (advisor, right-hand man), has been his best friend, his honorary brother, the son of the man who took him in and gave him his first job; but Genco is dying, and it is suspected that Tom Hagen, Vito Corleone's "adopted" son, will be taking over as counselor. Vito's eldest child, Sonny, operates one of the three principal divisions or regimes of the family. The other two division leaders (*capo-regimes*), Tessio and Clemenza, are *compari* of Vito, godparents to his children as he is to theirs. Fredo, the second son, serves as his father's bodyguard and executive secretary. Michael, the youngest son, is the black sheep of the family and has nothing to do with its business. By tradition, the women are "civilians." But Connie's groom, Carlo Rizzi (Sonny's boyhood chum), expects to rise quickly in the syndicate through his marriage.

The network of nuclear family, extended kin by blood or marriage, and honorary kinship is not simply a structural convenience. The ideology of family operates not as false consciousness in the vulgar sense nor as rhetoric that is entirely and self-consciously hypocritical. Rather, the rhetoric of solidarity works to organize the Corleone syndicate because of its hold over the imaginations and passions of the leaders and the common ranks alike. As Cohen explains it, ethnic symbols function in lieu of formal structures precisely because of their transutilitarian emotional appeal. The dual nature of this symbolization is illustrated especially well in Puzo's depiction of Tom Hagen's admission into the Corleone syndicate.

Sonny Corleone had brought Tom Hagen, an orphaned waif of German-Irish extraction, into the Corleone household, where he was allowed to remain. "In all this the Don acted not as a father but rather as a guardian." Only after Hagen goes to work for Don Corleone is he treated as a fourth son:

> After he passed the bar exam, Hagen married to start his own family. The bride was a young Italian girl from New Jersey, rare at that time for being a college graduate. After the wedding, which was of course held in the home of Don Corleone, the Don offered to support Hagen in any undertaking he desired, to send him law clients, furnish his office, start him in real estate.
>
> Tom Hagen had bowed his head and said to the Don, "I would like to work for you."
>
> The Don was surprised, yet pleased. "You know who I am?" he asked.
>
> Hagen nodded. . . . "I would work for you like your sons," Hagen said, meaning with complete loyalty, with complete acceptance of the Don's parental divinity. The Don, with that understanding which was even then building the legend of his greatness, showed the young man the first mark of fatherly affection since he had come into his household. He took Hagen into his arms for a quick embrace and afterward treated him more like a true son, though he would sometimes say, "Tom, never

forget your parents," as if he were reminding himself as well as Hagen. (51–52)

Hagen moves into the Don's inner circle, both into the inner realm of Don Vito's familial affections and into the ranks of his crime organization. Tom touches the Don's heart by volunteering, despite his origins, to submit himself to the Don's will and to risk his life and freedom in the company. By the same token, the Don rewards Tom's voluntary show of respect with a symbolic "adoption" that signifies the bond of loyalty upon which their futures as gangsters will depend. The symbol of paternity here works emotionally and pragmatically at the same time. Indeed, the father-son bonding is all the more powerful because of its economic component, while its utility depends, in the absence of biological paternity, quite precisely upon the psychological density of the tie.

So far I have been juxtaposing the sociology of ethnic and familial interest groups with various elements of *The Godfather*, treating the latter as if it were merely an illustration of the former, as if *The Godfather* were a kind of sociological tract or social work guide to the Mafia. Of course, *The Godfather* is not exposition but a novel, not sociology but story. Yet the fact that *The Godfather* is a fictional composition with mass appeal does not make it any less effective for implicating the ethnic family in capitalism than the scholarship of Cohen or Ianni. Puzo uses the resources of fiction—imagery and rhetoric, characterization, and, most of all, narrative—to make a case for the interpenetration of family and business.

In the instance of Tom Hagen's admission to the Corleone family, Puzo designs a set of circumstances and unfolds the event so that the strands of father-son emotion and corporate personnel management cannot be separated. Hagen's recruitment/initiation functions as a microcosm of the interpenetration of family and business in the narrative as a whole. Puzo inscribes the ethnic family within the capitalist economy while exploring the contributions ethnic culture and the rhetoric of ethnicity have made to illegitimate enterprise. He thereby subverts the reader's desire, in keeping with a purified notion of the family and a vilified notion of the economy, to subordinate one sphere to the other, as cause and effect, in any given instance. In *The Godfather*, one can never, or almost never, say that the syndicate uses family imagery merely to structure itself for lack of better alternatives, thereby "corrupting" the forms and values of an otherwise sacrosanct ethnic tribe. Nor can one say that the family engages in business simply to support itself, dirtying its hands to keep head and heart clean. Always the two phenomena are causally intermingled.

The story line is crucial to *The Godfather* to a greater extent than we perhaps have become used to in analyzing modernist, highbrow literature. Even the critics most hostile to Puzo admit that his great gift is storytelling. Not only has he created memorable characters but he has been able to generate and maintain suspense. His beginnings captivate, his middles keep you going, and his endings satisfy. In *The Godfather*, Puzo narrates two plots that come together in a single resounding conclusion.

When the novel opens, a breakdown in filial obedience exposes the Corleone syndicate to a hostile take-over bid from the Barzini-Tattaglia group. At the same time, business matters threaten the lives of Corleone family members and precipitate dissent among them. This double crisis is the hook that captures our attention: a business in trouble, a family in trouble. We crave a solution to both crises—nothing less will satisfy—and Puzo contrives brilliantly to give it to us. Both crises, potentially disastrous, are solved when Don Vito's youngest son Michael ascends to his father's place and successfully squelches the Barzini-Tattaglia threat. It is a stunning illustration of the structural logic of family business in narrative terms. The return of the prodigal son alleviates the problem of managerial succession while the resurrection of the syndicate's power base restores the primacy of family values and commitments. Puzo's story is dual in the sense that the ethnic symbols of the Mafia are dual, and that Tom Hagen's adoption as a Corleone is dual. Puzo's plot is so tightly constructed around the theme of duality that the denouement of the novel seems inevitable. To save the business, you must regroup the family; to save the family, you must regroup the business.

Puzo uses Connie Corleone's wedding to illustrate the overlapping structures of family and business in the American Mafia of the 1940s. In *The Godfather* film (the lens of which con-

stantly obscures our view of the novel), Coppola plays with the
contrast between the beneficent private life of the Corleones
(the sunlit wedding feast) and their business escapades (inside the darkened house, inside their hearts of darkness).
Coppola's moral allegory reifies the distinction between the
private and the corporate, home and work, that the novel explicitly undermines. In Puzo's design, business associates are
the proper wedding guests, because one's family and friends
are one's proper coworkers and retainers. The specter of communal solidarity embodied in the wedding marks a plateau of
harmonious unity from which the Corleones are about to fall.
As Puzo introduces the members of the Corleone family at
Connie's wedding and in their familiar environment, he
not only reveals the functional interdependence of family and
business but foreshadows a disturbance in the family-
business equilibrium, which will become the central crisis in
the narrative. As Puzo imagines it, the incipient threat to
the Corleone empire is inseparable from the breakdown in
the familial solidarity of the syndicate—including Genco's
death, the Don's creeping senility, Sonny's disobedience, the
disloyalty of Carlo and Tessio, and Michael's rebellion. At
the same time, tensions in the family arise directly out of its
members' involvement in the business of crime.

At the beginning of the novel, Don Corleone is nearing
retirement, and he justifiably worries about the leadership of
the syndicate. In standard corporate management, such a
problem would be handled either by promotion of the best
available personnel from within the company ranks or by
recruitment from outside the company (intercorporate "raid-
ing"). But for the Corleones, of course, the problem of the
company executive is strictly a family matter, and that makes
it a problem indeed. The right-hand man, Genco Abbandando, dies on the day of the wedding, leaving Don Corleone
no choice but to promote Tom Hagen, an adopted son whose
German-Irish descent precludes consideration for the top post
of don. Both Clemenza and Tessio, the two *capo-regimes*, are
nearing retirement themselves; also they are not quite family
enough. Of the Don's own sons, neither Sonny nor Fredo
seems finally to have the mettle to be don, while Michael, once
favored to head the family, is now an outcast. Sonny

did not have his father's humility but instead a quick, hot temper that led him into errors of judgment. Though he was a great help in his father's business, there were many who doubted that he would become the heir to it.

The second son, Frederico . . . did not have that personal magnetism, that animal force, so necessary for a leader of men, and he too was not expected to inherit the family business.

The third son, Michael Corleone, did not stand with his father and his two brothers but sat at a table in the most secluded corner of the garden. (17)

The leadership vacuum, familially engendered, is the weak link that tempts the Barzini-Tattaglia consortium (fronted by Sollozzo the drug dealer) to take over the Corleone rackets. Weaknesses in the character of family members and in their relations with one another expose the Corleone family, quite literally, to a hostile takeover bid.

At the same time, business tensions have precipitated disputes within the intimate family circle. Michael has fallen out with his family because he objects to the way they make a living; he commits himself instead to the defense of his country and the "straight arrow" mobility of a Dartmouth education. Connie's old-fashioned Sicilian wedding seems to symbolize the unity of the Corleone generations, yet the garden celebration actually masks the dissent between Connie and her father, traceable to Corleone involvement in the rackets. "Connie had consented to a 'guinea' wedding to please her father because she had so displeasured him in her choice of a husband" (20). The persistence of the Corleone syndicate means that one of the qualifications for a Corleone son-in-law is the potential for criminal leadership. Don Vito objects to Carlo Rizzi as his daughter's husband not necessarily because he doubts Carlo's qualities as a mate, but because he questions Carlo's ability and trustworthiness as a gangster. Carlo marries Connie not only for love; he also hopes to rise in the Corleone syndicate. When Don Vito violates the principle of familial promotion, providing Carlo with a living but not with an executive role, Carlo seeks revenge on his father-in-law and the family. He sets up the assassination of Sonny, bringing the syndicate to the brink of disaster. As this instance shows, any analysis of family-business disrepair comes full circle in Puzo's novel: we trace family problems to business questions, only to find that the way business has intruded into family life has returned to haunt the business.

Carlo's betrayal, like that of Paulie Gatto and ultimately of Tessio, illustrates the point of vulnerability in a family business operating within a competitive market. The principles of maximizing profits and employing insiders are not always compatible. Syndicate leaders are tempted, for the sake of performance, to slight certain inept family members while syndicate members are tempted, for personal gain, to betray their organization. As long as a doctrine of familial loyalty is obeyed to the letter, neither temptation constitutes too much of a threat; but when family principles break down, the company is in danger.

The leadership vacuum in the Corleone syndicate is filled when Michael returns to his family, his descent culture, and his filial "destiny." As John Cawelti notes, the crisis of managerial succession in *The Godfather* is a crisis of "family succession," which can only be solved familially.[17] Puzo resolves the dual crisis by having Michael develop a familial conscience and an ethnic consciousness, mandating his ascension to his father's position as patriarch. When the novel opens, Michael is a family pariah—*scomunicato,* excommunicated. Before the war, Michael had been the chosen heir to his father's regime, but he later refuses to have anything to do with the business and barely anything to do with the members of his family. He courts an "Adams" for a wife. Puzo's narrative counteracts the seeming decline of the Corleone syndicate by charting Michael's rebirth as a Corleone family member and a businessman of crime.

Michael's return as a once-prodigal son is enacted in a step-like progression that mirrors the rhythms of religious initiation: baptism, confirmation, the sacrament of marriage or the priesthood. By killing Sollozzo and the police captain, Michael simultaneously commits himself to his father's honor and a life of crime. In Sicily, he is symbolically rebaptized a Sicilian, learning the history of the Italian Mafia, converting to the old traditions, even taking a local wife (who subsequently gets killed). Back in America, he is apprenticed to his father. When Don Corleone dies, Michael takes over the business and the family, becoming godfather to Connie's firstborn and "Don Michael" to his business associates. As Coppola depicts it in the film, while Michael's godson is being christened, his henchmen are executing a series of murders that restore the internal solidarity of the Corleone syndicate and enlarge its boundaries and standing. Acting his father's part, Michael's face even begins to resemble Don Vito's in his prime. Puzo's drama of monarchical, Oedipal succession reverses the familiar convention of second-generation "orphanhood" with which the novel begins.

Any attempt to separate what Michael does out of an emotional recommitment to his father or to his ethnic past from what he accomplishes out of a pragmatic enlistment in his father's company is doomed. Readers even vaguely familiar with *The Godfather* narrative know that the brutal killings at the end of the novel reestablish and indeed improve the Corleones' standing in the American Mafia. But it is less well recognized, and the film downplays, how the ending reintegrates the Corleone household. Critics argue that Puzo deploys family imagery only to win sympathy for Michael's otherwise morally egregious plans. They likewise misconstrue the strategies of the novel when they subordinate the familial pleadings of the narrative to its capitalist melodrama, as if the reintegration of the family were merely an ideological cover for the reincorporation of the syndicate. The two structures are interrelated; neither can be subordinated to the other.

Standing godfather to his nephew, Michael accepts family leadership and embodies family unity, literalizing his newly won title as patriarch of an extended family. Michael, crowned "Don," tightens the family circle around him. Hagen returns from Nevada. Traitors to family honor—Gatto, Rizzi, Tessio—are eliminated. Michael's success in restoring the Corleone empire is as much the act of a truly obedient son as his godfatherhood is a basis for taking over the syndicate, since the crime organization becomes the ground on which the Corleones are reunited. Coppola's film version leaves us with a trace of dissent, since it ends with Kay's recognition of

Michael's ruthless criminality. In the novel, Puzo restores the equanimity of husband and wife, symbolically extending it to the Corleone family at large. Tom Hagen explains to Kay why it was necessary, from the standpoint of their ethos, for Michael to order the executions of Carlo Rizzi, Tessio, and the others. Kay acquiesces to Hagen's explanation and Michael's desire that she come home. She undergoes a rite of cultural self-transformation to make herself into the kind of Italian-American woman the criminal environment expects. Whereas the film ends with Kay's anguish, the novel ends with Kay's conversion to Catholicism. Every morning she goes to Mass with her mother-in-law, there to say, in the final words of the novel, "the necessary prayers for the soul of Michael Corleone" (446). The peace of the Corleones is thereby restored. Michael doesn't mend matters with Kay simply to make the company perform better any more than he restores the power of the syndicate simply to win his wife back and reintegrate his family. As Puzo has rigged the plot, the two go hand in hand.

The Godfather would warrant attention from scholars for the way it depicts an ethnic subculture that functions as an interest group even if, like Puzo's Fortunate Pilgrim (1964), it had disappeared into obscurity upon publication. But the novel has had a major impact on popular culture. The figure of "the godfather" outstrips all but the most ubiquitous cultural symbols, falling somewhere between Huckleberry Finn and Superman, better known, perhaps, than Uncle Sam himself.[18] By 1971, when the first film was released, there were over one million hardcover copies of the book in circulation—multiple copies in every library in every town in America—and at least ten million more paperbacks.[19] Historically, the reading of the novel framed the film; not, as in academic criticism, the other way around. By the early 1980s, the book had become the best-selling novel in history, and it continues to sell steadily even outside the United States.

The most immediate spin-offs of the novel were the two films, versions of those films rearranged for television, and the video format, in which the two films plus outtakes are combined as The Godfather Epic. By 1975, 260 more books on the

Mafia theme had been released, principally of the hard-boiled variety.[20] In 1984, Puzo himself tried again with his fictional account of Salvatore Giuliano, *The Sicilian*. Ethnicity in crime has figured in many major films, including *The Cotton Club* (co-scripted by Coppola, Puzo, and William Kennedy), *The Gang Who Couldn't Shoot Straight, Broadway Danny Rose, Heart of the Dragon, Scarface, Once upon a Time in America, Miller's Crossing*, and *Goodfellas*, Martin Scorsese's reply to Coppola. During the 1980s, the popularity of family-dynasty sagas, especially in their many ethnic varieties, can be traced in part to Puzo's model. Most telling has been the ceaseless production of *God-father* clones, emphasizing the fusion of family and crime. Now a genre of its own, the proliferation includes (auto)biographical works such as Gay Talese's *Honor Thy Father*, Joseph Bonanno's *Man of Honor*, and Antoinette Giancana's *Mafia Princess*; novels such as Vincent Patrick's *Family Business* and Richard Condon's trilogy of the Prizzi family; and a legion of films and teleplays, including "Our Family Honor" (ABC's ill-fated attempt to combine Italian-American gangsters with Irish-American cops), *Married to the Mob* (which picks up on the feminist themes in Condon), the "Wiseguy" series (an affecting drama of homoerotic underpinnings in the mob), *China Girl* (Abel Ferrara restages *Romeo and Juliet* between Italian and Chinese mobsters), and *The Freshman* (Brando parodies his portrayal of Vito Corleone). *The Godfather Part III* was released on Christmas in 1990.

What are we to make of the lasting fascination with *The Godfather?* Since its appearance, scholars have recognized *The Godfather* as an artifact of the "new ethnicity." The timing of the novel and its immediate offspring, from publication of the novel in 1969 to the television miniseries in the late 1970s, corresponds to an upturn in Americans embracing ethnic identity. This celebration included not only groups that were by and large still marginal—Native Americans, the descendants of Southern slaves, the newest comers from the Caribbean, the Hispanic Americas, and the Far East—but also the descendants of European immigrants, including the Italians, who were well on their way to middle-class security. Necessarily, the connections drawn between the increased salience of ethnicity and popularity of *The Godfather* have been premised on construing *The Godfather* as a two-part fantasy in which family sanctuary and successful corporate enterprise are polar opposites. My reading of *The Godfather*, which emphasizes the complicity of family and business, calls for a reexamination of the role of the novel in the new ethnic self-consciousness. Both the popularity of *The Godfather* and the celebration of ethnicity are complex phenomena, reflecting myriad attitudes toward race, class, and gender as well as ethnicity, attitudes that often conflict with one another. By claiming that *The Godfather* articulates the business of family, I do not wish to mute these other voices but to point the way toward situating the voice of family-business within the larger cacophony of debate.

Scholars such as Jameson and Cawelti, who work within the frame of traditional *Godfather* interpretation, seek to locate within the novel an anticapitalist energy—not an overt critique so much as an impulse, the energy of a potential critique partially veiled and misdirected. Both critics argue that Puzo portrays the Mafia as the center of a capitalist conspiracy and, simultaneously and irreconcilably, as a refuge from the conspiracy of capitalism. Because Puzo's Mafia functions as "the mirror-image of big business," its brutality provides a focus for anticapitalist anxiety and an outlet for anticapitalist anger. Similarly, the equally powerful image of the family reflects, in Jameson's terms, a "Utopian longing" for escape from the prison house of capitalism. "The 'family' is a fantasy of tribal belongingness," echoes Cawelti, "that protects and supports the individual as opposed to the coldness and indifference of the modern business or government bureaucracy."[21]

In the standard view, the putative double fantasy of *The Godfather* reflects the misdirected energies of the new ethnicity. The new ethnicity arises from frustration with capitalism yet mutes its resistance in clamor about the decline of the family and traditional values. My analysis of *The Godfather* suggests we might hesitate before we accept the majority opinion that the family in the novel embodies a refuge from capitalism. We need to question whether a case for the subversive nature of *The Godfather* can rest on the myth of the Italian-American family as a precapitalist collectivity, particularly when Puzo uses all his forces to undermine this false dichotomy. The representation of the Southern Italian family in *The Godfather* is not the kind of saccharine portrayal of innocent harmony, the haven in a heartless world, that scholars take as the benchmark of ethnic nostalgia. In *The Godfather*, capitalism is shown to accommodate, absorb, and indeed accentuate the structures of family and ethnicity. Americans respond to *The Godfather* because it presents the ethnic family not as a sacrosanct European institution reproduced on the margins of America, but as a fundamental American structure of power, successful and bloodied.

Scholars' desire to identify ethnic piety as a locus of anticapitalist energy has blinded them to the existence of an alliance between the new ethnicity and the procapitalist celebration of the family. This alliance is an insufficiently recognized strain within recent popular culture. At least until World War II, and perhaps into the 1970s, the dominant attitude was that the ethnic family in the United States was incompatible with capitalism, whether ethnicity was favored or not. The rabid Americanizers of the early decades attempted to strip immigrant workers of their familial and cultural loyalties. Many of the immigrants themselves feared that the price of upward mobility might be a loss of family solidarity, even as most relied on the family as a basis for group enterprise and mutual financial support. And intellectuals, who were partly or wholly skeptical of capitalism, based one strand of their critique on the damage that capitalism supposedly inflicted upon traditional family cultures. We hear less and less frequently from these nativist Americanizers and guardians of ethnic tradition, but the nostalgia among scholars remains pervasive nonetheless. The general public, however, increasingly has come to accept and indeed to welcome the idea of compatibility between ethnicity and capitalism. In the case of Italian Americans, for instance, public figures ranging from Lee Iacocca to Geraldine Ferraro and Mario Cuomo emphasize the role family values have played in their own success stories, occasionally stretching our imaginations.[22] Similar rhetoric appears in the reemerging critique of the black family, in the widespread lauding of Asian- and Caribbean-American merchants and their schoolchildren, and in the general appeal for a new American work ethic. In this light, *The Godfather* helped to introduce and continues to feed upon a strain of American rhetoric and expectation that has reached full salience in the last decade.

Perhaps no artifact of American culture, popular or serious, has made the case for the business of family with quite the force of *The Godfather*. At no time in United States history has ethnicity enjoyed the vogue that it first achieved in the years of *The Godfather*'s greatest popularity and, in large measure, now maintains. The convergence is no coincidence. While *The Godfather* does participate in the new ethnicity by celebrating the ethnic family, the Mafia achieves its romantic luster not because Puzo portrays the Italian-American family as a separate sphere lying outside of capitalism, but because the Italian-American family emerges as a potent structure within it. The ethnic family in *The Godfather* feeds off a market sensibility rather than undermines it.[23] The Corleones can provide protection from the market only because they have mastered it. Indeed, Puzo reaches the height of romance in *The Godfather* by choosing the Mafia as a model for family enterprise, for illegal family enterprises are capable of growing and expanding to an extent that the structure and regulation of legitimate capitalism ultimately will not support.

If *The Godfather* does indeed harbor anticapitalist energies, as a thorough reading of the novel might suggest, then perhaps scholars have been looking for that energy in the wrong places. Jameson concludes:

> When indeed we reflect on an organized conspiracy against the public, one which reaches into every corner of our daily lives and our political structures to exercise a wanton and genocidal violence at the behest of distant decision-makers and in the name of an abstract conception of profit—surely it is not about the Mafia, but rather about American business itself that we are thinking, American capitalism in its most systematized and computerized, dehumanized, "multinational" and corporate form.[24]

Jameson and the others may be correct in insisting that fascination with *The Godfather* is motivated, at a deeper level, by anticapitalist anxiety. But the real scare *The Godfather* entertains, however much suppressed, is about capitalism, not in its "most systematized and computerized, dehumanized" form but rather in its more "intimate" varieties—ethnic, familial, personal. My reading of *The Godfather* suggests that if we wish to press charges against capitalism, we must press charges against family and ethnicity, too.

One strand of rhetoric in twentieth-century America, dating as far back as Howells's *Hazard of New Fortunes* and surveyed by Christopher Lasch in *Haven in a Heartless World* (1977), urges Americans to go home to escape the specter of capitalism. Professionals often complain about taking work home with them, mentally if not literally. How much more frightening, then, is the alternative Puzo represents: when some Americans go home to papa, they end up confronting the boss. Critics have been quick to interpret the brutality of the Mafia as a symbol for the violence to the individual inherent in capitalism, and to assume that the family represents an escape from that violence. Yet the melodrama of *The Godfather* implicates the family not only in the success of the Corleone empire but in its cycle of self-destructive violence as well. Michael reintegrates the family business only after burying a brother, murdering a brother-in-law, alienating a sister, and betraying his wife's trust. For Americans who experience family and economy as interwoven pressures (if not actual combined enterprises), the Mafia genre may allow them to focus their resentments, even if, inevitably, a Mafia analogy overstates them. For the cost of employing blood in the marketplace is finding "The Company" at home.

My speculations notwithstanding, there is no direct way to study popular opinion and pinpoint the popular interpretation of *The Godfather*. Indeed, it would be a mistake to assume there is any singular interpretation, any more than there is a singular "mind of the masses." The great strength of popular literature may be its ability to entertain different, even contrary readings. But at least we can consider how other American artists catering to mass audiences have read the message of Puzo's novel. Two of the best offspring of the novel—the film *The Godfather Part II* (1974) and the novel *Prizzi's Honor* (1982) by Richard Condon—illuminate the way Puzo's novel has been received. Although he receives credit for the *Godfather II* screenplay along with Coppola, the film offers a very different perspective on the Corleones than either the novel or the first *Godfather* film. Pauline Kael gives Coppola almost all the credit for *Godfather II:* "This second film . . . doesn't appear to derive from the book as much as from what Coppola learned while he was making the first."[25] It is not essential for us to assign praise or blame, but simply to note that the film differs significantly enough from the original narrative to constitute a "rereading" of it, even if it is, in part, Puzo's own. Whereas the original *Godfather* intertwines the fates of the Corleone family and the Corleone business, Coppola's *Godfather II* separates them. In *Prizzi's Honor*, on the other hand, Richard Condon uses all the devices in Puzo's novel, plus some of his own, to bond family and business tighter than ever. *Prizzi's Honor* retrieves Puzo's theme from beneath his excesses and Coppola's sermonizing and exposes it to a scintillating parody. The greatest testament to *The Godfather* has been paid not by critics or scholars but by Condon (and by John Huston, who directed the 1985 film version from Condon's screenplay). Together, *Godfather II* and *Prizzi's Honor* can be construed as leading voices in a debate about the meaning of Puzo's novel and the future of the genre in which all three works participate.

> This time I really set out to destroy the family. And I wanted to punish Michael.
>
> Francis Coppola[26]

Scholars and film critics commonly regard *Godfather II* as a greater work of art than the first *Godfather* movie, and as infinitely preferable to the novel. In the standard interpretation, the second film strips the Mafia of its sentimental familial wrappings and reveals it for what it is and perhaps always has been: capitalistic enterprise in its most vicious form. Kael interprets this act of unveiling moralistically: *Godfather II* is to be praised for eliminating the illusion that there might be anything desirable about the Corleone crime family.[27] Jameson stresses the historicity of *Godfather II*, claiming that the film explodes the illusion of the Mafia's "ethnicity" by attributing its origins to social arrangements in "backward and feudal" Sicily and its growth in America to the advanced stages of capitalism. The second film, according to Jameson, submits the themes of the first "to a patient deconstruction that will in the end leave its ideological content undisguised and its displacements visible to the naked eye."[28] For both Kael and Jameson, the deconstruction of the family and the ethnic group is a precondition for truth. But to my mind, it is they, along with Coppola himself, not Puzo, who run the greatest risk of romanticizing the Sicilian-American family.

Godfather II narrates the further adventures of Michael Corleone, interspersed with flashbacks to the early days of his gangster father, Don Vito Corleone. The film is a political morality tale with a vengeance. In the original narrative, as Don Vito's business goes, so goes his family: their fates are intertwined. But in *Godfather II*, Michael promotes his criminal enterprise at the expense of his immediate family, group solidarity, and the Italian-American heritage. The central plot is a Byzantine series of maneuvers between Michael Corleone and the Jewish gangster Hyman Roth (modeled on Meyer Lansky). In their struggles, both Michael and Roth use a Corleone *capo-regime*, Pentangeli, who now lives in the old Corleone house on Long Island, as a pawn. To counter Roth, Michael manipulates the imagery of the criminal "family"—Roth as Michael's "father," Pentangeli as his "godson"—with complete cynicism. He succeeds by using the language of family and ethnic solidarity in its shallowest sense, using it as a short-term (and shortsighted) instrument in a (transethnic, transfamilial) quest for power.

In the process, Michael's multinational crime outfit is reduced to a mere conglomerate of illegal enterprises: the network of ties with his father's retainers back in New York City unravels; his nuclear family falls apart completely; and the Southern Italian ethos that structured his father's world is vanquished entirely. Michael's evil is measured on a scale marked out in emphatically familial and ethnic units. The detail is endless. At the end of the movie, Michael arranges the deaths not only of Roth (his "father") and Pentangeli (his "son"), but of Fredo, his own brother by blood. Fredo has traded information with Roth, but he has also served as the only real father Michael's children have ever known. Michael wins the trust of his partners and underlings only by blackmail, bribery, and the promise of mutual profit. Such trust lasts only as long as it is convenient for all parties, and such relations frequently end in death as well as dissolution. The Corleones' family and community have disintegrated. In the opening scene, the band at Michael's son's first communion party cannot play a tarantella but, under Pentangeli's frustrated urgings, comes up with "Pop Goes the Weasel." In his portrayal of Michael, Coppola draws upon one of the most familiar of ethnic themes—second-generation infidelity—and chastises him accordingly.

The loss of family/ethnicity, coupled with the consummation of Michael's business deals, can mean only one thing: Michael has Americanized. The Corleone empire has become, as Hyman Roth says, "bigger than General Motors and AT&T." But it has cost Michael and his people their inheritance. It is an old story, magnificently updated. By the end of film, Coppola will have used Michael to restage Abraham Cahan's *Rise of David Levinsky*, outfitting the Russian Jewish merchant as a 1970s CEO in Sicilian garb. Like Levinsky, Michael trades his roots for rubles. The film exploits that peculiarly American paranoia of cultural and social orphanhood amidst fortune and fame. Isaac Rosenfeld wrote of Cahan's novel, "it is . . . an exemplary treatment of one of the dominant myths of American capitalism—that the millionaire finds nothing but emptiness at the top of the heap."[29] Reviewing *Godfather II* in *Commentary*, William Pechter concluded that Michael was "another instance of that unrevivably exhausted cliché: it's lonely at the top."[30]

In comparison, Michael's father had found the top of his heap quite rewarding:

> And even Don Corleone, that most modest of men, could not help feeling a sense of pride. He was taking care of his world, his people. He had not failed those who depended on him and gave him the sweat of their brows, risked their freedom and their lives in his service. (215)

At the end of the original narrative, Michael has lost his brother Sonny and the enforcer Luca Brasi to the five-family war; his *capo-regime* Tessio and brother-in-law Carlo Rizzi to treachery; and, possibly, his sister Connie, because of Carlo. But a new family regime coalesces around him: his mother, his new wife Kay, Fredo, Tom Hagen, Clemenza and his men, the new *capo* Rocco Lampone and his men, and Albert Neri. In Puzo's *Godfather,* family and business work in tandem, although with no guarantee of perfect profits or perfect harmony; not so in *Godfather II.*

Ironically, *Godfather II* would seem to have been more hospitable than the original narrative to the twin appetites identified by Cawelti, Jameson, and other critics. Formal analysis suggests that if Americans in the 1970s needed to vent rage at capitalism or to fantasize about ethnic solidarity, then *Godfather II* would have been the better vehicle for doing it. In the original story, the "mirror-image corporate capitalism" thesis is compromised, as Stanley Kaufmann notes, by the unconventional "blood-bonds of loyalty" in the Mafia.[31] In *Godfather II,* those bonds are broken, and Michael Corleone's operations are identified as mainstream, big-time capitalism. In the original story, the Corleones' criminal enterprise compromises nostalgia about the Italian-American family. In *Godfather II,* the linear narrative of assimilation feeds a yearning for a time when the Sicilian family withstood the ravages of individualism, personal greed, and the capitalist dynamic. Intermittent flashbacks bathe the youth and young manhood of Vito Corleone (played by Robert De Niro) in sepia light: a time when an ascent into murder, thievery, and extortion was justifiable, in Sicily and in Hell's Kitchen at least, on the grounds of supporting a family and protecting the neighborhood. For the *Godfather* television specials and subsequent multivideo "epic," Coppola recut the two films into chronological order (Vito's early days from *Part II,* Vito's maturity and Michael's rise from *Part I,* Michael's maturity from *Part II*), neatly literalizing this romantic revision.

The professional film community—from directors to actors to critics—gave *Godfather II* rave reviews, hailing it as a sign that Hollywood could still produce art and rewarding the movie with the "Best Picture" Oscar for 1974. Yet the public reacted with surprising indifference, especially given the unparalleled success of the novel and first film as well as the usual appetite for sequels. William Pechter accurately noted at the time, "I know of no one except movie critics who likes *Part II* as much as part one."[32] Public coldness to *Godfather II* has, if anything, deepened over the years. Curiosity brought millions into the theaters to see *Godfather II* the first time around, but most viewers told their friends not to bother, nor did they return for a second showing. America's notorious disdain for unhappy endings may account for the unpopularity of the film. Yet, having said so, we still need to specify what, after all, makes Michael's conquest over his enemies, both Hyman Roth and the Senate Investigation Commission, so unsatisfying for so many.

If *Godfather II* reasserts in unmistakable terms an antithesis between ethnic familial solidarity and success in capitalist enterprise, then perhaps the unpopularity of the film signals, in part, a resistance to this delusive dichotomy. Many intellectuals favor the film because they cling to the idea of a naturalistic, precapitalistic family. But most other Americans increasingly believe in the compatibility between family values (which ethnics are now thought to epitomize) and the capitalist system. The original narrative promotes changing expectations; the sequel disappoints them. Certainly, the general audience resents the condescension in *Godfather II*: Coppola assumes he must strip the Corleones of all redeeming value in order to communicate the social costs of their megalomania. Moviegoers are unhappy less with the villainy of Michael's empire, which they acknowledge, than with the film's underlying regressive sociology: that the breakup of family life is a necessary precondition for syndicate expansion. We no longer tend to underestimate the compatibility of the ethnic family and capitalism. Rather we now overestimate, and hence romanticize, the growth potential and structural flexibility of the ethnic family business. In the final analysis, *Godfather II* strips the original narrative of its populist sociology, returning to the well-worn conventions of up-from-the-ghetto novels. In *Prizzi's Honor*, on the other hand, Richard Condon restores the Mafia genre to its original source of strength, the icon of family-business. In doing so, he creates a parody of Puzo's novel that is also an interrogation of the business of family.[33]

Prizzi's Honor, like *The Godfather*, begins with a wedding as an occasion to bring the Prizzis together and explain the structure of their syndicate and their relations with other families:

Corrado Prizzi's granddaughter was married before the baroque altar of Santa Grazia di Traghetto, the

lucky church of the Prizzi family. . . . Don Corrado
Prizzi, eighty-four, sat on the aisle in the front pew,
right side of the church. . . . Beside Don Corrado
sat his eldest son, Vincent, father of the bride, a cu-
bically heavy man. . . . Beside Vincent was his
brother, Eduardo, and his third "natural" wife,
Baby. . . . Directly behind Don Corrado sat Angelo
Partanna, his oldest friend and the family's counselor. . . . Behind the first two rows on the right
side of the church, captured like pheromones in the
thickening smell of hundreds of burning beeswax
candles, in serried ranks, row upon row, were
lesser Prizzis, one more Partanna [Charley], and
many, many Sesteros and Garrones.[34]

Men from these four families—Prizzis, Partannas, Sesteros,
and Garrones—constitute the upper levels of the Prizzi organization.

On the inside cover of the hardcover (immediately following
the epigraph page of the Berkley paperback), the web of command is diagrammed in a chart reminiscent of Francis A. J.
Ianni's breakdown of the Lupullo family. This structural dia-
gram combines genealogy with company organization, suggesting that not only corporate leadership but the relation
between the units themselves is familial. A web of marriage
unites the Prizzis with other Mafia families. "Heavily larded
among them were relatives from most of the principal families
of the fratellanza in the United States. Sal Prizzi had married
Virgi Licamarito, sister of Augie "Angles" Licamarito, Boss of
the Detroit Family" (12). Condon explains the system of "profitable repair" operating between the Prizzis and the noncriminal
sector of society—"the New York City Police Department . . .
the multinational conglomerates, the Papal Nuncio, the national union leaders, . . . the best and brightest minds of the
media, the district attorney's office, the attorney general's office, and the White House staff"—all of whom are represented
at the wedding (12–13). To an even greater degree than Puzo,
with more irony yet more telling detail, Condon explicates the
mechanisms of power, responsibility, cash flow, and production: precisely how the semiretired Don, counselor Angelo

Partanna, boss Vincent (chief operating officer), underboss Charley, who is in disfavor with Vincent but not with the Don, are related; how Eduardo heads up the legitimate side of their operations, which does the laundering for the rackets; in what ways the Prizzis differ from other Mafia crime outfits; and so forth. "They took a poll and sixty-seven percent of the American people think that what they all call the Mafia is the most efficiently run business organization in the whole country," quips one of Condon's characters (122).

At times in *The Godfather*, Puzo's narrative commentary suggests a tongue-in-cheek guide to the manners and mores of the Mafia. *Prizzi's Honor* serves the Mafia as Lisa Birnbach's *Preppy Handbook* serves the old-boy, old-money networks of the Northeast. Although the Prizzis call themselves a brotherhood, *fratellanza*, they do not mean a coterie of equals but a male hierarchy: "You must obey your superiors, to death if necessary, without question," swears the initiate, "for it will be for the good of the brotherhood" (43). The Prizzis operate as a unit both in their personal and their business lives. Decisions are controlled from the top and always with a mind to "Prizzi's honor." The characterization of the main protagonist, Charley Partanna (played by Jack Nicholson in the film) personifies the system. In the opening scenes of the film, we see in quick succession, Charley's birth and baptism, the brass knuckles he is given for a birthday present as a boy, and his blood rite initiation into the Prizzis. Charley's father is Don Corrado's *consigliere*.[35] Charley is the Don's godson. Charley calls Don Corrado "*padrino*" ("little father"), a diminutive meaning "godfather." At seventeen, Charley becomes a "made" man in the family; in his thirties, he becomes the enforcer and underboss; in his mid-forties, he becomes heir apparent to the family, after the Don's son Vincent (Domenic in the film) and the Don himself. "As we protect you, so you must protect Prizzi Honor" is the Mafia creed (42). There is no functional distinction, as the Prizzis understand it, between Charley's "birth" into the Prizzis and his "initiation" into it. From birth he has been destined to be, in turn, a dependent of this clan, a soldier, its chief executive in charge of security, and ultimately boss and don. "Both men, father and son, had been bred to serve their feudal lords" (53). There is no more distinction between

Charley's biological descent and cultural election than there is between the familial and professional nature of the Prizzi organization.

Condon focuses throughout the novel on the interdependence of family and business, the personal and the professional, basing his comedy on the tensions between them. No pretense of separation is maintained. Boss Vincent resents underboss Charley for a scandal caused by his own daughter, Maerose, so Vincent does not deal through Charley, as custom dictates, but through his father, Angelo. The personal penetrates the professional, and vice versa. Business is conducted in homes as well as offices, and frequently over meals. Don Corrado lives in a grand old city mansion, "as befitted a business executive," but owns neither the home nor any of its contents, out of respect for both "the rules of humility and austerity" and the diligence of the Internal Revenue Service. Don Corrado's house is his business quarters. The lack of private lives is underscored by the virtual absence of women within the inner sanctum of the Prizzi family, a literalization of both Mafia mythology and Puzo's narrative precedent.[36]

The structural hierarchy, male bonding, and Sicilian cult of honor provide the context for the action of the novel. On the level of plot, *Prizzi's Honor* has much in common with *The Godfather*, including: a botched caper that exposes the Prizzis to hostile maneuvers by the other New York families and leads to a crisis of managerial/familial succession; familial doublecrosses, with Charley acting Michael's role as the prodigal son who temporarily turns against the family; and a murderous resolution that brings the appointed heir to power, restores the primacy of the crime organization, and resolidifies the nuclear and extended family of the new Don. The details in Condon's novel and in Huston's film echo those of Puzo and Coppola in an amusing game of one-upmanship. Both works begin with a wedding, but Puzo and Coppola produce an ad man's fantasy of a Sicilian garden party while Condon and Huston produce a credible representation of an actual Brooklyn wedding: the women dressed in black, not white; a VFW hall rather than a garden; Sinatra tunes as well as old folk songs; and so forth. Condon not only refines the cultural milieu of *The Godfather*, he develops a brilliant plot conceit that highlights and at the same time satirizes the family-business mentality of the Prizzis.

Prizzi's Honor is, in the words of a *Playboy* reviewer, "the best episode of *As the Underworld Turns* since Puzo's *Fool's Die*."[37] The reference to the soap opera is not gratuitous, since the action of *Prizzi's Honor* involves a problem marriage between its central characters, Charley and Irene (née Maida Walcewicz) Walker, who is a free-lance assassin, or "contractor," in the occasional employ of the Prizzis. Charley and Irene's marriage violates the sanctity of the Prizzis' family business. Irene is a Catholic Pole whose former husband (murdered by Charley on orders from the Don) is a Russian Jew. "How come you aren't a wop and I meet you at Teresa Prizzi's wedding?" asks Charley, who falls in love and marries her against that logic (33). Irene's non-Italian background is a symbol for her real outsider status. "You and this woman see everything with the same kind of eyes," Maerose tells Charley, knowing better and setting Charley up for a fall (96). True, both Charley and Irene kill people for the mob; otherwise, though, their operations are like night and day. "Let's see how it goes," warns Angelo. "A mixed marriage" (144).

The film plays up the comedy of middle-class manners between Charley, an Italian chauvinist, and Irene, who wants to keep working after marriage. In the novel, Irene's sexual autonomy is, quite explicitly, a corollary of her independence in the marketplace of crime. Irene is a loner, a one-woman company, an entrepreneur whose approach to business exemplifies the norms of a free market:

> The fantastic thing about Charley was that he *was* a Boy Scout. Charley paid his dues to his life. Charley believed. . . . Charley knew he was serving a purpose, not a buck. . . . It was different for [Irene]. . . . She wasn't locked into any family, she was a straight, commercial freelance who couldn't expect any protection from anybody if she didn't do the job right. (117–18)

While Charley is a *sotto-capo*, Irene is a *contractor*. The idiom is perfect. Irene makes deals independently, strictly on a cash

basis, accepting no retainer and maintaining no ties to any particular outfit. As a cover, Irene is a tax consultant. To her the
world operates simply as the circulation of dollars; loyalty is
simply a matter of the origin of the next paycheck. She is therefore the perfect foil to a family-business mentality.

Just prior to the denouement of the novel, the Prizzis appear
to be in shambles. No money is coming in, the Filargi caper has
soured, and the other families are maneuvering to take over
the entire business. Vincent has been assassinated, and
Charley is turning traitor. The Prizzis suffer as the Corleones
suffer after Sonny's death. Condon resolves the crisis by
duplicating one strand of *The Godfather*'s narrative logic, turning the family over to the rightful heir—in this case, Charley.
Don Corrado offers Charley the position of boss, second in
command, with the promise that he will become don after Don
Corrado's death. The Prizzis need Charley, yet Charley needs
to earn that promotion. Charley must repair the family's relations with the other syndicates and with the police; and, in the
dual logic that organizes these narratives, Charley must prove
his fidelity to the family. The price is steep: he must deliver
Irene to the cops himself—dead. The borderline in Charley's
decision is clearly demarcated. Will he honor his contract with
Irene or the Prizzis' ethic of familial loyalty?

"The family were what he had been since Sicily started
breeding people. They were his food. They had been with him
forever. There were hundreds of thousands of them, most of
them ghosts, some of them bodies. They were all staring at
him, waiting to know what he would do" (296). The weight of
all the Prizzi tradition, his respect for his *padrino* and father
who are waiting for his decision, and Charley's training and
dreams overdetermine the decision:

> He thought of becoming Boss of the Prizzi family.
> His entire life had pointed him toward that. He had
> trained for that since he was thirteen years old and
> now it could happen. He could feel the power as if it
> were the texture of fine, strong cloth between his
> fingers. He could taste it as if his mother had come
> back to cook one more glorious meal for him. He
> thought of the money . . . eight million dollars a

year, every dime tax free, every dime safe in
Switzerland. (269)

Becoming boss means filling his father's shoes, his mother's
expectations: family is money is destiny when you are born
into the Prizzis. Eight million dollars and Mom's home cooking, too! In *Prizzi's Honor* as in *The Godfather*, the working out of
the Oedipal crisis prompts the return of the prodigal son and
the reintegration of the crime family. Charley's quest for power
follows the path of filial obedience; the strength of the Prizzis
depends on Charley's urgency to obey. Being asked to become
don is for Charley, as it was for Michael, an offer he can't refuse.

Charley sets Irene up for the kill by telling her that the Don
accepted her terms of settlement, paying all she asked. Irene
knows that Charley is lying, because the Don would never
settle the Las Vegas score by returning the money she stole
from the Prizzis. She considers the love match canceled. In ac-
cordance with her own methods, she prepares to kill him,
transmuting the marriage contract into a murder contract in
her mind: "She didn't feel the grief anymore. Charley was a
contract she had put out herself, and had given to herself; full
fee" (305). In contrast to Irene's cold-bloodedness, Charley
feels the righteous conviction of Prizzi duty. Irene

> had a different, much paler, thinner meaning when
> he judged her beside the total meaning he got from
> his family. He was now Boss of the family. He had to
> set an example that would be remembered as long
> as the family stood. He saw dimly that it was right to
> sacrifice the woman he loved so that the family
> could go on and on fulfilling its honor, which was
> its meaning. He suddenly saw clearly that Irene had
> stepped so far out of line that there was nothing left
> to do but to whack her. (300)

Charley kills Irene before Irene is able to kill him. Charley wins
not because he is technically more proficient or luckier but because he has the emotion of Prizzi honor motivating him and
the full force of the Prizzi clan backing him up.

However much the business of family causes friction (the

"grinding, double-crossing mass of their families"), still there is a corporate front (103). Irene dies because she stands alone, without a family, without protection. The structural equivalent in *The Godfather* is the death of Carlo Rizzi, kin by marriage, but an outsider, a traitor. At the end of each novel, the integrity of the crime family is reinstated by sacrificing a "family" member whose membership had been suspect in the first place and compromised by that member's activities. The murder of Irene is also an ironic footnote, highlighted in the film, on the conventions of romantic love so favored in American popular culture.

"The surprise ending will knock your reading glasses off!" runs a blurb on the paperback, credited to the *New York Times*. Yet the elimination of Irene, and the fact that Charley has to do it, is a perfect culmination for a novel that insists on playing feudal capitalism off against free-market independence. Charley and Irene could have fled the Prizzis together to Hong Kong, where they would be outfitted with new identities (Irene's past misdeeds, and the current difficulties with the police, preclude Irene's remaining with the family). This alternative ending would require a conversion in Charley's character, to the point where he could see himself turning his back on history for autonomy and romantic love. But at least such an ending would remain true to the hypothesis of the narrative—namely, that feudal capitalism, which dominates the American underworld, operates by sacrificing individualism to the group. Readers and film viewers are surprised because they expect a dreamy ending in which Charley gets his family and Irene too. Such an ending, however, violates the business of family in the world of the Prizzis. The principle of family honor precludes romantic love because romance presumes a free-market logic of one-to-one relationships. In the film, the overlay of Rossini and the casting of Nicholson as Charley tips expectations in the direction of a romanticized ending. To conclude with Charley as the don, while still happily married to Irene, would be to entertain a fantasy of irreconcilables (of the sort characteristically misattributed by scholars to *The Godfather*). In the final chapter, Charley calls up Maerose, initiating their reconciliation. Maerose and Charley are now both outcasts who have returned to the family. Maerose's claim on

Charley is ethnic. As she reminds him in the film, "We grew up together, Charley. We are the same people." By marrying Maerose, Charley reunites the Prizzis and Partannas in the incestuous bond that maintains the power of their family.

As Puzo does in *The Godfather*, Condon makes it clear from start to finish that *the* theme to be pursued in a Mafia narrative is the question of business and family. Condon's comedy is effective because we, as readers, already understand the structural interdependence of business and family in the Mafia, and we accept it as basic truth. Whereas Puzo insinuates tragedy through narrative irony, Condon adds layer upon layer of satire, usually comic but occasionally courting a grimmer dimension as well. From start to finish, Puzo eliminates no more than a dozen or so mobsters, who deserve it anyway. Condon burns down the Palermo Gardens nightclub, leaving eighty-nine people dead, 217 severely burned, and four blinded, most of them innocent guests and "civilians." Condon also corners his main character into killing his wife.

Both *Godfather II* and *Prizzi's Honor* submit the Mafia to moral scrutiny. *Godfather II* depends on a romanticized ideology of family for its critique, so that Coppola, in the final analysis, is caught within a family-business hermeneutic circle. *Prizzi's Honor* adopts a position truly contrary to that of the family-business mentality: it assumes, in the figure of Irene, the possibility of a free marketplace, in which individuals function independent of one another and the realm of the personal is uncluttered by the operations of business. In so doing, Condon (like Puzo in the novel) is able to question the naïveté of free-market spokesmen and ethnic romantics, who think that the domain of "family" and the "group" are extraeconomic. But Condon pushes his point ever further than Puzo in *The Godfather* or Coppola in *Godfather II:* he charts the special costs of doing business familially.

In *Prizzi's Honor*, the family business exceeds its members' need for wealth, annexing their freedom to its own dynamic, the growth of the syndicate. "Money, beyond a point that they had left long before, was only grease for the chariot" (103). The Prizzi organization empowers its members, but it also imprisons them, psychologically and literally. While more legitimate forms of family business may not police their boundaries with quite the brutality of the Prizzis, they may not prosper to such a degree either. In *The Godfather,* the Corleones' loss of individual liberty, however implicit, is buried beneath the glorification of familial loyalty, whereas Condon's carefully developed "surprise" ending etches in the popular consciousness a nightmarish image of familial tyranny: Charley hurling a knife into Irene's throat, from their marriage bed.

As an analysis of the mechanics of family capitalism and a critique of its appeal, *Prizzi's Honor* supersedes *The Godfather.* Saying this, however, is not to forget that Puzo paved the way for Condon's accomplishment. Puzo is often maligned for exploiting the stereotype of Italian-American criminality, which has long been used to discriminate against the general Italian-American population. But, in the final analysis, *The Godfather* does not so much rehash an old tale, whatever its strands of inheritance, as tell a new one. In *The Godfather,* Puzo refashions the gangster genre into a vehicle for overturning the traditional antithesis between ties of blood and the American marketplace. He thus transforms the stock character of the Italian-American outlaw into the representative super(business)man, and transforms the lingering image of immigrant huddled masses into the first family of American capitalism.

2

"Working Ourselves Up": Middle-Class Realism and the Reproduction of Patriarchy in *Bread Givers*

From 1920 through 1932, Anzia Yezierska, an American Jew of Russian-Polish origin, produced four novels, two collections of short fiction, and dozens of miscellaneous sketches, reviews, and occasional pieces. All of her books relied heavily on conventions of immigrant realism and were promoted as insider's guides to "how the other half lives."[1] She was awarded a national literary prize, front-page reviews, audiences in Europe with Joseph Conrad and Gertrude Stein, and a year as writer-in-residence at the University of Wisconsin. Her more energetic promoters included short-story czar Edmund J. O'Brien, syndicated columnist Frank Crane, Yale professor William Lyon Phelps, and fellow novelists Zona Gale and Dorothy Canfield Fisher; her publishers included the nation's most distinguished house, Houghton Mifflin, and one of its most innovative, Boni and Liveright.[2] Samuel Goldwyn made two of her books into films, paying handsomely and giving her significant billing.

Despite Yezierska's reputation as "the recognized mouthpiece of New York's Jewish East Side," sales of her books were disappointingly low, and critical reception became increasingly antagonistic, especially among those with competing claims to ethnic authority.[3] From the beginning, it had been easy to assume that her fiction primarily served the purposes of minority protest and self-congratulation, and soon would be outdated. In 1925, a coterie of Jewish-American men—Alter Brody, Samson Raphaelson, Yosef Gaer, and Johan Smertenko—lambasted *Bread Givers* as yet another up-from-the-ghetto tract. They found it cartoonish in plot and characterization, assimilationist in drive, anti-Semitic in effect if not in intent.[4]

During the later years of the Depression, anthologizers working to document America's oppressed masses often chose one of Yezierska's shorter pieces. At the same time, her novels disappeared from circulation, and the new Jewish-American intelligentsia, if it remembered her at all, consigned her work to its ghetto past. "They were not really good stories," explained Irving Howe.[5]

In the early 1970s, however, when scholars began searching our literary archives for documents of immigrant experience, Yezierska was proclaimed a major rediscovery, and *Bread Givers* was hailed as her finest text.[6] Scholars today continue to argue that Yezierska's writing merits renewed attention. They locate her work at the juncture where Russian Jewish migration, women's experience, and labor history meet, that is, in a terrain of authentic otherness removed from the dominant culture by ethnicity, gender, and class.[7] In returning *Bread Givers* to print, editor Alice Kessler-Harris writes that Yezierska's novel is more revealing of the complexities of triple marginality than anything else now available: "she offers unparalleled ability to bring life to a neglected aspect of Yiddish culture, plunging us directly into the woman's experience of immigration."[8] In this formulation, Yezierska's partisans resuscitate and politicize her original sponsorship, in which her fiction was advertised for showing "immigrant life in the raw—as it really is to-day."[9]

The reception, both laudatory and skeptical, of Yezierska's prose has been almost entirely a function of the cult of Lower East Side authenticity that enveloped her in the 1920s and continues to frame our portrait of her. Proclaimed as a rags-to-literary-riches heroine, "the Cinderella of the Tenements," Yezierska took center stage at press banquets in her honor, spun fantastic accounts of herself for the Sunday color supplements of East Coast tabloids and national magazines, and even played the role of screenwriter-starlet for the publicity machinery of Goldwyn's Hollywood. It was not the immigrant fiction that commanded attention, then, but the immigrant writer herself: Yezierska as the unassimilated "Russian Jewess," fairygodmothered into professional authorship as if she had not left the Lower East Side at all. The recurrent invocation of Cinderella notwithstanding, the most crucial contribution to the mythology of Yezierska was her pretense, tirelessly reiterated, that the transition from the Lower East Side to Washington Square involved nothing more than a short afternoon stroll.[10]

Yezierska was born, around 1880 (to the best of her biographers' reconstruction), in a town called Ploch, along the Vistula River in the Polish part of Russia. As a young child, she emigrated with her family to the neighborhood of Hester Street. As "Hattie Mayer," she worked the pushcarts and the garment shops, encountering English in the streets, in the factories, and under the less-than-ideal conditions of night school.[11] Yezierska left the Lower East Side at age twenty; her second published story, "Fat of the Land," gained her national recognition when she was thirty-nine. Absent in Yezierska's accounts of herself are a dozen years of middle-class experience: college, teaching in the public schools, marriage, and motherhood. Absent, too, are a half-dozen years of apprenticeship in the business of writing, during which she courageously acquired, late in her life but ahead of her time, rooms of her own.

In 1900, having finagled a scholarship in domestic science to Columbia Teacher's College, Yezierska entered what she called "the uptown ghetto" of Riverside Drive and the Bronx suburbs, where successful immigrants and especially their children took up the professions and pastimes of American modernity. Four years later, graduation and certification as a cooking instructor won Yezierska the interim independence of the college-educated. Frustrated by teaching, she turned away from the horizon of "new womanhood" and toward the temptations of upscale domesticity, parlaying her education into two "enviable" marriages: the first in 1910 to a prosperous lawyer, Jacob Gordon, who sued for and won annulment; the second in 1911 to Gordon's best friend Arnold Levitas, a school principal and author of textbooks, with whom she lived for several years and with whom she had her only child.

In the mid-1910s, Yezierska began positioning herself to become a writer. She left the security of her marriage, breaking the bonds of the oldest of conventions by leaving her daughter to the care of Levitas. In 1918, she talked her way into a graduate seminar taught by John Dewey, possibly the country's foremost intellectual, who fell in love with her. Dewey gave Yezierska her first typewriter, employed her as translator on a sociology project among Polish Jews in Philadelphia, and insisted that she transfer the focus of her literary ambitions from Emersonian philosophy to East Side testimonials.[12] On the strength of a single published manuscript, she gained admission to Dorothy Scarborough's creative writing classes at Columbia, where she drafted the stories that soon would appear in *The New Republic, The Nation, Scribner's,* and so forth.

Although biographers have begun to analyze the catch-22s of Yezierska's self-promotion in the 1920s, no critic seems to have recognized the dangers of resurrecting that mystique in our own time. With the publication of both Mary V. Dearborn's *Love in the Promised Land: The Story of Anzia Yezierska and John Dewey* and Louise Levitas Henricksen's account of her mother, *Anzia Yezierska: A Writer's Life,* in 1988, Yezierska comes before us once again as a starlet, implicated in a tragic love affair with a famous man, now memorialized by the neglected but adoring daughter.[13] That is, she comes before us not as a novelist whose work compels our scrutiny but as an ethnic literary personality whose encounter with America is the better story.

Following seminal work by Carol Schoen and Jo Ann Boydston, Dearborn and Henricksen have filled the gaps that Yezierska left open, at times making effective use of the autobiographical resonances in her fiction. But using Yezierska's fiction to reconstruct her life is not the same as using her life to reorient our approach to her fiction. The neglected "middle" of Yezierska's life, so flagrantly absent from interview and autobiography, resurfaces in her most important fiction, especially in the novels. *Salome of the Tenements* (1923) depicts the 1905 marriage of Yezierska's close friend, Rose Pastor, another former denizen of the Lower East Side; *Arrogant Beggar* (1927) is set in the charity world she experienced during her Columbia years and later; and *All I Could Never Be* (1932) focuses on Dewey and the Philadelphia sociology project. For all that Yezierska's other novels have to tell us about Jewish America during this period, however, in *Bread Givers* she fictionalized the most significant, because most representative, forms of her uptown life.

Yezierska divides *Bread Givers* into three sections (she calls them books)—"Hester Street," "Between Two Worlds," and "The New World"—thereby underscoring that her heroine Sara Smolinsky does indeed, in the course of the novel, escape from the downtown ghetto. In fact, Sara rises, or is offered the opportunity to rise, four times. In book 1, Sara's employment in her family's suburban grocery story reflects Yezierska's exposure to that classic path of limited mobility, petty entrepreneurship. In book 2, Sara's engagement to a real estate magnate offering leisure and conspicuous consumption draws upon, among other sources, Yezierska's short marriage to Jacob Gordon. Bridging books 2 and 3, Sara's march from night school to ivy-walled college to salaried teaching replays, in schematic and glorified form, Yezierska's education and entry into the professions. At the close of the novel, Sara's proposal for a new kind of domesticity, one in which she and the principal of her school dedicate themselves to both a partnership of the mind and a renewal of their attachments to family and faith, is clearly modeled on Yezierska's longer tie to Levitas. The arena of conflict for all but the opening moments of the novel are the developing institutions of the Jewish middle classes, institutions allied with if not embedded within those of more established Americans. The point here is not to delineate the concordances and discordances between Yezierska's actual experience and its subsequent fictionalization—we may never have enough biographical information for that—but to challenge the still-prevailing identification of *Bread Givers* as solely an "other half" novel.

A dominant current in *Bread Givers* is protest against the pain, fears, and frustrations faced by those who emigrated as part of the Eastern European proletariat. The novel protests, above all, against poverty. It opens with the Smolinskys facing the threat of eviction: "I already saw all our things kicked out on the side-walk like a pile of junk. A plate of pennies like a beggar's hand reaching out of our bunch of rags. Each sigh of pity from the passers-by, each penny thrown into the plate was another stab into our burning shame."[14] To her credit, Yezierska insists that not all immigrants and their offspring had the opportunity to escape the round of work and worry on the Lower East Side (witness the eldest sister), that those who were able to fight often faced hunger or worse along the way (witness Sara's pursuit of an education), and that even those who did achieve a modicum of earning power risked losing such means in old age (witness Smolinsky's situation after his wife's death).[15] Far less nostalgically than Mike Gold, Yezierska underscores the fact that there were and remain "Jews without money," which was and remains an important qualifying footnote to the larger historical record.

Yet I believe there is more to *Bread Givers* than the protest that meets the eye. Despite its anti-Semitic potential, the identification of Jews with precocious achievement carries a truth of great relevance not only for the social history of the United States but also for its literature. If the mainstream realism of the Gilded Age can be characterized as an inquiry into the formation of the middle class, then the kind of immigrant realism that developed later must be understood as an inquiry into the contribution ethnicity has made to the triumphant reformation of that middle class. In its earliest forms, ethnic realism included texts by representatives of other admirably successful groups, such as O. E. Rolvaag's classic trilogy about Lutheran Norwegians, but the best circulated and most influential texts were by the offspring of Jews: Cahan's *Rise of David Levinsky,* the generational epics of Daniel Fuchs and Meyer Levin, as well as the inspirational autobiographies of Mary Antin, Marcus Ravage, and Ludwig Lewisohn. Among these Jewish novels were the works of Yezierska, especially *Bread Givers* in its more mysterious and vexing dimensions.

During the 1980s, a wave of revisionist scholarship sharpened appreciation of realism as a response to the deep transformations of the Gilded Age, especially the transfer of cultural authority from family to corporation, the transfer of women's energies from home-based production and wage labor to household management and competitive consumption, and the advent of a professional-managerial system that sped the divorce of public and private, shifted emphasis from skills to accreditation, and plunged individuals headlong into marketing themselves.[16] Despite the seminal accomplishments of William Dean Howells, Kate Chopin, and Theodore Dreiser, and despite the claims of her modernist peers, Yezierska intuited that the realist chapter on modern American culture had not been closed. For Yezierska recognized that new populations with legacies and agendas of their own were encountering American institutions and their attendant problems for the first time. In portraying her "own people," she saw her duty as going beyond immigrant protest; she needed to investigate the reciprocal reshaping taking place between Eastern European folk Judaism and twentieth-century American structures of opportunity.

Because life among upwardly mobile second-generation Jews still felt Jewish, hence neither entirely different nor radically "free," Yezierska assumed that she hadn't really made it, that she hadn't found "the real America." Meanwhile, diverse combinations of economic ascendency and ethnic persistence were transforming Anglo-Saxon middle America into a transnational mosaic. In narrating the search for real Americans and the quest for Emersonian self-determination, Yezierska was able to explore, sotto voce, the competing pathways through which Russian-Polish Jews were making themselves, in the words of social historian Deborah Dash Moore, "at home in America."[17] In *Bread Givers*, Yezierska paid particular attention to what the varieties of "incorporation" within the United States meant for immigrant daughters.

Both in print and in off-the-record conversation, scholars have continued to testify to Yezierska's unparalleled capacity to speak for Russian Jewish women, especially the generation of immigrants, only to qualify their enthusiasm by affirming some version of the long-standing judgment on her fiction: it may be important history, but it's not really literature. The most frequent criticism is that the high pitch of emotion animating Yezierska's narrative voice marks it as irrevocably unreflective, albeit touching in its "defenselessness" and "helpless candor."[18] To demonstrate how *Bread Givers* is *not* transparent is to demonstrate why it is not innocuous and why it is anything but unthinking. When read as an inquiry on behalf of upscale daughters, the novel takes us down unexplored pathways of ethnic self-knowledge. What makes *Bread Givers* worth rereading, to my mind, is its irreverence, which is to say, its chutzpah.

In the "Hester Street" section of *Bread Givers*, Sara Smolinsky narrates three events as the stepping stones in her coming of age as the youngest of four girls in the Smolinsky household. First, her father, Reb Smolinsky, a Talmudic scholar and would-be instructor of Hebrew, is tried and acquitted for assaulting his landlord's collection agent, becoming a local hero whose reputation promotes the family boardinghouse. Second, Smolinsky interdicts the love affairs of his three eldest daughters, arranges marriages for two of them through a traditional matchmaker, then brokers the marriage of his third daughter himself, pocketing a combined finder's fee and bride-price. Finally, he purchases a suburban grocery store, only to discover that he has been swindled, yet, with his wife and Sara, he eventually makes a going proposition of the store. Given that *Bread Givers* has been celebrated almost exclusively for its representation of its narrator, the self-willed Sara, we need to ask why Yezierska focuses so obsessively on the father in the first third of the novel. If we wish to presume that Smolinsky embodies the heritage of Orthodox Jewish patriarchy against which Sara must struggle, then we need to ask why Yezierska represents that culture not in terms of the scholar at work but rather in terms of a courtroom melodrama, the brokering of a daughter, and ethnic family (greengrocer) capitalism.

The three events of "Hester Street" tell the story of the family's modest progress from poverty to varying forms of security, especially petit-bourgeois security. Whereas Sara's mother is a vocal advocate of pursuing prosperity, and all four daughters contribute to and benefit from the process, it is Smolinsky who dictates (with increasing enthusiasm) the methods of what Bessie, the eldest daughter, calls " 'working ourselves up' " (38). At first with a kind of bumbling luck, then with less fortunate deliberation, Reb Smolinsky seeks to make Orthodox tradition and upscale enterprise mutually supportive: to deploy the patriarchal family and Eastern European folkways in order to run one or another small-scale business as well as to use the activities and profits of such businesses in order to keep the family together, subsidize the Jewish poor, and supply much-needed support for Talmudic studies. Throughout "Hester Street," Sara participates in a profoundly ethnic version of the American dream. In the interstices of *Bread Givers* lies a provocative revision of the up-from-the-ghetto novel, what might be called, after Howells and Cahan, "The Rise of Reb Smolinsky's Family." Whereas Cahan made Silas Lapham a Jew only to deny him his heritage, Yezierska envisions a specifically Eastern European form of success in America and thus raises to the second power the capacity for cultural dissent of the immigrant novel.

To understand what the Smolinskys face in America requires that we understand what happened in Europe. Mrs. Smolinsky was the daughter of a prosperous merchant, evidently nouveau riche, who respected the kind of prestige that only learning could bring. She was given in marriage to a young scholar of renown, who also received from her father a "big dowry," years of room and board, and a handsome deathbed bequest. During the fierce upturn in anti-Semitism of the 1870s and 1880s, pogroms took Jewish lives, robbed Jews of their possessions, and destoyed the sense that, in spite of its restrictions, the Pale of Jewish settlement was at least a temporary home.[19] Several million Jews emigrated, three million to the United States, Reb and Mrs. Smolinsky among them. Not only were Reb and Mrs. Smolinsky stripped of their birthright and European class status, but upon arrival Reb Smolinsky was placed in the seemingly untenable situation of having to support a family while still being committed, body and soul, to his religious-scholarly vocation.

The novel opens an unspecified number of years after the family has emigrated, when Sara is ten years old, when the fight for survival seems further away from being won than ever, and when the family's patience with Reb Smolinsky's devotion is at the breaking point. One Friday evening, as Smolinsky recites the Sabbath devotions, the "collector lady" for his landlord barges into the apartment and demands overdue rent. Annoyed by Smolinsky's excuses and self-absorption, she snaps his Bible shut with such force that it falls "at her feet." Enraged by her sacrilege, "Father slapped the landlady on one cheek, then on the other, till the blood rushed from her nose" (18). As Smolinsky is brought to trial on assault charges, the neighborhood pools funds for "the best American-born lawyer" and rushes into the courtroom to testify and intimidate on Smolinsky's behalf. The defense portrays the accused as a defender of his faith staving off the parasitic capitalist trust, symbolized by the collection agent who is identified metonymically with the landlord. Backing the lawyer's populist eloquence is a crucial piece of evidence: the collection agent's footprint on Reb Smolinsky's Bible. Smolinsky is acquitted and carried home on the shoulders of the crowd, who project their exaltation onto him.

It is disturbing and mysterious that Sara is swept up so uncritically into her father's victory. Mary Dearborn asks: Why does Sara not side with the collection agent who, like herself, is ethnic, female, and working class?[20] The original assault, notes Dearborn, lends itself easily to a feminist reading: invoking the sacred, a Jewish patriarch bloodies a daughter of the faith who is, like his own daughters, merely trying to eke out a living. Why does Yezierska, who elsewhere is so imaginative in exposing Reb Smolinsky's chauvinism, invent the footprint (there is no trace of it in the original scene of assault) and thereby silence the collection agent on his behalf?

In the opening pages of *Bread Givers,* Smolinsky has embraced Judaic asceticism as a stay against the American Protestant interpretation of worldly success as the sign of God's favor. Yet the five women he lives with (who hear stories of more and more learned men abandoning study to make money) have been applying increasing pressure on him to enter the marketplace and do well there: " 'You're so busy working for Heaven that I have to suffer here such bitter hell,' " declares Sara's mother (10). For Smolinsky, women's desire and capitalism have always seemed to pose a threat to the sacred calling. This threat is brought to life when the "agent of capitalism," the impoverished Jewish female, intrudes upon his prayers.

Yezierska designs the courtroom trial as a scene of instruction in which Smolinsky learns a lesson about capitalizing on his reputation as a saintly man among the prodigal. His dedication to the sacred texts may have always been a minor point of honor in the community, but during the trial, because of the timing of the agent's intrusion and the symbolically trodden Bible, it becomes something much more. Crucially, the crowd does not direct its anger toward capitalism per se, but toward the sort of parasitism practiced by the agent (who is said to "insult . . . her own religion") and by the Riverside

Drive landlord, who is compared to a pawnbroker. Whereas the agent and landlord's commitment to capitalism is viewed as working against their people, Smolinsky is hailed for combining his sacred calling with the community's fight against exploitation, marking the latter with the sanction of the former. "Not only did he work for the next world, but he was even fighting for the people their fight in this world" (26). In the aftermath of the courtroom scene, Smolinsky realizes that it may be possible to enter the marketplace as a Jewish patriarch after all, to put his new reputation to profitable use immediately.

Since he settled in the United States, Smolinsky had resisted the temptation to sell his services as a rabbi because he disdained the processes of secularization and modernization, refusing as he puts it, to become "a false prophet to the Americanized Jews" (111). The publicity of his trial permits him to abstract his piety into a lucrative symbol while preserving the rigor of traditional study:

> And so it kept on. And the arguments always ended with, "Long years on Reb Smolinsky to fight the landlords for the people!"
> Soon everybody from all around knew us so well, it got easy for us to rent the front room. First one came, then another, and then a third. . . . Things began to get better with us. (28)

To accommodate more boarders, Smolinsky moves his books out of the front room, their place of honor, into the kitchen. He agrees to this symbolic demotion on the understanding, however, that the women will do the actual work of running the boardinghouse, as they would have in Eastern Europe, leaving him undisturbed to pursue religious study as well as his Jewish men's lodge and his charities. Mrs. Smolinsky complains about the arrangement, the traditional prerogative of Jewish women who sacrificed for their men to such a degree, but she respects her husband's commitments.

The girls, in contrast, are unsympathetic and resentful, their hearts and minds increasingly absorbed by American habits of acquisition and raiment. The production of income permits consumption, which Yezierska portrays as the most important development in the affairs of the Smolinsky household:

> Mother began to fix up the house like other
> people. The instalment man trusted us now. We got
> a new table with four feet that were so solid it
> didn't spill the soup all over the place. Mashah got a
> new looking glass from the second-hand man. . . .
> Mother even bought regular towels. . . . We no
> sooner got used to regular towels than we began to
> want toothbrushes. (28–29)

In the first chapter, older sister Mashah's determination to prettify herself—"like the dressed-up doll from the shop window of the grandest department store" (4)—was depicted as a form of antifamilial selfishness. Now Mrs. Smolinsky, who once "tore her hair" when she found that Mashah had wasted money on a toothbrush, takes the lead in household improvement. At the same time, all the Smolinsky women begin to attend to personal hygiene and appearance—"each for himself like Mashah"—so that consumer-driven individualization receives, paradoxically, the family seal of approval. "More and more we wanted more things," recalls Sara with insight worthy of Dreiser, "and really needed more things the more we got them" (29).

In chapter 7, "Father Becomes a Business Man in America," Yezierska collapses the Smolinskys' ambitions as entrepreneurs and consumers into the single image of buying a grocery store in Elizabeth, New Jersey. On the one hand, the store represents increasing confidence in family business as the pathway into the middle class. On the other hand, the Smolinskys' anticipation of consumption is so mesmerizing that the purchase of the store seems like an end in itself, the first step in an orgy of buying:

> Father began dancing around the store crazy with
> joy. "And such a bargain! Look only around this
> full-packed store! Who would not grab such a
> chance, quick? Think only! Seventy-eight dollars
> and eighty-nine cents in one day! In one week,
> seven times seventy-eight dollars and eighty-nine
> cents. *Shah!* We will have to hire a bookkeeper to
> count up for us all our profits in a year." (116)

The family rapidly conflates the goods they must sell and the goods they wish to buy, the work that affords middle-class consumption and consumption itself. A "bought store" anticipates, prematurely, a "bought house." " 'And with seventy-eight dollars and eighty-nine cents coming in every day,' " Sara chimes in, " 'we'll soon be able to buy a piano and I'll begin to take piano lessons' " (118).

With ownership comes a new aesthetic. Sara's newly minted sense of order is upset by a missing box in the "great pile of oatmeal boxes," which interrupts the clean lines of the "fancy pyramid" she admires (118). When she goes to realign the pyramid, the pyramid tumbles over, instantaneously and with nary a sound. Reb Smolinsky wonders if the boxes marked oatmeal really hold " 'that feathery puffed rice,' " but his wife confirms Sara's startling discovery:

> "Business man! What have you! You got air in your hand," and she tore open the box and held emptiness before Father's eyes.
> "How could they be empty?" said he, puzzled. "Didn't I see him selling them?"
> "Fool!" Mother turned upon him. "Couldn't he have had full ones on the top of the pile to sell from?" . . . And she and I began tearing around the store to examine the stock, while Father stared blankly at us.
> The shelves had goods only in the front row. The whole space behind was empty. . . .
> Half the night we worked to see the extent of the great business deal that Father snatched with such mad haste. (119–20)

Lifted out of context, Yezierska's conceit of "shelves faked with emptiness" and "windows full of dummies" constitutes a merciless visual pun that is once again Dreiserian: Let the newcomer beware; when you buy into America, the boxes may be empty.

In *Bread Givers*, however, it is not consumption in the abstract that trips the Smolinskys up, for Sara and her family enjoy tremendously whatever they buy for themselves or the house. The emptiness of the boxes suggests not the vacuity of the American dream but the cost of participation in it. If there is just enough of Eastern Europe in seventeen-year-old Sara so that she is able to resign herself to her father's minimalist participation in the drudgery of the grocery business, there is enough of the United States in her that she becomes increasingly impatient with him when he does exercise his authority, ineptly and self-righteously, in the store.

It is such an incursion that leads to Sara's departure from Elizabeth, despite the fact that the family is making "a go" of the business. One day Smolinsky ridicules a customer's request for cereal (in Shnipishock, bran was fed to livestock), then castigates Sara for extending two cents of credit to a girl from across the street. Silenced by the double bind of her subordinate position as both daughter and employee, Sara declares that she is going to leave her parents to find work and residence back in New York, by which she means the Lower East Side. When her father rages about the Torah's injunction— " 'only through a man has a woman an existence,' " " 'in olden times the whole city would have stoned you' "—Sara counters with the rhetoric of individualism: " 'Thank God, I'm not living in olden times. Thank God, I'm living in America! . . . I'm going to make my own life!' " (137–38). In their mutual justifications and recriminations, Sara and her father adopt "olden times" and "America" not as cultural essences but as rhetorical positions for negotiating how prosperity is to be earned and its rewards distributed.

Sara talks as though she were just now finding the courage to pursue "an American dream," but, in fact, she has participated for almost half the novel in achieving a still potent (if underrepresented and too little studied) form of upward mobility. Entry into small-scale, family-based retail trades is a strategy of adaptation that Jews and their fellow immigrants in large numbers have begun to seek but which her family is not especially adept at, and that Sara, as the wage labor force without the wages, bitterly resents. She has risen with her parents into the precarious lower reaches of the middle class, but she ultimately decides that the prospect of a piano is not worth the physical and psychological strains of laboring under her father's rule.

Abrupt and histrionic, Sara's departure from home initiates

a chain of ambitious alliances—from her sisters to a real estate magnate to one of her professors, and so on—reminiscent of Sister Carrie's march from Minnie to Drouet to Hurstwood to Ames. At first glance, Sara's self-reorientation may seem even more capricious and compulsive than Carrie's, but a careful review of Carrie's upward wanderlust reveals just how tutored and strategic Sara's decisions actually are. Carrie drives herself from lover to lover through recurring acts of consuming vision, what Rachel Bowlby terms "just looking."[21] Carrie becomes dissatisfied with her current state of affairs only after taking a look around and discovering a higher step on the social ladder. For Sara, unrest precedes the look around. Invariably, at each stage in her progress, Sara's gaze is focused precisely on where she is at the moment. Carrie moves forward because something calls to her—that "vast persuasion"—as being better than what she already has. Sara moves forward because she has discovered the limits of the social arrangements in which she currently is embedded; in subsequently scouting around, she identifies alternative forms of mobility that will allow her to address these new concerns.

Paradoxically, Sara's desire is both less and more of what Philip Fisher calls "anticipatory" than Carrie's.[22] Sara's desire is less anticipatory because it is stimulated by a critical insight into the present. It is more anticipatory because Sara embarks on new endeavors, not, like Carrie, in a vague quest for happiness but in an attempt to ameliorate quite specific forms of social oppression—poverty, professional isolation, the culture of consumption that threatens to consume Carrie, and, of course, various forms of patriarchy.

Since the early 1970s, students of *Bread Givers* have stressed its uncompromising critique of Jewish patriarchy. Carol Schoen writes that Sara "succeed[s] in making her break from the Old World past" because she learns to challenge her father's "right under Jewish law to control her." Alice Kessler-Harris notes that Yezierska "freed herself from a tradition few of her countrywomen could ignore in that first generation, and she did it against the heaviest odds."[23] When critics praise *Bread Givers* for undermining Jewish "tradition," they turn our attention toward the past and away from Sara's increasingly prosperous circumstances. They thus risk limiting the capacity for cultural criticism in the novel to the immigrant way of life that, by 1925, was facing near extinction (as well as to the way of life now preserved in the United States by the Orthodox few).

It seems to me that *Bread Givers* excites feminist interest because it does more than challenge Sara's inheritance. While using the up-from-the-ghetto narrative model, Yezierska also demonstrates the continuity between Europe and the United States. She depicts two incompatible cultural worlds, but she also recognizes that Judaism is not static but adaptive. Indeed, one of its strongest forms of adaptation, because it is supported by mainstream culture, is patriarchy. If we look back through book 1 with this in mind, we realize that Reb Smolinsky the matchmaker has already begun outfitting Jewish fatherhood for American life. If we follow Sara into book 2, where she investigates the marriages of her three sisters and almost makes one herself, we see how wifely subordination has been reconstituted within the new Jewish-American middle classes. Wherever we look, we see the Old World/New World dichotomy challenged by the eerie correspondences of patriarchal persistence.

In arranging marriages for his daughters, Smolinsky redeploys Jewish patriarchy within the American marriage market to take advantage of its intersection with the larger capitalist economy. In the Russia-Poland of Mrs. Smolinsky's memory, fathers exercise nearly complete authority over their daughters' marriages, but they are obligated to provide as opulent a dowry as possible. In the United States, where daughters earn their own wages and attract suitors who are upwardly mobile, the relation between marriage market and political economy encourages a shift away from dowries toward bride wealth and its equivalent in the currency of social prestige. While deriving his authority to intervene from tradition, Smolinsky reinterprets the obligation to provide a dowry as an opportunity to secure economic peace. In a relentless exercise of paternal authority, Smolinsky interferes with the love affairs of his three eldest daughters and arranges, one after another, three disastrous marriages.

Bessie and Mashah both represent valuable commodities, but in illuminatingly different ways. Bessie brings home the largest wage, envelope unopened, whereas Mashah spends almost every penny she makes on herself. Bessie's dumpy looks and advanced age make her undesirable except to an upwardly mobile man who puts a premium on her work ethic and self-effacement, whereas Mashah's attention to her looks and consumer expertise make her attractive to a man whose position is already secure. Bessie wants to marry Berel Bernstein, a fellow garment worker, who plans to open his own sweatshop and work his way up from there. Mashah is in love with Jacob Novak, the son of a wealthy Grand Street department store owner, who has been studying to become a concert pianist and raise his family's respectability.

When Bernstein comes calling, Smolinsky determines what he already suspects: that Bernstein expects to put Bessie to work in his own sweatshop. Smolinsky demands cash in trade for Bessie's income-producing labor. Taken by surprise, Bernstein rejects Smolinsky's hard bargain. Bernstein knows he can find other Hester Street fathers, inured by the dowry system, who will part with a strong-backed daughter for far less than Smolinsky. He appeals to Bessie to defy her father and marry him anyway, but she refuses. Breaking up the engagement, Smolinsky uses his daughter's loyalty against her. Indeed, he acts less traditionally in demanding bride wealth than Bessie does in acquiescing to his authority.

Bessie's value to Smolinsky is directly monetary. Mashah, on the other hand, because she has acquired middle-class looks and manners, represents a long-term investment, an investment that must be recouped in an equally long-term alliance with a wealthier, better established family. Pleased that Jacob Novak offers such an alliance, Smolinsky provides encouragement without demanding money or even questioning Novak's piety. It is the groom's father, the Grand Street merchant, who puts a halt to marriage: "All Mashah's beauty couldn't stop the cash-register look in his eyes, that we and our whole house weren't worth one of his cuff buttons" (58).

Despite the cultural and economic distances separating the Novaks from the Smolinskys, both patriarchs identify themselves as Jews and manipulate their children's lives in the name of familial upward mobility. By placing Smolinsky's interventions in the shadow of Mr. Novak's, Yezierska suggests how close the Lower East Side already is to Riverside Drive. Smolinsky hires a traditional matchmaker and marries

Mashah (whose spirit he has broken) to a jewelry store clerk whom he mistakes for a diamond merchant. The calculable value of daughters is emphasized further when he forbids his daughter Fania's promising engagement to an aspiring poet (on the grounds of his poverty) and packs her off to a prosperous West Coast garment manufacturer, reveling in what he takes to be a great success.

The relationship between the transformation of marital traditions and the larger economy is necessarily reciprocal. In trying to profit from his daughters' marriages, Smolinsky has been trying to turn fatherhood itself into a source of profit. When Yezierska represents Smolinsky's negotiation of Bessie's marriage, she hits upon an astonishing image for the capitalization of Jewish fatherhood. Smolinsky becomes a professional matchmaker, brokers the marriage of Bessie to Zalmon the fish peddler, and claims a five hundred-dollar commission as replacement for bride wealth, which he then uses to buy the grocery store in New Jersey. Acting as the agent for his own daughter's marriage, Smolinsky makes money both as a representative of traditional authority and as an individual father, literally selling off his daughter.

Sara counts the cost of making capital out of Jewish marriage traditions: "More and more I began to see that Father . . . was as a tyrant more terrible than the Tsar from Russia. As he drove away Bessie's man, so he drove away Mashah's lover. And each time he killed the heart from one of his children" (64–65). In book 2, "Between Two Worlds," Yezierska assesses the damage. Her scene of interrogation shifts from the paternal forces fashioning the marriages of the Smolinsky daughters to the sexism within them. Sara visits Bessie and Mashah in their new homes, sees Fania when she returns East, and becomes engaged to a man who warrants her father's approval. These scenes allow Yezierska to investigate Jewish-American marriages across a significant class range. As each sister testifies to feeling trapped in marriage and subordinated to male authority, Yezierska reveals how reestablishing patriarchy produces in ethnic women the uncanny sensation of never having left their ghetto home.

Married to an immigrant old enough to be her father and charged with the care of six stepchildren, Bessie is still living, literally and figuratively, on Hester Street. Married to a dash-

ing entrepreneur and comfortably established in the foothills
of Los Angeles, Fania has traveled about as far from the Lower
East Side as it is possible for Sara, at this point, to imagine.
"What a picture of poverty and riches! Bessie in her old fish-
store clothes, a ragged *kooshenierkeh*; Fania, like a Queen of
Sheba, shining with silks and sparkling with diamonds" (174).

In comparing Fania of Beverly Hills to a Lower East Side
yenta, Yezierska represents the continuity of women's position in marriage, running from the actual slums (Mrs.
Smolinsky, Bessie) to the blue-collar neighborhoods (Mashah)
to the far suburbs (Fania). In an economy of conspicuous
consumption, male control of purse strings becomes a height-
ened source of tension, especially in the upper classes where
women face husbands who demand both economic discipline
and acquisitive display. Fania therefore badgers her husband
for money while complaining to her sisters about his stingi-
ness, hypocrisy, and poor consumer judgment. The ancient
ghetto of women's marital subordination is reproduced in the
American suburbs. " 'Then I'm better off than you married
people!' " Sara concludes. " 'It's not a picnic to live alone. But at
least I've no boss of a husband to crush the spirit in me' " (177).

Sara's resolution to stay single is tested by a romance with
Max Goldstein, a department store owner and real estate in-
vestor. For weeks Goldstein wines and dines Sara, who at first
is thrilled by the attention she has never experienced, but she
becomes increasingly suspicious about its ramifications. One
evening, after reading a story to him, Sara realizes that
Goldstein hasn't been paying attention to her at all, except to
admire her beauty. Otherwise, his mind has been strictly on
business:

> The man seemed to turn into a talking roll of dol-
> lar bills right there before my eyes. His smile. He
> could buy everything. That's what laughed in his
> eyes. He could buy everything. To him, a wife
> would only be another piece of property. I grew
> cold at the thought how near I had been to marrying
> him. (199–200)

Although Sara sees Novak Sr.'s "cash-register look" in Max
Goldstein's eyes, she is disillusioned not by business per se but
by its impact on relations between men and women. Sara sees

how male control of income reinforces hierarchy within marriage, how a culture of competitive consumption can turn wives into household goods, and how the division of labor pulls couples apart. Taking full stock of such dangers, Sara decides to go to college and earn her own ticket into the middle classes.

Scholars have often viewed Sara's pursuit of higher education and professional status as just another aspect of the traditional polarity between ethnicity and mobility, an interpretive perspective that reduces Sara's protofeminism to the struggle to make an adequate living. Yet her decision to defy her father occurs after the establishment of the Smolinsky family store, and her decision to earn her own living occurs after Goldstein's offer of instant riches. For Sara, it is mobility itself that allows her to see the differences between having access to wealth and social position through men and commanding that wealth and position on one's own. Independence is a powerful enough lure that Sara is willing to pay the price, risking both security and comfort to begin again, economically speaking, at ground zero.

Yezierska outlines the marriages of Sara's three sisters not simply to explain why Sara is so motivated toward independence but to assign responsibility for the damage done to immigrant daughters, ultimately redistributing blame from Smolinsky and his sons-in-law to his daughters. Yezierska's investigative technique is juxtaposition: Sara rebels even from the prospect of marriage whereas each of her sisters acquiesces, even after the fact. Sara's anger at the way patriarchy is reinscribed is channeled into personal recriminations against her three sisters. Yezierska thereby underscores a liberal construction of free will (each sister held personally culpable for her own predicament) at the same time that her context, with its hyperboles of caricature and repetition, hints at the social construction underlying seeming acquiescence (the predicament of the sisters as class variations of the reproduction of Jewish patriarchy).

Although *Bread Givers* does not fully delineate female-to-female recrimination, the novel gradually assigns responsibility to the women themselves. Sara's mother elicits more curiosity than anger. Responsibility within Sara's generation is marked as a function of cultural distance, economic mobility, and the passage of time away from her mother's situation. Yezierska expects less of women raised in Russia than of those raised in America, less of working-class women than of those who have made it into the middle classes, and less of women who came of age before the turn of the century than of those who did so in her own time. Sara's three sisters are arrayed along a continuum running from Mrs. Smolinsky to Sara, and Yezierska's impatience increases accordingly. As these women move from fathers to husbands Yezierska expects them to be educated in desire, to refuse to tolerate from their husbands what they once thought was natural in their fathers.

Bessie, the oldest of the sisters, was probably raised in Europe and has spent the better part of her twenties supporting the family. In a comic routine in which Bessie dons Mashah's party dress and splits it wide open, Yezierska suggests that Bessie is, culturally speaking, unfit for the Americanized middle classes. It is not so much Smolinsky and his co-conspirators who trap Bessie into marrying Zalmon as it is Bessie's own internalization of the maternal "bread-giving" ethos. Bessie resists Zalmon as a lover and resists her father for conceiving the marriage but, at the same time, she is unable to resist taking care of Zalmon's unkempt youngest child, Benny. Although Bessie's capitulation reveals how women's inclination to nurture works against them, Yezierska doesn't hold Bessie personally responsible. Bessie's fate is the product of a historical irony that deserves our pity, not our anger: "When the wedding day came, she went quietly from our house to Zalmon's—the burden bearer had changed her burden" (110).

Mashah's marriage to Mirsky represents a very different historical marker for Yezierska. Men must still hold the burden of responsibility for the marriage: Smolinsky arranged it; Mirsky misrepresented himself as a wealthy diamond merchant in order to win Mashah, and he now spends the little he does make on himself rather than on her. Yet Yezierska registers impatience with Mashah. Sara remembers how self-display and independence of spirit were allied in Mashah, but now her love of beauty is channeled into domestic order and cleanliness, her self-determination drained in the process. "The soda with which she had scrubbed the floor so clean, and laundered her rags to white, had burned in and eaten the beauty out of her hands" (147). Concluding that Mashah doesn't have the courage to speak or act against Mirsky, Sara determines to speak on her behalf: " 'If you were my husband, I'd kill you. I'd scrub floors sooner than live with a thing like you' " (150). When Sara visited Bessie, Zalmon threw Sara out. This time, Sara marches out herself, melodramatically illustrating what Mashah is unwilling to do. In portraying Mashah's refusal to act, Yezierska implicates second-generation women in the persistence of marital misery.

It is possible that Sara gives up on her sister too quickly, but it is more likely that she is simply demanding too much. Mashah's independence is proscribed not only by custom but by the fact that her only marketable skill, cleaning the house, now serves as her last remaining stay of pleasure and self-esteem. Asking far too much of Mashah given her circumstances, Yezierska continues to use a criterion of individual responsibility that is itself implicated in maintaining the lower middle-class culture she is interrogating. Yet the higher Sara moves up the ladder of wealth and assimilation, the more reasonable her demand for some kind of protofeminist enlightenment becomes, reasonable not as a transcendence of middle-class culture but as a 1920s cultural imperative, the logical extension of Emersonian self-making to "the second sex."

If we understand Fania as the test case for sisterly support, we can see why Yezierska goes to the awkward trouble of creating a Los Angeles marriage. In visiting the New York homes of Bessie and Mashah, Sara comes face to face with husbands whose presences are so dominating that she finds it difficult to direct any anger at their wives. But by shuttling Fania three thousand miles away from her husband, Yezierska isolates the youngest, wealthiest, and most assimilated of Sara's sisters as a test case for sibling solidarity. Away from her husband's circle of influence, yet testifying to his tyranny, Fania is better placed to encourage Sara in her effort to educate herself. Yezierska grants Fania this opportunity to emphasize the failure of a generation of married women to support the ambitions of their younger sisters.

Although each sister has been victimized by Smolinsky's matchmaking, each still identifies with and values marriage. Indeed it is Sara's sisters who take the lead in finding her a husband. The scene in which Fania reveals the bitter entrapment of her marriage ends, ironically, with her chastising Sara for wanting to stay single. Sara looks to Fania for intragenerational sanction and sisterly solidarity, only to find her father's drive to marry her off reproduced in her sibling. Fania and Bessie uphold an alternative solidarity, that of sisters in marriage. For, of course, they not only mean to help Sara by guaranteeing her a modicum of security, they also recognize that being married allows them to maintain ties with their female ancestors as well as with each other. " 'Put on your hat and coat and come with us to Mother,' " they urge (178). Sara thinks of her sisters in terms of the old adage "misery loves company," but the text indicates that Sara's ascent into individualism threatens an older form of women's strength, that of mutual support.

It is Fania who, upon returning to Los Angeles, sends Goldstein back East to seduce Sara out of independence. Adopting Reb Smolinsky's role as matchmaker, she writes:

> Max Goldstein, the man I told you about, is coming special to New York to see you. From what I told him about you he thinks you're just the wife he needs. . . .
>
> Think only! You'll have your own house and garden. Your own car. You'll have servants do all your work for you. You'll be able to wear the best stylish clothes that money can buy. (185)

In Yezierska's version of the temptation narrative, Adam offers Eve the apple, but the snake is Eve's sister. When Sara later grows "cold" at the thought of how close she came to taking more than a bite, the text throws the guilt back at Fania, who, given her own marriage, should have known better.

In replacing Smolinsky the matchmaker with Fania, Yezierska is not equating Fania with patriarchy. Rather, Fania's conspiratorial efforts are a mere addendum to Goldstein's influence as lover or Smolinsky's influence as father. While Fania does appeal to Sara to come join the fun, trying to throw a blanket of sisterly communion over courtship and marriage, the power of female seduction is depicted as supplemental to the hegemony of patriarchally sponsored heterosexuality. In the final analysis, men not only victimize women but their power overshadows that of their female allies. To prevent such misreading, Yezierska follows Sara's rejection of Goldstein with another melodramatic confrontation with her father. Smolinsky makes his first visit to Sara's New York apartment and berates her for rejecting " 'the one chance of [her] life' " (204). It is easy to mistake this scene as another variation on a well-worn theme unless one recognizes that Reb Smolinsky could only have found out about Goldstein's proposal and Sara's refusal if one of her sisters, probably Fania herself, had told him.

The small mystery—who told Reb Smolinsky about Max? who betrayed Sara?—is a haunting note from Yezierska, who incriminates ethnic women for collaborating in the middle-class reinscription of patriarchy. She laces her conventional intergenerational melodrama with a thread of *intra*generational tragedy: "So this is what it cost, daring to follow the urge in me. No father. No lover. No family. No friend. I must go on and on. And I must go on—alone" (208). In the interstices between "family" and "friends," implicated but not named, are Sara's sisters. Underneath Yezierska's rebellion against the generation of fathers lies a challenge to the generation of daughters, her own generation.

But how historical, how prophetic has Yezierska been in envisioning an end to sisterly solidarity? After all, it is Yezierska who writes Sara into this either-or bind—either loyalty to her sisters or to getting an education—just as it is she who creates the mystery of Reb Smolinsky's informant. By the end of the novel, Sara will have passed through a series of recoveries that do not include reconciliation with *any* of her three sisters. Does not the guilt leveled through Sara at Bessie, Mashah, and especially Fania reflect something of Yezierska's own self-recrimination for what she has done, as the author, to Sara? Perhaps the tensions between female bonding and female self-determination being dramatized in the text are more difficult for Yezierska to mediate in her imagination, taken as it is by

Emersonian individualism, than they have been in social practice.

In book 3, "The New World," Sara responds to the disillusionment of new womanhood by designing a rapprochement with her past. Although the first two books expose the complicity of Jewish tradition with middle-class culture to permit dissent from that complicity, the third book seems to rationalize—to discover as both "reasonable" and "reasoned," practical and justifiable—a partial recovery of those very values.

Finding education as a profession both tedious and lonely, Sara commits herself in marriage to the principal of her school, Hugo Seelig, who in many ways is an exemplary "new man," compassionate with children and drawn to intelligent women. In response to her mother's deathbed request that she care for her father, in light of her own cultural empowerment, and in view of Seelig's willingness to help, she agrees to rescue her remarried father from his exploitive second wife and take him into her home. Sara analyzes her options with great care and makes a decision that is not only defensible but persuasive: to seek freedom within a (changing) community rather than outside of it. Yet the terms, the tone, and especially the imagery of Sara's rapprochement suggest that she has conceded too much.

In one of the strange narrative conceits demanding explanation, Yezierska separates Sara and her family for six years, from the moment she rejects Goldstein until she has achieved her education, secured a job, and reaped material prosperity. Sara's rationalization for the long delay is a pragmatic calculus rendered in specifically economic terms: "Would they understand that my silent aloofness for so long had been a necessity and not selfish indifference? . . . I had no great riches to bring them" (242). It is tempting to accept the rationale for the degree of practical truth it contains. It is likewise tempting to attribute the economic idiom in which that truth is couched to the American "mainstream" that Sara, by this time, is in the process of joining. But the idiom too closely recalls the rhetoric of obligation in which Reb Smolinsky insists on his investment in his daughters. It prompts us to consider, too, the capitalist language in which Sara's mother, whose sacrifices Sara finds persuasive, expresses her support for Sara's educational plans. Throughout the narrative, the Smolinskys have socialized Sara through a language of transaction, not simply establishing an economy of psychological energy in a general sense but organizing part of her psyche as an economy. Sara understands that her parents are "investing" material support and tacit approval in the upward mobility of their seemingly prodigal daughter in exchange for the reproduction of the bread-giving ethos after she has earned her degree. In the wake of the implicit agreement with her mother that returns to haunt her, Sara finds herself driven back into the fold of Eastern European Jewish femininity. The discourse of economics has promoted the reproduction of women's oppression, just as that oppression, in turn, has supported economic gain.

For Yezierska, the linkage between mother and daughter is nearly as fundamental as the alliance of father and son-in-law in the intergenerational reproduction of women's subordination. Since she began to rebel, Sara has felt the urgent claim of the past, particularly as that claim was mediated through and by her mother. Late one winter evening, when Sara is too tired and cold to do her night school homework, Mrs. Smolinsky arrives with food and a highly prized feather bed. She makes the usual appeals to tradition—calling for more attention to the family, questioning the purpose of college, and telling Sara that spinsterhood is " 'good enough for *Goyim'* " but not for her. Sara argues with her mother, " 'I could see you later. But I can't go to college later' " (172, 171). Mrs. Smolinsky neither expresses approval nor demands compliance; unlike her husband, she seems to offer Sara freedom of choice. But Mrs. Smolinsky makes an unspoken pact with her daughter, symbolized by the feather bed, that not only supports Sara's quest for education (it promises to supply warmth and sleep) but implicates her in a rhetoric of debt. Sara says that her obligation is to "visit" her mother at a future date, implying that a deal has been struck, but the real deal is much more serious. After achieving an education, that is, attempting to fill her father's role in secularized form, Sara is to repay her mother by returning, if only partially, and taking up, however figuratively, her mother's place in her father's (feather)bed.

Sara does not see her mother again for at least six years. Wanting to "share" her hard-earned prosperity, she finally "pays" a long "overdue" visit to her parents, only to find her mother dying. In the ensuing melodrama, Yezierska signifies how Mrs. Smolinsky's debt-credit arithmetic has implanted guilt within her and awakened desire for the "motherly" role that, in the context of upward mobility and partial assimilation, borders upon the self-destructive. " 'Are you already a finished *teacherin?'* " asks Mrs. Smolinsky, claiming her own contribution to that victory in order to announce the terms of repayment:

> "Be good to Father," she begged. "I'm leaving him in his old age when he needs me most. Helpless as a child he is. No one understands his holiness as I. Only promise me that you'll take good care of him, and I can close my eyes in peace." (245)

Sara experiences her mother's death as an inhalation of the spirit: "I felt literally Mother's soul enter my soul like a miracle" (252).

Sara claims mother-daughter unity, but her sense of sublimity indicates an asymmetry of power. For psychological peace, Sara must accept her own powerlessness and accede to her mother's deathbed demand. In the chapters that follow, Sara will be haunted by the ghost of her mother's memory until she takes up the traditional Russian-Polish domestic role. To underscore this process, Yezierska effects another narrative sleight of hand. As Mrs. Smolinsky is dying, Yezierska produces a suitor for Smolinsky, the "fat widow" Mrs. Feinstein, who has already begun giving the Reb his meals in hopes of marrying him as soon as he collects on Mrs. Smolinsky's life insurance.

In addition to reiterating the cruel insensitivity of men to women, the appearance of Mrs. Feinstein the fortune hunter allows Yezierska to alienate Smolinsky from Sara's sisters and to establish a rival to Sara in the matter of taking care of her father. Having given Sara her feather bed, Mrs. Smolinsky's ghost insists that Sara stave off the threat of Mrs. Feinstein by assuming her mother's role in all but the sexual sense. The overtones of the classical paradigm of incest emphasize how powerfully the repression of debt to the mother, a repression inculcated as debt, drives Sara to her father. In the final analysis, Yezierska implies, daughters owe it to their mothers to preserve their mothers' investment in men—if not, someone like Mrs. Feinstein is going to run off with the "goods."

Just as Sara's visit to her parents began as an act of free will only to be implicated in a long-standing psychology of daughterly debt, so her falling in love with Hugo Seelig seems to be a free-willed act of romance but is implicated in long-term socialization: the father criticizes the daughter, eventually driving the daughter to seek the approval of the father. To the extent that Sara is ready to compromise her independence as a new woman, Seelig's Deweyite qualities of compassion and sensitivity make him a logical, indeed compelling choice—an exemplar of the "new man." Yet Yezierska makes it plain that Seelig is multiply reminiscent of Sara's father: they come from European villages only miles apart; Sara speaks of her father just prior to Seelig's appearance, then makes explicit comparisons; and, most important, as Smolinsky is a respected rabbi, so Seelig is an older, more established figure in a professional hierarchy of knowing, learning, and teaching.

When Seelig visits Sara's pronunciation class, he listens to Sara correcting the children and hears her "slipping back into the vernacular." As he shows her what must be done to pronounce the "g" in "sing" correctly, the intimacy of shared teaching turns to physical intimacy with the teacher: "He watched me as I blundered on. The next moment he was close beside me, the tips of his cool fingers on my throat. 'Keep those muscles still until you have stopped. Now say it again,' he commanded" (272). No matter how gently and constructively he admonishes and corrects Sara, Seelig necessarily does so from a platform of forbidding authority constituted in his job as principal, substantiated by the social norms of the times, and made sacred by Sara's and the community's respect. Assiduously blinding herself to her embarrassment, Sara is mesmerized by Seelig's public tutelage because he is repeating the primal scene of paternal chastisement without her father's badgering, self-righteous, obviously self-interested tone. Sara's suppression of her embarrassment prepares her to respond with outsized enthusiasm to Seelig's subsequent praise and willing ear, gestures of appreciation and acceptance that stir Sara's love by animating a not-so-dormant form of incestuous desire.

Yezierska empowers Seelig's strategy of seduction by placing in his hands a letter from Sara's father, a letter in which Smolinsky accuses Sara of daughterly neglect. Seelig brandishes the letter: "Gravely, without even a word of greeting, he handed me an opened letter. 'Perhaps you had better read this'" (273). Reb Smolinsky appears to be giving away family secrets here, but, as Yezierska insinuates, he is actually demonstrating how he has already authorized Seelig's conquest by the time-honored technique of bashing women's esteem.

The next day, Seelig pursues Sara with words of praise and understanding she finds "magical," metamorphosing her shame into sexual attraction. She hopes that Seelig has not been alienated by the letter from her father, which hangs unmentioned over their conversation. When Sara invites him into her apartment (a loaded invitation among immigrant Jews in the 1920s, never mind the 1890s), she fears that her self-exposure, symbolized by the emptiness of her apartment, might undermine the "enveloping friendliness." But it is precisely her accumulating anxiety (anxiety that he himself has had no small hand in producing) that Seelig is able to manipulate, consciously or not, into a sexual charge.

Sara spills her past to him in a rush of oral preliminaries to the implied physical consummation: "All the secret places of my heart opened at the moment. And then the whole story of my life poured itself out of me to him. Father, Mother, my sisters. And Father's wife, with her greed for diamond earrings" (278). Through imagery of penetration and discharge, Sara represents her exposure of family secrets (skeletons and jewels in the closet) as the conduit and sanction for physical intimacy, but, of course, Seelig is already privy to the Smolinsky melodrama. When she finally mentions her father's letter, Seelig testifies to knowing "'just the kind of old Jew he is,'" which Sara experiences as a thrilling stroke of interpersonal sensitivity (279). Sara speaks, but there is no indication that Seelig is actually listening; he does not need to hear her "secret" in order to gain access to her "secret places."

Tutored by the letter and empowered by the cultural heritage it symbolizes, Seelig is not so much paving a new road to intimacy as taking an old man's cue and following, whether he realizes it or not, a well-worn path into the affections of the opposite sex. "All differences dropped away," rejoices Sara, "we talked one language" (278). Yezierska demonstrates what Sara herself cannot quite understand: that her father has authorized Seelig's seduction by socializing her through recrimination. In the final chapter Seelig will return *his* "debt" to the fathers by tapping into dormant forms of femininity that work to the advantage of Jewish men, especially fathers.

Reb Smolinsky's case for Sara's renewed attention and support seems sufficiently strong without the need of blackmail, but the letter underscores his claim. As an attempt to exercise patriarchal authority in a realm where it is inappropriate, the letter dramatizes how Smolinsky's income has fallen below Sara's, how his cultural authority (symbolized by his lack of linguistic facility) does not extend as far as hers does, and how his precarious situation pales in comparison to her newly won security. Still, Sara resists the appeal for help until she appraises her father's domestic situation and realizes that it was the new Mrs. Smolinsky who had badgered him into writing the letter. It takes a visit to her father's new home, where she watches her stepmother tie his shoes, before she is willing to contribute financially; it takes a visit to a retirement facility for her to realize that the "nurturing" of a woman is, in fact, indispensable. Most important, it takes the intervention of Seelig before she is finally willing to fulfill the spirit as well as the letter of her promise to her mother.

Seelig's most important act as Sara's school principal, her "teacher," is to reflect the worshipful appreciation Sara directs at him back onto her father. When Seelig asks Reb Smolinsky to teach him Hebrew, he rekindles the old man's self-esteem, which in turn rekindles Sara's filial respect: "Father leaned back in his chair. The old dream look came back into his glowing eyes . . . [which] grew soft and moist" (293). As Sara responds warmly to the spark of friendship between the men, the scene taps into the attractions of masculine learning and spirituality that have, in fact, implicitly underwritten Sara's attitude toward Seelig all along.

What is most provocative about Yezierska's interrogation is not that she identifies a psychologically operative patriarchy, but that she shows how a specifically Jewish and feminine socialization allows patriarchy to catch up with even the most rebellious of daughters. Here we are reminded of the scene in the first chapter that establishes Smolinsky's religious authority and instigates the antipatriarchal energy of the entire novel. As Reb Smolinsky chants from the Psalms, the Smolinsky women look on in rapture:

> Silent, breathless, we peeked in through the open crack in the door. The black satin skullcap tipped on the side of his head set off his red hair and his long red beard. And his ragged satin coat from Europe made him look as if he just stepped out of the Bible. . . . "Is there any music on earth like this?" Mother whispered. (16)

For the scholars of Orthodoxy, the regime of prayer and of study was often energizing, but it could also be tedious or worse: Mary Antin reports the stultifying results of her father trying to keep up a scholarly pretense.[24] But Yezierska illustrates what is gained as well as lost for women in not knowing the tedium from within. "Mother licked up Father's every little word, like honey" (12). It is this energy of spectatorship that is rekindled when Sara witnesses Seelig and her father bonding over the text. "Delighted with the outcome I turned to Father . . . 'Would you care to live with me?'" (294–95). It is to recover these feelings of communion and pleasure that Sara makes her ultimate compromise.

Manifesting "the full force of his unbending spirit" (295), Smolinsky insists that Sara take up the Jewish woman's traditional domestic responsibilities as the terms of his moving in, terms that she accepts. Although full arrangements are not negotiated (we do not know, for instance, if Sara must follow menstrual rituals), in her acquiescence to Orthodox "housekeeping" Sara seems to relinquish one of her most important agendas. She had protested in the very first chapter:

> Women had no brains for the study of God's Torah,
> but they could be the servants of men who studied
> the Torah. Only if they cooked for the men, and
> washed for the men, and didn't nag or curse the
> men out of their homes; only if they let the men
> study the Torah in peace, then, maybe, they could
> push themselves into Heaven with the men, to wait
> on them there. (9–10)

Yezierska, of course, hasn't "forgotten" this insight. In the final moments of the novel, Sara is allowed to question the wisdom of assuming the traditional female role of domestic handmaiden, even if she does not quite understand why she feels compelled to make the compromise. She speaks of her past under male Orthodox rule as a barrier between herself and a hypothetical Emersonian freedom. The dominant imagery of the last chapter is that of a ghostly haunting. Sara's middle-class sanctuary is penetrated by the claims of the Lower East Side, which insinuate themselves through the medium of conscience. The culture of the past works through internalization of its norms; the vehicle of Smolinsky's hold over Sara is guilt.

Symbolic of the past, particularly its patriarchal burden, Sara's father literally stands before her in the penultimate scene of the novel. Sara experiences the claim he exercises upon her at this moment not as legitimate or affordable or attractive but as a return of the repressed:

> Just as I was beginning to feel safe and free to go on
> to a new life with Hugo, the old burden dragged me
> back by the hair. Was there no place in the world for
> Father? My home! Must I give it up to him? But with
> him there, it would not be home for me. I suddenly
> realized that I had come back to where I had started
> twenty years ago when I began my fight for free-
> dom. But in my rebellious youth, I thought I could
> escape by running away. And now I realized that
> the shadow of the burden was always following
> me, and here I stood face to face with it again. (295)

The trope of ghostly shadows is compounded by the cartoonish image of incestuous desire—a primitive man drawing back a rebellious woman to the tribal cave. Sara feels caught in a vicious cycle of guilt: guilt for resisting the paternal culture, whose hold over her is figured as the desire of father for daughter; guilt for capitulating to her own incestuous desire, hence abandoning the struggle for self-determination.

> So there it was, the problem before us—the problem of Father—still unsolved.
> In the hall, we paused, held by the sorrowful cadences of Father's voice.
> *"Man born of woman is of few days and full of trouble."*
> The voice lowered and grew fainter till we could not hear the words any more. Still we lingered for the mere music of the fading chant. Then Hugo's grip tightened on my arm and we walked on. But I felt the shadow still there, over me. It wasn't just my father, but the generations who made my father whose weight was still upon me. (296–97)

Sara's own sorrowful cadence, in ironic counterpoint to Reb Smolinsky's scriptural recitation, suggests that men give women the greater trouble; or, taking "men" generically, that the tradition of Scripture itself, having created the culture of the generations, should be held responsible for giving mankind its greatest burden. Sara cannot escape her past because the cultural construction of her desire ("the mere music of the . . . chant") will not let her.

Few novelists have ever identified with their heroines as closely as Yezierska does with Sara. Yet, in her concluding conceit, Yezierska distinguishes Sara's story, which ends with surrender, from her own project, which is being renewed in Sara's aftermath. In the final lines of *Bread Givers*, I hear an especially Jamesian double irony, reminiscent of the conclusion to *The Golden Bowl*. There, Maggie's victorious preservation of her marriage is undercut by her despair at its consolidation, and that despair is undercut in turn by James's own exultation in rendering her victory hollow. Whereas Sara (like Maggie) uses the idiom of defeat to retreat from the battle, Yezierska (like James) revels in the renewal of her own energy wrought by the production of the novel itself. Sara's melancholy cry of regret consolidates upscale Jewish-American life around the reinscription of patriarchy, but Yezierska renews her resistance to a heritage that continues to threaten her.

Sara says, "And now I realized that the shadow of the burden was always following me, and here I stood face to face with it again" (295). In narrating Sara's life story, Yezierska seems as drawn as her protagonist is to a conservative denouement: it is Yezierska, after all, who overdetermines Sara's destiny, who seems incapable of imagining any other solution to the disappointments of teaching. But if we insist on interpreting the plot of *Bread Givers* as evidence of the continuing hold of Eastern European Jewish tradition over Yezierska's imagination, we must also have recourse to our knowledge of Yezierska's subsequent biography. Whether Yezierska means us to see Sara's marriage as a victory or a defeat, as a workable compromise or as doomed from the start, we know that she herself never returned to Levitas, never remarried, and never renewed responsibility either for her own father or her daughter. We know, too, that she continued to write and publish: novels in 1927 and 1932, minor contributions to the Federal Writers' Project, an autobiography in 1950, and intermittent short stories until her death in 1969. Unlike Sara, Yezierska sought "the real America" not within the relatively comfortable institutions of her successful peers but within a more tenuous community of writers and readers, a transnational community whose common ground would be to deromanticize immigrant experience and which failed to coalesce in her lifetime.

3

Oedipus in Brownsville: Parricide, a House Divided, and *Call It Sleep*

> At some point in the fifties it would become clear that the problem we faced was no longer how to fight for modernism, it was to consider why the fight for it had ended in so unnerving, almost unseemly a triumph.
>
> Irving Howe[1]

In the late 1920s, a young Lionel Trilling wrote a series of book reviews for *The Menorah Journal* in which he criticized his fellow American Jews for producing immigrant novels "without poetry, without imagination . . . without sophistication." Distinguishing between form and content, Trilling made it clear that he did not oppose the fictional topoi of migration and mobility as much as he did the techniques of "realistic" fiction, what he called "the shoddy prose of Sinclair Lewis, Theodore Dreiser, and Upton Sinclair."[2] A half-dozen years later, Joseph Wolf used the cutting-edge *Partisan Review* as a forum to hail the beginning of a post-Dreiser era in American-Jewish fiction: "The author [of today] has been a student of the best in modern literature; he has read Joyce and Proust, he is familiar with Symbolist poetry."[3] From the late 1920s through the mid-1930s, Delmore Schwartz, Daniel Fuchs, Meyer Levin, Charles Reznikoff, and others were praised for "more mature" treatments of immigrant subjects.[4] Reviewing *By the Waters of Manhattan*, Trilling himself claimed Reznikoff's first novel "not merely a finer but a truer story than previous attempts in the field of American-Jewish immigrant fiction."[5]

For Wolf, the cutting edge in 1935 meant one novel: Henry

Roth's autobiographical tour de force, *Call It Sleep*. "*Call It Sleep*
is more than the best novel of Jewish-American life to appear
up to the present time," concluded Wolf. "This first novel by
Henry Roth can easily take its place as one of the most out-
standing books of the past ten years. *Call It Sleep* is the most
promising novel since Joyce's *A Portrait of the Artist as a Young
Man*."⁶ Although several critics of the 1930s echoed Wolf's
praise, the novel went out of print almost immediately and
was by and large lost to memory as well, that is, until it was
"rediscovered" in 1957, when both Alfred Kazin and Leslie
Fiedler nominated it as one of the most neglected books of the
previous twenty-five years.⁷ At the height of its renewed salience, R. W. B. Lewis judged *Call It Sleep* "incomparably the
best" of immigrant narratives and "indeed, to speak without
equivocation, one of the classic American novels."⁸

Call It Sleep follows an Austrian Jewish immigrant boy from
age six to eight as he deciphers, tries to escape from, and yet
only succeeds in exacerbating an Oedipal triangle more than
coincidentally reminiscent of Eugene O'Neill's threesomes
in *The Great God Brown*: a lone male child, terrified of sex yet
driven to an increasingly hallucinatory probing of his parents'
troubled sexuality; the father economically and culturally
disenfranchised, prone to impotence and a compensatory paternal rage, feeling increasingly isolated from wife and child;
the mother betrayed in her marriage, turning vengefully to the
affection of the son, exposing him to the ultimate divergence of
his awakening desire and her growing need. If it was O'Neill
who confirmed and organized Roth's Oedipal suspicions, it
was the narrative techniques of James Joyce (stream of consciousness, Freudian and Judeo-Christian symbolism, the psychological apportioning of narrative) that helped Roth to focus
not on late adolescence and early adulthood—the classic locus
of psychological fiction—but rather on early boyhood. The assault against lingering Victorian sensibilities marked the novel
as irredeemably modern. Eliot's influence can be felt throughout the novel as well, in what Howe praised as its "obligato of
lyricism," its stunning sensual impressionism, and its poetics
for redeeming the debris of the contemporary cityscape. Eliot
is climactically present in the visionary collage of Lower East

Side voices through which Roth himself seeks the anodyne his protagonist cannot find.

The point here is not to praise the novel for achieving a "sophistication" that realism putatively lacks, which would be to reiterate the way it originally was received and the way it was promoted in the 1960s. It is to recognize, rather, how modernist breakthroughs in figuration and meaning-making could serve a second-generation writer wishing to recover what Trilling calls the "solid, raw, sociological truth" of immigration.[9] "Roth's novel patiently enters and then wholly exhausts the immigrant milieu," writes Howe.[10] "It is a *specifically* Jewish book," adds Fiedler, "the best single book by a Jew about Jewishness written by an American, certainly through the thirties and perhaps ever."[11] Although these testaments date from the 1960s revival of the novel, *Call It Sleep* seems ideally suited for critics impatient with ethnic sentimentalism and committed to exploring the explosive, discomforting interactions of ethnicity, gender, and class. *Call It Sleep* identifies how masculine insecurities originating in Eastern Europe were exacerbated by stepwise migration (first the father, then the mother and children), by the transformation from rural stability to urban poverty-cum-mobility, and by the discordance between a boy's formal education in Judaic guilt and his informal one in Christian redemption. In so doing, the novel demonstrates the resiliency of Yiddish family culture, which reproduces itself (for better *and* for worse) through a psychological dynamic—across the generations, amidst the ebbing of Orthodox Judaism, and against the temptations of middle-class conformity.

After a small flurry of attention in the 1960s and early 1970s, professional interest in *Call It Sleep* seems to have all but evaporated. The novel is represented in none of the plethora of state-of-the-art anthologies (not even in the much-lauded Heath omnibus), each of which has been published in the last four years and each of which lays claim to multiculturalism and canon revision.[12] Jewish immigrant realists—Abraham Cahan, Mike Gold, and even Anzia Yezierska—are figured prominently in the *Columbia Literary History of the United States*, but Roth is mentioned only in passing, as if his warrant upon our attention did not extend beyond the mandate of pluralistic inclusiveness itself.[13] Although we have learned to be as wary of countercanons as of canons themselves, I wonder if *Call It Sleep* might deserve to be named, once again, one of "the most neglected books of the past 25 years."

It is curious that we would have any hesitation at all in teaching and studying *Call It Sleep*. On the one hand, we can invoke the term "high modernism" with a great degree of rigor. "T. S. Eliot, James Joyce and Eugene O'Neill were the writers of major stature that interested me back then," recalls Roth.[14] *Call It Sleep* welcomes New Critical analysis and is also quite hospitable to the thematic concerns characteristically employed in the name of formalism. At the same time—and this is what is most surprising about its poor salience recently—*Call It Sleep* envelops the reader in the world of the Lower East Side as thoroughly as any narrative before or since. As Wai-chee Dimock reports, American literary studies are making a move away from "the local, the verifiable, and the unique" and toward "the speculative and the relational."[15] One would expect *Call It Sleep* to be a source of great interest, then, because it invites speculation across the boundaries between immigrating and expatriating, between canonization and relative obscurity, between the United States and Europe, and between fiction and the genres of poetry and drama.

That *Call It Sleep* continues to fall through the cracks of academic reception is a function of its capacity to continue to frustrate our terms of critical inquiry. During the postwar years when the American canon was being formulated, critics praised *Call It Sleep* for breaking down the barriers of realism, yet the novel ran aground of their insistence that to ascend to modernist technique requires dispelling the politics of an ethnic agenda. Too much was at stake in the interdependent modernist notions of aesthetic transcendence and humanist universalism for critics to deal fully with the insistent Jewishness of Roth's novel. Since the early 1970s, *Call It Sleep* has been noted for its unapologetic saturation in urban Jewish folk life, but it now founders on the assumption that to write of marginal experience is to write outside of mainstream aesthetics. Too much is now at stake in the notions of ethnocultural authenticity for critics to deal with its insistent high modernism.

How impolitic it has become to speak of a minority writer's interest in canonical aesthetics is illustrated by the state of the exemplary minority criticism of our time, criticism concerned with African-American literature. Robert Stepto writes that contemporary critics have become apprehensive of acknowledging how black writers necessarily use and often self-consciously celebrate established forms of Anglo-American literary practice. It is as if these critics fear discovering in writerly engagement with mainstream aesthetics evidence "of black writers 'escaping' from their culture and 'passing' into the world of Art," "of black writers pouring 'black content' into 'white forms,'" and "of the subjugation of the Afro-American or the near-colonization of his or her critical intelligence."[16] It is this wariness, shared by students of other minority traditions, that has frustrated the critical recovery of a work as enabled by high modernism as *Call It Sleep*.

Given present-day suspicions of assimilation, one of the daunting facts about ethnic modernists is how many of them understood themselves to be engaged in Emersonian remaking, both culturally and socially. Leslie Fiedler writes that, for those who started out in the 1930s, the typifying figure was "a second generation Jew . . . trying to find his identity in the pages of *transition*."[17] "Most of the New York writers," recalls Howe, possessed "a strong drive to both break out of the ghetto and leave the bonds of Jewishness entirely. . . . They meant to declare themselves citizens of the world."[18] They did not seek assimilation in the sense of a blind naturalization into the U.S. middle class; instead they sought entry into what Daniel Aaron has called "the universal republic" of letters, a multinational community of self-marginalized intellectuals reaching for aesthetic achievement.[19] Not only entering but "opening up" this republic, the New York intellectuals gave the reception of high modernism an Eastern European bent; first they reworked literary journalism, then contemporary literature, and finally the academy according to received senses of spiritual value and social purpose, including (paradoxically) the strain of universalism within Jewish thought itself. What is perplexing, then, is not that the New York intellectuals abandoned all of their cultural heritage in a rush to embrace modernism (how would anyone succeed at total self-transformation?), but that many of them were motivated by the prospect of self-transcendence, and many of the rest were savvy enough, in the face of anti-Semitism, to talk as if they were.

Roth abandoned his parents upon matriculating at City College in favor of an international family, a network of artists and critics obsessed with European experimentation.[20] He replaced Judaic observance with the creed of "art for art's sake," which he absorbed in tutelage to his live-in lover, New York University professor Eda Lou Walton. "Like so many first generation American Jewish youth, I had already come to disassociate from family, Judaism, the whole thing—and to embrace the American scene, the new American attitudes."[21] He turned to Eliot, Joyce, and O'Neill, a Catholic literary trinity:

> Eliot's *Waste Land* had a devastating effect on me, I felt stunned by the vastness of its conception. . . . Some of the plays of Eugene O'Neill left a deep imprint. I went to see *The Great God Brown* . . . and came away feeling that I had been listening to the inner voice of a man. I had already read Joyce as a freshman in college, and a copy of *Ulysses* . . . introduced me to an entirely new way of seeing things. I felt I could see doors swing open on untried possibilities in literature.[22]

In *Call It Sleep,* Roth looked back at his boyhood with a model of intrafamilial intercourse derived from the grandson of Irish Catholic immigrants, with technologies for investigating precocious forms of sexuality and religious mysticism derived from the most influential literary Irishman of the century, and with a commitment to the receptive power of the word derived from an expatriated old-stock American on his way to the most insistent of all Catholicisms—that of conversion.

In large measure, then, Roth did undergo something like a religioaesthetic conversion. Yet there remains the fact of his novel: in *Call It Sleep* he returned imaginatively to the Lower East Side, and in returning he recast his struggle for self-universalization in a highly particularistic light. In 1972, when Bonnie Lyons asked Roth what he had learned from *Ulysses*, he replied, "What I gained was this awed realization that you didn't have to go anywhere at all except around the corner to flesh out a literary work. . . . In stream of consciousness I saw that my own continual dialogue with myself could be made into literature."[23] What clearer provocation could there have been to experiment with Jewish stream of consciousness than the fact that Joyce centered *Ulysses* upon Leopold Bloom?

The version of *Call It Sleep* we have received from the 1960s shows Roth breaking through realist sociology to achieve genuine literary merit. Fiedler writes, "Cued by whatever fears, Roth's turning to childhood enables him to render his story as dream and nightmare, fantasy and myth—to escape the limits of that realism which makes of other accounts of ghetto childhood documents rather than poetry."[24] At every opportunity, Roth has described his novel as an impressionist tone poem that achieves univocal expressiveness at the expense of social insight:

> In sticking to the child and patterning the world around him, I was able to use all my lyrical impulses. And therefore the whole texture of the novel is like that of a long poem or metaphor. . . .
> When I think of novelists like Bellow or Philip Roth, social commentary seems to be the most important aspect of their books. In *Call It Sleep*, social commentary was anything but. What *was* important was the sensuous world that kind of flowed and the subjective reaction to this sensuous world.[25]

Roth's characterization of the novel as a "long poem or metaphor" has led critics to focus, in the fashion of high formalism, on its "symbolic structure" or its "use of motifs."[26] Within the lyric density of Roth's prose await surprises for all of us smitten with language and in his unpacking of boyhood phantasmagoria lie insights for those of us interested in developmental psychology, particularly young male sexuality. But to acknowledge that the novel seduces with linguistic pleasures or presses beyond ethnic parochialism is not to discount—Roth's own testimony to the contrary, notwithstanding—its contribution to reconstructing immigrant experience.

For Fiedler and Roth, the key to transcending "social commentary" was the turn to boyhood—as if the "dreams and myths" of Jewish sons had not helped to make the Lower East Side what it was, as if challenging those dreams and myths were not integral to comprehending the social world in which they lived. To my mind, the formula they have left us is backwards. *Call It Sleep* is valuable to us because its boy's-eye view provides special insight into especially Jewish concerns. Its high modernism neither guarantees transcendence nor signifies a kind of extraethnic literary bonus. The Freudianism that Roth derived from O'Neill, the narrative strategies he gleaned from Joyce, and the lyricism he modeled upon Eliot are indispensable to the ethnic perspective of the novel, doing sociohistorical recovery work that has not and probably could not be done as well in any other way.

Mario Puzo writes of the urge to "retrospective falsification" that bears down upon adults trying to recollect immigrant experience.[27] Mediating recollection is not only time, not only maturity, but the guilt and glory, the pride and prejudice of having escaped immigrant confines to become a writer in English. In returning to his childhood, Roth works to penetrate the barriers of rationalization and repression that falsify memory, and he does so by investigating the forces at work within the immigrant family that erect those barriers in the first place.

"The whole substance of the novel is presented as what happens inside the small haunted head of David," writes Fiedler, "aside from a prelude, in which the arrival of David and his mother in America is objectively narrated."[28] Roth wrote what he himself called a "prologue" after drafting the novel. It is often praised for being able to stand on its own and anthologized as if to underscore the point. In light of Roth's recollections of his own parents, it seems to function as a chastening reminder to himself that his own father's tendency to violence was, after all, fairly minor and his mother's maternalism more defensive than impassioned. But Roth's opening gesture is neither as autonomous nor as self-indulgent as it might seem. Functioning as the reader's port of entry into the novel, the prologue dramatizes how the dislocations of migration— economic disappointment, marital separation, and ethno- linguistic disenfranchisement—converge to spark and fuel familial psychodynamics. *Call It Sleep* has been celebrated for "transcending" the putative confines of its Brownsville/Lower East Side setting, however Roth introduces the Schearls under the shadow of the Statue of Liberty not in order to leave the issues of Ellis Island behind but to reexamine them through the lens of Oedipus.

The situation and melodramatic conceit of Roth's prologue is so established a set piece that it seems to be taken directly from *Yekl*, Abraham Cahan's 1896 novel that made his reputation as a novelist. *Yekl* is widely accepted as the founding text of English-language immigrant realism. Here is the shared sce- nario: Two to three years before the opening of the novel, a young Jewish man of Eastern European extraction migrated to the United States, leaving behind a bride who is pregnant or has just given birth for the first time. He now goes to claim his wife, dimly remembered, and his son, even less known, at Ellis Island. Hyperconscious about his family's evident for- eignness, he insists upon the removal of a telltale piece of headgear: the wife's Orthodox wig in *Yekl* and the son's polka- dot hat in *Call It Sleep*. The wife is disconcerted by her hus- band's "Yankeeness" and alerted to what in intervening years might have come between them. In both instances, the boy is frightened, cries, and seeks refuge in his mother's arms.

The Ellis Island reunion has become a set piece not only be- cause it is representative—with the exception of the Irish, the men came first—but because the conceit of stepped migration puts into temporal relief the diverging settlements of men and women, particularly emphasizing the male experience of that divergence. For all the refutation of Oscar Handlin's central metaphor of being "uprooted," the image still basically ap- plies: there has been a journey from a village or town, poised at some juncture between feudalism and capitalism, to New York City, which was, by 1890, *the* metropolis, synonymous with multinational industrial capitalism. New York, New York: where wage labor presents unprecedented opportunities for success yet also unprecedentedly brutalizing forms of failure; where intergroup competition and seduction begins with those of neighboring regions and moves increasingly beyond boundaries of nation, language, and faith; and where traditional forms of valuation (especially self-valuation), rooted in pre-Enlightenment religions, suffer before both the still-potent Protestant self-justification and the increasingly persuasive culture of consumption.

More is at issue in the debate over dress than the mild stigma of "greenhorn." Just below the surface are exchanges of meaning and contests of will, initiated though by no means fully orchestrated by the settled yet vulnerable male. In the conceit of stepped migration, it is the young man who has put his understanding of himself as an individual, a husband, and a father on the line. He reaps the rewards of interpreting how to proceed and incurs the dangers of its consequences. Upon him lies the new task of cultural mediator for the family. As he explains changing cultural traditions to his wife, he is, in effect, working to recruit her to his way of looking at America. He presents a brief on behalf of his past actions (at once a plea for solace and a gambit for praise) as well as a policy statement for proceedings that are to include the wife and implicate the only son.

Although there are portents of dissent in *Yekl*, the reunion goes well enough and is credited by Cahan to his title character's felt success. In the three years preceding the arrival of his wife and child, Yekl, who now calls himself "Jake," has won promotions in the garment trades, enjoyed the camaraderie of his fellow workers, and become something of a favorite on the playing fields and at the dance halls after work. Taken aback by Gitl's "bonnetless, wigged, dowdyish little greenhorn" appearance, Jake adopts the roles of reunited lover and native informant, a winsome combination to coax Gitl into replacing her wig with a kerchief. When Jake realizes that the kerchief makes her look like "an Italian woman of Mulberry Street," he accepts disappointment with good humor and gracefully drops the subject. At the end of the scene, Gitl pokes fun at Jake, which is her way of lending reserved approval and of affirming their prospects as a family in America.[29]

Roth sets his reunion in 1907, "the year that was destined to bring the greatest number of immigrants to the shores of the United States." Yet he distinguishes his threesome, saying,

"The truth was there was something quite untypical about their behavior."[30] If Roth follows Cahan in taking the experienced young male as the cultural mediator for young women and children, he departs from Cahan in choosing a figure who has undergone a much more frustrating, apparently less characteristic, settlement. As he boards the ferry to Brooklyn with his wife Genya and son David, Albert feels that he has failed them in the effort to become reestablished in the new land, and he listens defensively for any sign that Genya judges him harshly. Meanwhile, Genya wonders whether the possibility of economic gain has been worth the cost of parting from her husband shortly after marriage and of raising their child for two years without him.

The prologue of *Call It Sleep* presents a wealth of technical tip-offs suggesting Roth's immersion in the psychodrama of O'Neill. First and foremost, he seems to have "staged" the reunion as much as possible without jettisoning the form of the novel entirely. We do not see the moment when the family members first meet. Instead we come upon the threesome, discussion in progress, as they board a ferry bound for Manhattan. Not only is the narrative of the prologue entirely limited to their actions during the crossing (as if it were a single dramatic scene), but the boat motif is exactly the kind of staging device that O'Neill, the ex-sailor, used so prominently in his early plays. To introduce the Schearls, Roth describes dress and posture but lets character reveal itself by speech and gesture. He sets the scene at dusk on a late spring day, giving us directions of light and atmosphere as O'Neill always does; he directs mother and son to stare, wondrously, at the Statue of Liberty, a melodramatic backdrop, as heavy-handedly laden with Freudian and Christologic imagery as anything in O'Neill. Even the audience is inscribed in the text, in the form of a peddler woman and some "overalled men in the stern" who watch and respond to the reunion.

Roth's favorite O'Neill play, *The Great God Brown*, also features what O'Neill had called a "prologue." In their respective prologues, O'Neill and Roth each introduce father-mother-son families (O'Neill actually has two of them) at moments of socioeconomic transition, yet both press beneath their planning for mobility to uncover "irrational" and primarily sexual moti-

vations. Both foreground the parental battle in order to demonstrate how the son is inserted into an Oedipal triangle,
exposing him as a victim at the outset. Both writers thereby
prepare their readers for an investigation of the son's response, his manifestations of need and desire, several years
down the road. Seven years have passed when the curtain
rises for act 1 of *The Great God Brown;* it is four years later when
chapter I of *Call It Sleep* discovers David Schearl at his kitchen
sink.[31]

Two small skirmishes reveal the trouble between Genya and
Albert. When she fails to identify him to the Ellis Island super-
visor as her husband, he construes a breach of trust. She then
answers by noting how "haggard" and "thin" he looks.
" 'You've gone without food,' " she chides (12). Albert's resentment seems to reflect a preoccupation with performance and
fear of exposure, and leads to a second round of chastising
Genya. At his request she attempts to procure an infant-priced
ferry ticket for their son, David, who is several months older
than the requisite two years. When her awkward lie fails, he
takes the small embarrassment personally, suggesting that he
came up with the idea more to test her allegiance than to save
money, squandering her support in her first gesture of offering
it. At the same time, Albert seems overly preoccupied with the
size and maturity of his son, insisting simultaneously that
David is both small for his age and " 'big enough to stand on his
own feet' " (13), as if the boy were old enough to be held accountable for the kind of self-reliance that he fears is missing in
himself.

Although wary of speech, Albert signals his anxieties loudly
and has done so in advance of the actual reunion. Genya's
alertness to David comes at the price of near obliviousness to
the deeper strains in her husband's embarrassment. Given
that he went to the trouble to supply Genya with American
clothing, and given how he has already behaved on the ferry, it
is surprising that she fails to anticipate his irritation at David's
outlandish hat:

> "Pretty? Do you still ask? His lean jaws hardly
> moved as he spoke. "Can't you see that those idiots
> lying back there are watching us already? They're

mocking us! What will the others do on the train?
He looks like a clown in it. He's the cause of all this
trouble anyway!" (15)

Albert demands that Genya remove the hat. The bickering
frightens David, who intuits not only their impatience with
each other but Albert's impatience with him.

When Genya invokes the boy's susceptibility to the chilly
weather, she makes a show of just the kind of overprotective-
ness that Albert has made a point of questioning. He therefore
feels justified in interpreting her refusal as auguring resistance
to his efforts to establish paternal and husbandly authority.
"While his wife looked on aghast, his long fingers scooped the
hat from the child's head. The next instant it was sailing over
the ship's side to the green waters below" (15). If he intends the
act not simply as revenge (a small sad test of his potence) but
as a "second chance" for her to welcome him as the patriarch,
it fails completely. His eruption into violence at the defense-
less child confirms to her that he is not ready to take either
of them into custody. "She lifted the sobbing child to her
breast, pressed him against her. With a vacant stunned expression, her gaze wandered from the grim smouldering face of
her husband to the stern of the ship. . . . Tears sprang to her
eyes" (15). On one side stands father, alone, jaw tightened in
delusory self-justification; on the other stand mother and
child, united in a community of teary apprehension.

It is in Albert's nature to feel the burdens of being a husband
and a father more deeply than most. If we understand the
home to be in many ways the center of premodern cultures like
Eastern European Judaism, then women like Genya, who do
not work outside the home and who move only among those
who speak her dialect, are granted a special privilege: dispen-
sation from the rigors not only of industrial labor but of interethnic contact. "'Within this pale is my America,'" notes
Genya in the fourth chapter of the novel, "and if I ventured
further I should be lost'" (33). As they shuttle between work
and home, men must of necessity negotiate change more than
women need do, and it is the men who take the lead in in-
structing the young, especially boys, in the terms of such negotiations. By tearing off the polka-dot hat, Albert signals a

dreadful, and dread-filled, impatience at the responsibilities that lie before him. Directed at Genya, the gesture is a tantrum of self-pity for her refusal to grant him instantaneous inviolability and an expression of resentment that he must earn her respect and affection by sponsoring their way on this side of the Atlantic. Directed at David, it is a grotesque parody of cultural mediation and paternal instruction, premature and self-defeating.

Venting his own anxieties by scapegoating the child he does not know, Albert takes a first, prototypical step toward locking himself and his son in a vicious circle of paranoia and preemptive betrayal. Albert's action seems to accuse David (absurdly) of something like a failure of filial duty and toddler masculinity, but, of course, it is Albert himself who has sent David into tearful retreat and thus failed as protector and role model. Although David is too young to comprehend and remember in ordinary terms, his crying not only voices a short-term complaint against his father's abrupt intercession but also registers, in the recesses of unconscious memory, a sense of the origin and purpose of this peculiar form of paternal violence. At a deep level, David is being educated into the pattern of suspicion and anticipatory redress that epitomizes his father's behavior. It is not only a recurrent personal threat; it is his primary illustration of what it means to be a male of Jewish descent in America.

If David's unmistakable precursor is Stephen Dedalus, especially during the latter's first years at Closgrow, David is even more of a mama's boy than Stephen, his nascent sexuality is more directly and importantly implicated in Oedipal struggle, and that struggle is at least as carefully contextualized in immigrant New York as Stephen's is in Dublin. In interviews, Roth says he assumed while writing *Call It Sleep* that David was "almost completely victimized, passive," and that only after much personal "maturing," well after completing the novel, did he "come to see the child as much more active, not victimized but on the contrary doing his own share of victimizing."[32] Roth may have been feeling sorry for himself while writing the novel, but the portrait of David that emerges from the instinctual operations of his pen is more skeptical than he credits.

One way of looking at *Call It Sleep* is to see it as Roth's effort to trace the roots of antiassimilationist rhetoric in his own experience and to deal with the two sides of its lingering legacy: on the one hand, to dispel the bitter feeling that he was pushed out of the fold of family and faith by his father; on the other hand, to absolve himself of the guilt that he actually goaded his father into doing the pushing. By patiently reconstructing early boyhood, Roth fingers neither father nor son but rather the dynamics of male assertion and doubt to which both are heir and through which they "victimize" each other. In thereby uncovering continuities in male self-conception and father-son interaction, Roth is able not simply to elude assigning responsibility for abandoning his past but, far more profoundly, to elude the informing presumption (shared by father and son, Jew and Gentile) that he has escaped it at all.

In the first chapter of the novel, David remembers one evening during dinner when Albert complained about being received with hostility at work. When Genya declined to commiserate, Albert flung his plate to the floor. In trepidation, David now leaps from memory to prophesy:

> And other pictures came in its train, pictures of the door being kicked open and his father coming in looking pale and savage and sitting down like old men sit down, one trembling hand behind him groping for the chair. He wouldn't speak. His jaws, and even his joints, seemed to have become fused together by a withering rage. David often dreamed of his father's footsteps booming on the stairs, of the glistening doorknob turning, and of himself clutching at knives he couldn't lift from the table. (22)

David is his father's son, meaning that he is all too prepared to anticipate a slight and to strike out, prematurely, against it. Despite his tendency to suspect David of following in the path of his own failures, and despite his tendency to get into scuffles with other men at work, Albert, at this point, has never laid a hand on his son. It is David who wills his father's anxiousness into actual paternal violence; it is David who, imagining such a result, reaches for knives to rend his father's flesh asunder; and it is David who wakes up from this self-fulfilling reverie apprehensive that he cannot move quickly and strongly enough to the attack.

Freud understood how parricidal desire is born of filial fear, and O'Neill understood at least as well as Freud how the chain of suspicion can fulfill itself, emotionally if not literally, through the psychological games families play. Roth follows Freud in taking sexual investigation to be the primary manifestation of filial suspicion, and he follows O'Neill in charting the provocations that ensue from the act of inquiry itself. *Call It Sleep* is divided into four titled sections. In section 1, "The Cellar," David investigates with zeal and not a small degree of accuracy the efforts of his father's first and only "friend" in America, a man called Luter, to sleep with Genya. It is an extraordinary pastime for a boy still several months shy of his sixth birthday. By attributing to his father a murderous invulnerability, David works himself into a state of hyperattention in which he so intolerantly and self-indulgently probes Albert's masculinity that he provokes paternal rage, drives a wedge between Albert and Genya, and thus claims Genya (heretofore held guilty as "overprotective") for himself.

Luter, Albert's foreman at the print shop, is from the same region of Austria as the Schearls and a bachelor in need of a place to board. When Albert invites Luter to take suppers with his family, Luter accepts with a mind toward seducing Genya. While Albert is enjoying an evening of vaudeville, Luter treats Genya to veiled propositions that animate her in a way David has never noticed before. On a subsequent theater night, Genya avoids Luter by taking David to visit Yussie and his family. Not only is David confirmed in his sense of danger, but Yussie's older sister Annie tricks David into "playing bad," which horrifies him and sharpens his comprehension. As David investigates Luter's advances, he poses and acts upon a series of questions—will his mother play bad with Luter? does his father not care or not know? what will happen if he finds out?—that channel filial doubt into an Oedipal challenge of breathtaking sophistication.

David attributes to his father a super-potency against which he must struggle to legitimate himself, which accounts for the surface rivalry over Genya. But he also contrarily (and this is what makes for overdetermination) construes his father's vulnerability as tantamount to paternal abdication, which lends yet further justification to his Oedipal rebellion. From the moment in which he takes Luter's prospects seriously, David works to unseat his father sexually and to cast himself in his father's stead (though not quite in his father's bed) as his mother's white knight. When Luter withdraws because Genya ends the flirtation, David decides that he has actually made the conquest: "They would never be answered these questions of why his mother had let Luter do what Annie had tried to do; why she hadn't run away the second time as she had the first; why she hadn't told his father; or had she; or didn't he care" (115–16). *Or didn't Albert care:* although David's youth warrants mercy, his fantasized cuckolding of his father is still an extraordinary act of filial aggression.

Confused and distressed by Luter's withdrawal, lashing out rather than seeking an explanation, Albert beats David for the first time, with a clothes hanger, ostensibly for fighting with his playmates. " 'My blood warns me of this son!' " he cries, meeting hysteria with hysteria. More is at stake in his anxiety than his intuition that his son's imagination is in Oedipal overdrive. In the aftermath of the beating, Genya threatens Albert:

"Go out. Or I shall go."
"You?"
"Yes, both of us." (85)

Albert punishes David because he resents the boy's estrangement, yet the effect of his plea for recognition is to drive Genya and David into a tighter circle of mutual consolation. If what Albert fears is further alienation within the home, then his rage is as self-defeating as David's fantasy is self-fulfilling. Indeed, it tends toward the same end.

At the close of "The Cellar," in the immediate aftermath of these brutalizing disappointments, Albert bloodies his hand in a printing accident that Roth represents as a kind of symbolic self-castration. " 'I—I have no fortune with men,' " he says, but then he glares at David in such a way that David knows he is being held partly responsible. "Why?" David asks himself.

"What had he done? He didn't know. He didn't even want to know. It frightened him too much" (137). David represses his curiosity, sensing that he may find he *is* accountable for wounding his father. The combination of Albert's self-flagellation and David's self-restraint is initially salutary. Albert finds less stressful work as a night-shift milkman, and the family moves to the Lower East Side. During the following year's calm, as the Schearls begin to move from toleration to mutual enjoyment, the questions that David and Albert have raised of one another simmer below the surface awaiting aggravation.

In "The Picture," the second section of the novel, David eavesdrops on a conversation between his mother and his aunt Bertha, who challenge his ingenuity by speaking partly in Polish, a language he does not know. Back in Europe, six months before she met Albert, Genya had taken a lover, an organist in a local church. This man had betrayed her, first by marrying a wealthier woman and then by asking Genya to continue their affair. To David's ears, the crucial fact of his mother's violation—what pricks his curiosity, then transforms it into an obsession—is that her lover was a Gentile, or rather, in the term he now learns for the first time, a goy. "So he was a goy. A Christian. They didn't sound the same." Previously he had associated "Christians" with minor schoolboy enthusiasms (school vacation at Christmas) and with what he understood to be inconsequential adult belittlement ("Jesus Crotzmich, the grocery man said") (196). The new term, "goy," invokes the specter of the Other, the forbidden, the desired because despised, the despised because desired. Genya's "voice took on a throbbing richness now that David had never heard in it before. The very sound seemed to reverberate in his flesh sending pulse after pulse of a nameless, tingling excitement through his body" (197).

When Genya's father, a religious scholar, learned of the affair, he threatened to expel her from home on the grounds that she had, in effect, disinherited herself. His accusation of a moral violation—" 'you false slut!' "—is encompassed within the far larger sanction against exogamy, in which he accuses her of having deliberately forsaken her birthright as a Jew: " 'Esau's filth.' " " 'She's begun with goyim! Why should she stop!' " What David hears especially well is how readily his grandfather, in spite of all of his daughter's pain, took himself to be the real victim of the affair:

> "Somewhere, in some way I have sinned. Somehow,
> somewhere, Him I have offended. Him! Else why
> does He visit me with anguish great as this? . . .
> I tell you she'll bring me a 'Benkart' yet, shame me
> to the dust. How do you know there isn't one in that
> lewd belly already. . . !" (201–2)

Interpreting through the veils of language, foreign references, and adult experience, David assimilates this narrative of betrayal and revenge to his idiom of masculine power and frailty: for him, Judaic law is the responsibility of men, including the men of his own lineage, who are empowered by the sacredness of the Law within the Jewish community yet are made vulnerable to the energies of individual (particularly sexual, particularly filial) desire.

At the end of this section, Genya buys a picture of cornflowers, which reminds her of how she ultimately weathered her humiliations: with her self-esteem regenerated like the seasonal blossomings, Genya was reconstituted in the social order by Albert's proposal of marriage. Rather than hearing her relief and gratitude, however, David marches down a chain of Freudian significations from past to present: "What had happened? She liked somebody. Who? Lud—Ludwig, she said. A goy. An organeest. Father didn't like him, her father. And his too, maybe. Didn't want him to know? Gee! He knew more than his father. So she married a Jew" (205). It is crucial to David's misreading that his grandfather's suffering ("Father didn't like him, her father.") somehow be passed along to Albert ("And his too, maybe."), that Genya's transgression against her father should constitute in and of itself a preemptive strike against Albert.

Albert married, unwittingly and against masculine norms, an unchaste woman. In David's not quite articulated interpretation, Albert has been made to and continues to suffer the consequences of Genya's defiance (by David's illogic *has* been "cuckolded" before they were even married). Not only is Albert *still* unaware of the secret, but he embarrasses himself by not even trying to find out. David, in contrast, is both burdened and privileged to know "more than his father." For the next couple of years, David deposits "those curious secrets" in a back corner of his brain, where the issues they raise are suppressed but not vanquished, the information he has gleaned temporarily forsaken yet preserved for eventual use against Albert. What David represses most deeply is Genya's father's ultimate accusation: "Benkart, yes, benkart in belly, her father said. What did that mean? He almost knew" (205). As Marcus Klein notes, "according to [Freudian] formula, little David is allowed to suspect, continuously, that the father is not his real father."[33] I would add that David also feels compelled to suspect, through much of the novel, that his real father is not a Jew.

David suspects that he in and of himself constitutes an "abomination" to the faith, a suspicion that is fueled by and in turn fuels his struggle with Albert. In the third section of the novel, "The Coal," Roth explores David's Pyrrhic success at cheder (what the next generation will call "Hebrew school") to reveal the interweaving of intergenerational rivalry and American Jewish identity. Significantly, it is Albert who suggests that David enroll in cheder, where he feels tremendous pressure from the rabbi to excel and thus demonstrate the vitality of faith amidst the secularized American-born students. "'This one I call my child. This is memory. This is intellect,'" proclaims the rabbi, "'You may be a great rabbi yet—who knows!'" (233) Because religious maintenance is presented as a responsibility of maturing boys, questions of the sacred and of peoplehood contribute to David's felt need to prove himself. Yet because he identifies paternal authority with the letter of the law, transgression against the law, which leads ultimately to symbolic acts of disaffiliation, becomes an ideal medium for filial self-assertion. It therefore should come as no surprise that the step from recitation (for which David is praised) to actual religious instruction stirs in David "the old horror," reversing the intergenerational rapprochement that had begun (even Albert has been expressing quiet satisfaction) and setting David on the road to an insidious, insinuating retrieval of his mother's secret.

Reb Pankower instructs David in a doctrine of salvation contingent upon absolute purity and in a Canaanite notion of a righteous God, who moves amongst the wayward to dispense punishment. The revelation of Isaiah's uncleanliness plays into David's performance anxieties and provokes him to a new level of self-vigilance. "He [Isaiah] said dirty words, I bet. Shit, pee, fuckenbestit—Stop! You're sayin' it yourself. It's a sin again! That's why he—Gee! I didn't mean it" (231). Throughout the section, which takes place during Passover, David finds himself put to various tests: is it really a sin to light the gas after dusk on the Sabbath? can one use a Yiddish newspaper as toilet paper? what if an Italian street cleaner interferes in the ritual burning of leavened breads? David recurrently judges that he, and the boys and men around him (including Albert), will fail. In a final desperate effort to fulfill this Passover rite and thus redeem himself, David seeks to burn the wooden spoon that has held the leavened crumbs. Because Oedipal angst is integral to David's play for ethnoreligious self-justification, that struggle is bound to be self-imploding, at least as Roth represents it.

Down by the river, where David has gone with the spoon, he runs into three Gentile kids playing hooky, who immediately bait him into denying that he is Jewish. " 'I'm a Hungarian. My mudder 'n' fodder's Hungarian. We're de janitors,' " he protests (250). Urinating together, the threesome challenge David to do the same, brilliantly cornering him into both a de facto repetition of his lie and a de facto confession of his lineage:

> At the foot of the junk-heap, the lieutenant named Weasel stopped. "Waida minute," he announced, "I godda take a piss."
>
> "Me too," said the others halting as well. They unbuttoned. David edged away.
>
> "Lager beer," chanted Pedey as he tapped forehead, mouth, chest and naval, "comes from here—"
>
> "Ye see," Weasel pointed triumphantly at the shrinking David. "I tol' yuh he ain' w'ite. W'y don'tchiz piss?"
>
> "Don' wanna. I peed befaw."
>
> "Aw, hosschit." (251)

However much we wish to grant that displaying a circumcised penis before a gang of Gentile toughs is not a sensible act for a

Jewish boy, more is at stake here than exposing David to youthful anti-Semitism. Roth is also, indeed primarily, naturalizing a central Freudian metaphor within an interethnic context and thus restoring its psychosocial resonance and its aesthetic power.

Circumcision inscribes Judaism upon one's masculinity. Here David experiences Jewish identity as a burden demanding not only moral vigilance of oneself and others but also a particular kind of masculine courage, of performance among men. Fearful from the start of the novel that he may not be "up to" what is demanded of him, here he faces anti-Semitism as a challenge to, and for, his manhood—and he fails, "shrinking" before the boys. In one sense, David is unable to proclaim his patrimony because he lacks grace under pressure; he can't even say "piss," a sign of aspirations to maturity among pre-adolescents, only the juvenile "peed." Conversely, in failing to stand up to those who wish to strip him of his patrimony, David has been unable to meet an ideal of masculinity that he as a Jew (as a student of history) understands to be more profound than courage qua courage, that is, the public defense of Jewish peoplehood.

If "The Coal" section of *Call It Sleep* traces how the mandate of religious identity fuels David's filial fears and self-loathing, the final section of the novel traces how David, in seeking to combat that self-doubt, intuitively seizes upon the idiom of Jewish disavowal. One afternoon, David accompanies his father along an alternative milk route and fails at his assignment, which was to protect milk from being stolen. Albert runs down two men, whom he beats with a whip. Then he takes his frustration out on David, reiterating the old charge: "False son! You, the cause!" (282). What David finds particularly bewildering this time around is the "profound and incomprehensible contentment" he discovers in his mother late that same afternoon (297). The seemingly unprecedented fact of sexual reunion between his parents stirs David to jealousy, a rage exacerbated by his sense that, this time, his mother is in on the betrayal. If his father's all-too-evident sexual and emotional insecurities have long provoked resentment and self-questioning, now he is threatened, in the double bind of Freudian boyhood, by Albert's return to potency. On the one hand, David convicts himself of being a "cry baby! cry baby!" like his father; on the other, he interprets Albert's fulfillment of Genya as staking a claim against himself. In postcoital celebration, Albert buys a pair of bull's horns that remind him of Austria. David, however, "sensed only that in the horns, in the poised power of them lay a threat, a challenge he must answer, he must meet. But he didn't know how" (299).

David meets the challenge by befriending Leo Dugovka, a twelve-year-old Catholic Pole who flies kites on the roof of the tenement and spirits himself across neighborhoods on roller skates. "Leo wasn't afraid!" Leo gives the illusion of having transcended his boyhood, mastered the neighborhood, even conquered interethnic strife—" 'I et ev'y kind o' bread dey is. Aitalian bread-sticks, Dutch pummernickel, Jew rye' " (320)— yet for David to take Leo as a father surrogate is tantamount to Oedipus's decision to flee the prophesy of Tiresias. David attributes Leo's self-reliance to his Catholicism, in particular, to the medallion of Virgin and Child that he wears on a leather string. Leo "was not only free of his parents, but he also wore something about his neck that made him almost god-like" (305). Leo offers David male comradeship and a masculine role model without familial complications, just as the scapular Leo wears holds forth a promise of redemption. Underneath David's utopianism lies a paradoxically doubled drive *both* to wound his father as much as possible and to confess to all within hearing (but especially to his father) that he has, indeed, been plotting vengeance. " 'Jews is de Chris'-killers,' " Leo explained, showing David the first crucifix he has ever seen, " 'Dey put 'im up dere' " (323).

David's quest for an amulet like Leo's leads directly to reclaiming his mother's secret and putting it to work. In exchange for a broken rosary, David introduces Leo to a sexually active female stepcousin, who, unaware that she has been set up, does in fact indulge Leo. If one of the lessons of Genya's past is that Jewish men lay claim to the endogamy of "their women," then, in bartering his stepcousin to Leo, David is restaging what he understands to be the primal scene of his mother's disloyalty. " 'W'as's a orr—aorrghaneest?' " David asks Leo (321). In a fever of guilt for what he has done, David runs to Rabbi Pankower, where he reveals not only that the specter of Genya's first lover has returned to haunt him but that he has extrapolated from the event, deliriously, to create his Oedipal trump card: his father is not Albert but a church musician back in Austria.

David's imaginative defathering of himself is an effort both to enact what he imagines within the psychodrama of the family and to excoriate himself for his parricidal endeavors. When Pankower reveals David's fantasy to Albert, it plays into his father's long-standing insecurities about David's paternity and loyalty, instigating a resurgence of the antifilial rage that once again forces Genya to take a stand against Albert and with David. At the same time, David seeks the catharsis of revelation and penance: he confesses the story to Reb Pankower (who represents paternal authority) as Leo would to a priest, and he himself hands his father the whip, asking for his own punishment. Stunningly, the confession fails as an effort to dispel transgressive repercussions, precisely because Albert is just the kind of man to take the confession of disloyalty as the ultimate act of disloyalty, a fact that David has begun to comprehend at the deepest level of his consciousness.

As both catharsis and weapon, a significant element of David's fantasy confession is that he contains goyish blood, as if being born of a profanation against his faith has predetermined that he will believe and act profanely. By wearing the rosary, which tumbles out in the course of the beating, David makes sure his father gets the point. In taking the rosary as proof of David's story, Albert puts a sardonic literalizing twist on what is perhaps the most frequent leitmotif of immigrant literature (a theme already sounded by Genya's father), namely, the curse of the infidel child: "'God's own hand! A sign! A witness! . . . A proof of my word! The truth! Another's! A goy's! A cross! A sign of filth! Let me strangle him! Let me rid the world of a sin!'" (402). As the son is disinherited for his violation against the faith, so he is excised from the patrilineal ancestry. David not only disclaims his sonship; his father is only too willing to accept the disclaimer.

For Roth, there is great significance in David and Albert meeting on the common ground of David's betrayal. In the scene leading up to Albert's curse, we learn why Albert has been suspicious of David all this time. Albert has long felt accused, indeed has accused himself, of allowing his own father to be gored to death by a bull in the months preceding his marriage to Genya. On a pragmatic level, he has always wondered why Genya would allow herself to be married to a man with such a shadow hanging over him. He asks Genya, "'Didn't [my mother] tell you that my father and I had quarreled that morning, that he struck me, and I vowed I would repay him?" (390). Now he decides that Genya accepted his proposal because she was pregnant, and that David's "corrupting" presence in the household accounts for his prolonged impotence.

Under Albert's accusation that David was sired by another lies the more devastating fear that David, on the contrary, might be all too much his son. In David's filial anxiety and anger, Albert recognizes his own Oedipal paranoia. Is it any wonder then that he fears "insanely" for his life? Recall a much earlier curse: "'I'm harboring a fiend! . . . A butcher! And you're protecting him! Those hands of his will beat me yet! I know! My blood warns me of this son! This son!'" (85). If Albert can be said to intuit that the Oedipal cycle is itself a Schearl family tradition, then the novel can be said to have revealed how masculine culture (among these males at least) is reproduced not only despite but indeed through the mechanism of Jewish disaffiliation. In light of Albert's past, but more importantly in light of the unfolding psychodrama, David's disavowal of Albert constitutes not so much a relinquishing of his patrimony as a self-fulfilling tightening of the masculine knot that has, for two generations at least, bound Schearl father unhappily to Schearl son.

In his essays and lectures of the mid-1980s, Raymond Williams has argued, more strongly than anyone else I have read, that "the key cultural factor" shaping literary modernism was "the fact of immigration." In recent years, social historians have insisted that those whom we classically think of as immigrants, the poor who pursued wage labor, were able to reinstall their communities, languages, and folkways on foreign shores.[34] This was not so, says Williams, for "the restlessly mobile emigré or exile, the internationally anti-bourgeois artist." In Williams's estimation, the truly uprooted were the expatriated intellectuals—from Joyce and Eliot to Beckett and

Ionesco—who emigrated as individuals and made themselves strangers in strange lands. From the "endless border crossing" emerged the stereotypical figure of modernist autobiography, that "intense, singular narrative of unsettlement, homelessness, solitude and impoverished independence: the lonely writer gazing down on the unknowable city from his shabby apartment."[35]

Williams is not especially interested in migration as a theme, however. What fascinates him most is the contribution that migration has made to the sine qua non of modernism, the emphasis on literary form:

> But the decisive aesthetic effect is at a deeper level [than theme]. Liberated or breaking from their national or provincial cultures, placed in quite new relations to those other native languages or native visual traditions, encountering meanwhile a novel and dynamic common environment from which many of the older forms were obviously distant, the artists and writers and thinkers of this phase found the only community available to them: a community of the medium; of their own practices.[36]

Out of the ruins of the civilizations and folkways that these artists left behind rose the nearly universal obsession with innovations in form, an effort on the part of the dislocated to construct a common ground out of the material of writing itself. Following Williams's reasoning, writers like Roth, who first experienced migration and then self-conscious ethnic disaffiliation, ought to have found the allure of form as community especially potent.

The place in *Call It Sleep* to examine "the search for community through form" is its celebrated penultimate chapter. In a retreat from his father that is also a quest of his own, David runs, at night, through the East River warehouse district and out across the riverside flats, then pushes a zinc milk ladle into the slot between the trolley tracks that carries the live rail—to jolt himself, or so he thinks, into purity and grace. During the height of the novel's academic popularity, the twenty-two pages of chapter 21 were judged, in Allen Guttmann's words, "among the most remarkable in American literature, comparable perhaps to Captain Ahab's defiant worship of the fiery God who torments him."[37] Darkly lyrical, feverishly mythopoetic, David's monologue on the run, which is italicized and laid out in free verse, would have captured the imagination of postwar readers (trained in Eliot, steeped in existentialism) on its own, but there is more to the chapter than what David has to say to himself.

In a dramatic montage as richly multicultural as anything in the linguistic hybridizations of the recent "beyond ethnic boundaries" literatures, Roth crosscuts David's monologue with snippets of talk, only some of which the boy possibly could be hearing. We are presented with a stunning variety of street patois from a dozen or so voices representing immigrant New York, including Brits of various stripes as well as the usual, putatively more colorful descendants of Ireland, Italy, and Eastern Europe. As David approaches the trolley tracks, these conversations become more attenuated and difficult to differentiate, yielding a montage of phrases, traceable to their originating conversations yet heavily weighted, by repetition and contiguity, with images taken from Freud and Jung, the Cabala and the Mass, Zoroastrianism and *The Golden Bough*. When David at last reaches the third rail, throwing up a thunderous spark and electrocuting himself, the individual witnesses converge into a Samaritan crowd, running for a doctor, determining the boy's identity, and accompanying the ambulance home.

Chapter 21 comes upon the reader in just the same way, and with at least as much impact, as if the last section of Joyce's *Portrait of the Artist as a Young Man* had led without interruption into the first chapter of *Ulysses*. Symbolic to the point of vertigo, hallucinatory in effect if not in composition, the chapter welcomes the kind of patient exegesis proffered by Joyce in *Ulysses*, by Eliot in *The Waste Land*, and, most accurately, as Marcus Klein has noted, by Hart Crane in *The Bridge*.[38] The traditional interpretation has been to follow Roth's lead and read the chapter biographically, as the crossing of the final threshold between ethnic sociology and transethnic aesthetics: "The ending of *Call It Sleep* came as sort of an artistic accession or an assumption into artistry," reports Roth. "The whole process of development of the writer took place in *Call It Sleep*—starting from just an autobiography to a self-conscious literary person." The chapter itself seems to confirm Williams's thesis that the energy within modernism underlying the extravagant play of form was responsiveness to "the open and complex and dynamic social process" in literary innovation. "There is something positive in the writer striving for the broader awareness that enables him to interrelate many more disparate elements in an art form," comments Roth.[39]

The decisive formal effect in chapter 21 is a crosscutting among diverse voices. These voices echo each other's actual phrases (sometimes intentionally, sometimes by wild coincidence) and also share a kind of strobic speech pattern that alternates between down-and-dirty street witticism and a surreal, blasphemous spirituality. Let me illustrate by tracing one trail of reference, which branches out, roughly speaking, from the streetside proselytizing of a "goggle-eyed yid": " 'Only the laboring poor, only the masses embittered, bewildered, betrayed, in the day when the red cock crows, can free us!' " cries the revolutionary (417). The phrase "red cock crows" is picked up by Husky O'Toole, a "mick" who hangs out in Callahan's bar and whose surname is slang for the male sexual organ. O'Toole addresses another of the barflies, whose first name Peter is similarly allusive: " 'how many times'll your red cock crow, Peter, befaw y' gives up? T'ree?' " (418). O'Toole's playfully rhetorical question alludes to the apostle Peter's denial of Christ and is indicative of a kind of irreverence toward the Hebrew Bible and the New Testament that permeates the chapter: O'Toole calls himself " 'a fuckin' atheist,' " but the spirit of his blasphemy, like that of most of the others, is paradoxically good willed and expansive rather than a denial.

Throughout the section there is a sustained pun on card/cod/got/god, which points again both in the direction of sex (codpiece, card as a male dilettante, fish as female genitalia) and of the deity. Taking up this particular invitation to double entendre, one of the British sailors praises his national dish of fish-and-chips: " 'Christ knows how many chaps can be fed off of one bloody cod—' " (417). He refers, on the one hand, to the sexual servicing of several men by one woman, the word "bloody" hinting at both physical violation and menstrual phobia, while offering an even scarier reminder that the prostitutes in Callahan's bar are talking about an abortion performed with ice tongs. He refers, on the other hand, to Jesus' miracle at Bethsaida, where, according to Luke, the answer to how many people could be fed on one fish was an even five thousand.

There are more cross-references among the speakers I have named. And there are more speakers: Bill Whitney the watchman who mumbles to himself on his rounds; "a kindly face American woman" whose climb up the Statue of Liberty is rehearsed in unintended double entendre; and MacIntyre the motorman, who exchanges curses with an Armenian peddler blocking the tracks. Throughout the section, Roth brings together fragments from these conversations, repeating them in attenuated or revised form and introducing surprising echoes. The voices merge climatically into a single chorus:

> "Dere's a star fer yeh! Watch it! T'ree Kings I god.
> Dey came on huzzbeck! Yee! Hee Hee! Mary!
> Nawthin' to do but wait fer day light and go home.
> To a red cock crowin'. Over a statue of. A jerkin'.
> Cod. Clang! Clang! Oy! Machine! Liberty! Revolt!
> Redeem!" (418–19)

Roth reproduces the conflation of moments from different conversations as if it were a monologue, the apotheosis of his formal experiment.

Williams hesitates between affirming the play of the medium as a goal in itself and speculating that the particular kind of formalist experiment—encompassing fragmentation, montage, heteroglossia, and so forth—reflects the particular challenges facing the expatriated intellectual in the metropolis. He tempts us with a sense that social energies lie beneath what critics (Edmund Wilson and Malcolm Cowley on these shores) have long regarded as the turn against the social, but we are left with only the vaguest sense—"a community of the medium," "the only community available to them"—of where that social desire tended, never mind what it actually achieved. In the particular instance of Roth, the play of formalism readily suggests a symbolic act of figuration: a merging of peoples in

the tradition of American alchemy. In converging but not fus-
ing the vernaculars, Roth imagines a melting pot as that image
is traditionally used, not as an initiation rite into Anglo-
conformity but as a magic cauldron of syncretism.[40] We may
construe his representative figures as reflecting shame in his
origins, but the orgy of multivocality is as ambitious (and, I
think, as radically humane) as anything in the more poetic
strains of melting-pot utopianism.

Reading chapter 21 as a visionary social act, we acknowledge
that a forging of common ground is one of Roth's implicit
agendas in the concluding pages of *Call It Sleep*. But the
community is not necessarily the conjoining of "internationally anti-bourgeois" artists—"from Apollinaire and Joyce to
Beckett and Ionesco"—that Williams has principally in
mind.[41] It seems to me that Roth took the successful functioning of Walton's circle of modernist sympathizers as a given: if
he did not entirely disappear into it, he understood his res-
ervation to be an act of artistic distancing, not a product of
cultural anarchy and social fragmentation. More important,
one presses allegory too much (and in a dangerously self-
referential direction) to insist that the coterie of working-class
and underclass characters in chapter 21 are really stand-ins for
Roth's peer group. It is not coincidental that Roth drafted this
section of the novel in the dark months following the stock
market crash of 1929. The group Roth assembles can and
should be taken on their own terms, their convergence over
David's body constituting a rhapsody of proletarian camaraderie.

Whichever class configuration we settle upon, whether we
push beyond immigrant multiculturalism to emigré multiculturalism or not, we run the risk of discounting David. Roth
insists that he "left the child" and "wandered all over the city,"
but, of course, he held the child in the back of his mind all the
time.[42] It is not a coincidence that the author of the most extravagant, and serious, combination of graphic innuendo and
Judeo-Christian blasphemy in chapter 21 remains David himself: "*In the crack,/remember. In the crack be born*" (411). It is not a
coincidence that David reaches his climax, inserting the milk
ladle between the trolley tracks, just at the moment when the
collage of voices reaches its tightest focus. After the speech

merges into a single quotation, Roth cuts immediately to David's self-electrocution:

Power
Power! Power like a paw, titanic power,
ripped through his body and shackled him
where he stood. . . . he
writhed without motion in the clutch of
a fatal glory, and his brain swelled
and dilated till it dwarfed the galaxies
in a bubble of refulgence. (419)

As David is shocked, the individuals whose voices we have been overhearing are terrified. Gathered into a crowd over the still, small, burned frame of this nine-year-old boy, they stand riveted, breathless, in terror for David's life.

Not only does the commingling of voices occasion David's act of purification, but the crowd, in the raw humanism of its concern, carries him aloft symbolically (floating that "bubble of refulgence") before literally doing so. In the climax of the chapter, a young physician awakens David:

the interne glanced while he drew
    "Waddayuh say, Doc?"
a squat blue vial from his bag, grimaced, un-
        (*Zwank! Zwank! Nothingness beati-*
        fied reached out its hands. Not cold
        the ember was. Not scorching. But as
        if all eternity's caress were fused and
        granted in one instant. Silence)
corked it, expertly tilted it before
        (*struck that terrible voice upon the*
        height, stilled the whirling hammer.
        Horror and the night fell away. Ex-
        alted, he lifted his head and screamed
        to him among the wires—"Whistle,
        mister!Whistle!)
the quiet nostrils. The crowd fell silent, tensely watching.
    "Amonya."
                    "Smells strong!"
                "Stinks like in de shool on Yom Kippur."

> *(Mister! Whistle! Whistle! Whistle!*
> *Whistle, Mister! Yellow birds!)* (430–31)

David understands himself to be going through some process of contrition, penance, and second birth—the stilling of Oedipus's "whirling hammer"—which he associates with Pankower's Old Testament lessons, particularly Isaiah 6, and with Leo's misinstructions in Catholicism. But we understand David's accomplishment from a wider perspective that takes in the multitude whose concerted concern is epitomized in the intern. David's task—to extricate himself from the Oedipal struggle altogether—is too difficult for him to effect on his own, and the magical regimes of Judaism and Christianity are too much implicated as cause to function, hybridized, as a medium for psychological purification. Roth has elicited the folk of the city on David's behalf; they perform at his direction in a utopian rite of initiation that derives as much from his own reading of Joyce and Frazer as from David's immersion in cheder mysticism and street Catholicism. If heretofore we have wrestled with the temptation to speak of David as the mere occasion for a postmodern explosion of multivocality, the formula of means and ends here threatens to reverse itself, throwing new light on what has transpired previously. It is as if Roth has taken David's impossible struggle for psychological self-transcendence to heart and orchestrated a ritual of spiritual catharsis, a paganish chanting of Lower East Side peoples, to help him in ways he cannot help himself.

It is a measure of the ultimate force of the novel (and not just a New Critical drive toward "coherence") that, for all the praise heaped on the lyric inventions of chapter 21, the focus of critical debate is David's psychological state and prognosis after his self-induced "shock therapy." "Not pain, not terror, but strangest triumph, strangest acquiescence," concludes the novel. "One might as well call it sleep" (441). Walter Allen, in his afterword to the 1964 paperback, takes David's version of what he has been through at face value, attributing to the boy "a vision that unifies his fragmented world and, in a sense, reconciles him to his experience of that world" (447). The qualifying phrase, "in a sense," hedges Allen's bet. In the clearest statement of disagreement, Fiedler argues that "his intended sacrifice redeems no one": "The boy does not die, the world is not made clean." Pressed to resolve the dispute over whether David does or does not have a "private, internal transformation," Roth wisely waffles (why should he have to solve the dispute?), crediting David with a "triumph" of "intent": "The triumph he feels in the end was that he made the attempt, even though it is a failure."[43]

From the earlier cycles of preemptive betrayal with his father, David comprehends at some unconscious level that running away plays into his father's anxieties, thus constituting a gesture not of escape but of defiance. In chapter 19, during the ruckus of revelation at the apartment, David hands Albert a whip, asking to be beaten. However much he intends an act of penance, he floods the filled well of his father's guilt. Although he thinks he is pursuing transcendence, his act of self-electrocution is motivated as an act of revenge against his father for the very beating that he himself has had no small hand in soliciting. "Yuh dared me . . . Yuh double-dared me . . . Now I gotta. . . . *Now I gotta make it come out*" (409).

Competitive male display—father to son in the horns and the bullwhip, son to father in the cross of the rosary and now in the milk ladle—is signaled not only in the erotic language of David's explicit intent, to make it come out, but in his tallying, when the ambulance returns him home in chapter 23, of the effect upon his father:

> His father threw his chair back, sprang to his feet. His eyes bulged, his jaw dropped, he blanched.
>
> For the briefest moment David felt a shrill, wild surge of triumph whip within him, triumph that his father stood slack-mouthed, finger-clawing, stooped, and then the room suddenly darkened and revolved. He crumpled inertly against the cradling arms. (434)

For David, sleep is the irony that Oedipal victories are by their nature self-defeating. In his moment of shrill, wild triumph over his father (a feeling that is said to "whip" through David), it is not his father who crumples but David himself who crumples into his father's arms, an act that is, at one level of signification, not transcendence but the cradle of the Oedipal dilemma itself.

Yet Albert here blanches not with concern for himself (as it has always seemed he did before) but at last for David, and David, in relinquishing the spirit of struggle, collapses not into Genya's arms but into Albert's. If David's confession of sexual betrayal and of a wanderlust toward Christianity is finally as much a provocation (given his father's temperament) as a gesture for reconciliation, David's running away is a blatant provocation—watch me, father, I'm going to kill myself!—that, in practical terms, may improve the Schearls' day-to-day life. In bed, David reawakens to consciousness, listening as Albert leaves the apartment to purchase ointment for the burn on his son's foot: "A vague, remote pity stirred within his breast like a wreathing, raveling smoke, tenuously dispersed within his being, a kind of torpid heart-break he had felt sometimes in winter awakened deep in the night and hearing that dull tread descend the stairs" (440). Rather than returning to his fevered delusions, or to the eavesdropping that has caused so much of the trouble, David, like an "ordinary" small boy, simply seems to track the goings-on about him. I am unsure whether the pity he feels is for himself or for his father. If for Albert, as it may well be, then Roth has afforded David, just before his final sleep of the novel, an unprecedented insight. One need not rely upon an overreading of this moment, and indeed should not, for David is still a child and the burden of amelioration is not his to bear.

Nor will the burden of mediation fall on Genya alone, as it always has. For all the stark antipathy between Genya and Albert in chapter 19, the confrontation is now revealed to have opened the way to a reaffirmation of their marriage. Not only does Genya have a better understanding of the cycle of mutual fear and preemptive self-assertion that has joined father and son (the truth is fully out), but in the penultimate moment of the novel, after David's collapse, she goes beyond insisting that "none foresaw this" to confessing her own responsibility in keeping from Albert while revealing to David the secret of the cornflowers.

> "It—it's my fault you'd say. Is that it?"
> She shook her head wearily. "What use is there to

talk about faults, Albert? None foresaw this. No one
alone brought it on. And if it's faults we must talk
about it's mine as well. I never told you. I let him
listen to me months and months ago. I even drove
him downstairs to—to—"
    "To protect him—from me?"
    "Yes." (440)

Once again, Roth proves that he is a student of O'Neill. What
one carries away from the novel as the prognosis for the family
depends on how this exchange is performed. I prefer to credit
Albert with a conciliatory, expeditious will.

On the one hand, Albert is said to click his teeth at Genya's
stinging revelation. On the other hand, he himself has staged
this exchange, in a subtle but utterly crucial way. Immediately
prior to the exchange, he produces a slip of paper with the
name of an ointment for the burn on David's foot, which Genya
goes to take, assuming he wants her to play servant. He volunteers to go to the druggist himself. He reports the doctor's conviction that David will be better in a day or two, thereby
putting the danger into perspective and lowering the tension
level. Only then, after fairly well orchestrated preparation, be
it defensive or contrite, does Albert raise the question of guilt
and of his own guilt in particular.

I rest my case for hope, however, not on how Albert sets up
the exchange but on how he closes it. Before the mutual admissions, when Albert volunteered to go to the druggist, "his
preemptory tone lacked force as though he spoke out of custom, not conviction" (440). In the immediate aftermath of the
mutual admissions, he makes good on his promise, exiting
without a dance of self-congratulation to get the ointment. It is
an act of palliation not only for David but for Genya, and it is an
act, above all, that lends a tacit seal of approval to how David
and Genya care for one another. In leaving the apartment,
Albert allows Genya to go alone to David's bedside, making
possible the final exchange in the novel:

    "Perhaps you'll be hungry in a little while," his
    mother said persuasively. . . . "And then you'll go
    to sleep and forget it all." She paused. Her dark, un-
    swerving eyes sought his. "Sleepy, beloved?"
        "Yes, mama." (441)

Albert, meanwhile, has volunteered to be out on the street doing, albeit in a small way, what has to be done. In embracing the opportunity to provide, he makes a first step toward establishing his authority as a patriarch; in accepting a certain distance from the circle of mother and child, he makes a second tentative step toward securing himself in trust and ardor with Genya, and in respect and love with David, his only son.

4

The Old Man and the Boys in the Busheling Room: Form, Influence, and "The Tailor Shop"

My designation of Henry Miller as an ethnic writer will surprise most readers. Miller is not even mentioned in the bibliographies of German-American literature, including one that claims to be exhaustive.[1] Of two dozen anthologies devoted to "minorities in literature," I have seen only one that is imaginative and expansive enough (two volumes, over two hundred contributions) to include a selection by him.[2] Neither the Ethnic Studies Committee of the Modern Language Association nor the Society for the Multi-Ethnic Literature of the United States has published a paper or sponsored a talk, to my knowledge, in which Miller made a significant appearance. Although he is one of only a few major American writers whose most important work was produced during the 1930s, and although critics recently have turned to the 1930s in part because this time was a watershed for ethnic writers and ethnic themes, Miller has yet to be associated in any significant way with the literary production of the Great Depression.[3] The closest approaches have been made in passing by critics who expand party-line definitions of proletarian literature, such as Alfred Kazin and Marcus Klein.[4]

As the grandson of Protestant Germans who worked their way up from lower Manhattan to outer Brooklyn, Miller was too Teutonic and too fortunate to be certified, under current dispensations, as "the Other." Employed as a personnel boss for Western Union during the 1920s and expatriated to Paris in the wake of the stock market crash, he is judged to have forsaken whatever authenticity he merited as a plebe. As a writer who focused on challenging high modernist aesthetics, he is said to have dissipated his promise as a Dreiserian naturalist in a belated conversion to modernist formalism, the results of which (*Tropic of Cancer, Black Spring, Tropic of Capricorn*) have been impugned as self-indulgent, prurient, and, above all, apolitical. In Malcolm Cowley's still-prevailing terminology and periodization, Miller seems like an "exile" who, in departing late, failed to "return."[5]

In 1938, only two years after the French publication of *Tropic of Cancer*, Edmund Wilson, writing in *The New Republic*, anticipated the outline of nearly all subsequent debate over Miller's work when he distinguished between "the conventional critics," who were "too shocked . . . to deal with it," and "the Left-Wingers," who ignored the book on the ground that it was "merely a product of the decadent expatriate culture" and hence "of no interest to the socially minded and forward-looking present."[6] The first American editions of Miller's Paris narratives, published in the early 1960s, fueled the controversy over his sexual frankness and (a little later) his misogyny. Through the late 1970s, even his strongest sympathizers seemed uninterested in dispelling the other long-standing charge, that of political apathy or antipathy. Critics seeking to reappraise Miller's work of the 1930s in leftist political terms encounter a legacy in which he, like many others, is discounted for writing about "personal identity."[7]

More recently, rare but strong partisans have begun to reconstruct Miller's intentions and to place his accomplishments in the context of the struggle to universalize and institutionalize modernist aesthetics. They focus on the Paris trilogy as an attempt to create an alternative modernism: in its own time a deliberate response to the "revolution of the word" of the preceding decade, in retrospect (for the academy at least) a road of aesthetic possibility and valuation not taken. Wendy Steiner concludes her essay in the 1988 *Columbia Literary History of the United States*, "The Diversity of American Fiction, 1910–1945," with an homage to Miller, placing him at the cutting edge of the second wave of modernism, surprising praise given his still tenuous relationship to the academic canon.[8] More pointedly and at greater length, Raoul R. Ibarguen illuminates "the unsuspected density and coherence of Miller's narrative and aesthetic polemics" by analyzing the relation of the *Tropics* to

Ulysses, The Great Gatsby, and the discourse of the "new novel."
Ibarguen concludes, "Miller's radically digressive, free-flowing
prose style advances a post-realist/post-naturalist 'narrative
method' that closely pursues and disputes, almost point for
point, the then emerging 'mythic' consensus."[9]

It was part of the competitive edge of high modernism that
its practitioners understood themselves to have broken utterly
from the genres of realism, naturalism, and local color, genres
closely associated with the representation of ethnicity and so-
ciocultural mobility. Miller was no exception. In the 1920s, he
was a student of naturalism—Balzac, Zola, Dreiser, and Jack
London—committed to exposing the Horatio Alger myth.
Clipped Wings, his first full-length work, really his only major
production of the 1920s, was modeled directly upon Dreiser's
book of socially critical sketches, *Twelve Men.*[10] When Miller relocated to Paris, he was still thinking of reworking *Clipped
Wings* into publishable form.[11] But, as he reports in his letters,
he was "converted" to high modernism by several interlocking
circles of writers, including an overseas branch of expatriated
New York intellectuals as well as Anaïs Nin.[12] In essays he
wrote during the 1930s, Miller set an agenda for his books: to
outstrip Joyce, Eliot, and Proust in their outstripping of the
anachronistic conventions of nineteenth-century realism and
naturalism.[13]

Miller's polemical embrace of modernism is central to the
making and meaning of *Tropic of Cancer.* Yet to characterize the
Paris works as vanquishing naturalism is to run the risk of reiterating, or of seeming to reiterate, Miller's claim of total
rupture. Steiner declares, "What Miller devises is not the subversion of the Horatio Alger plot, as we have seen it subverted
from Jack London to John Dos Passos, but the end of that plot
altogether and the embracing of aesthetic possibilities explored
more in poetry than in prose."[14] By accenting Miller's formal
experimentation, Steiner preempts consideration of the *Tropics*
as a revision of his naturalist efforts in the 1920s and as a response, more generally, to the tradition of the Alger/anti-Alger
story running from Crane's *Maggie* and Dreiser's *Sister Carrie*
to Cahan's *Rise of David Levinsky* and Nathanael West's *Cool
Million.* Ibarguen, too, speaks of Miller's "post-realist/post-

naturalist 'narrative method,'" but does such a method mean what Steiner says it means, the end of the Horatio Alger plot altogether?

In developing his signature first-person narrative, Miller shook himself free of the techniques of realism and naturalism, but he sharpened the autobiographical specificity of his content and deepened the autobiographical wellspring of his form. Wherever we look in the *Tropics* we can find up-from-the-ghetto plottings, because wherever we look we find the fictionalized coming into voice of a writer of poor social credentials and dubious literary prospects who stylized himself, not incidentally, as "Gottlieb Leberecht Müller."

Miller was 100 percent Lutheran German by blood and brought up that way.[15] Although Miller's grandparents emigrated from Germany to the United States, Miller was raised within an extended family more typical of the second generation than the third. "Right on into the 1920s," one of Miller's biographers reminds us, "there were people living in Brooklyn who spoke nothing but German."[16] The Millers' lingua franca at home was, in fact, still German, so Henry Valentine experienced the typical immigrant offspring's shuttle between the foreign mother tongue and the English of school and public life. In 1901, when he was ten, the family made a crucial move from Williamsburg, a tough neighborhood of mixed immigration, to the more suburban neighborhood of Bushwick, which was then solidly blue and white collar and, as Miller would say, "stolidly" German American. For high school, he insisted on commuting back to the old neighborhood, where he embraced the community of Russian Jews and Southern Italians who had poured across the Williamsburg Bridge from the Lower East Side. After graduating second in his class in 1909, he applied for a scholarship to Cornell (to study German!) but was offered insufficient funding. So he enrolled in tuition-free City College. He would drop out after one semester, when *The Faerie Queene* disillusioned him and the Jewish majority made him feel like an outsider.[17]

Miller's most famous statement about his ancestry is his summary dismissal at the beginning of *Tropic of Capricorn:*

Wherever there is cold there are people who work
themselves to the bone and when they produce
young they preach to the young the gospel of
work—which is nothing, at bottom, but the
doctrine of inertia. My people were entirely Nordic,
which is to say *idiots*. Every wrong idea which has
ever been expounded was theirs. Among them was
the doctrine of cleanliness, to say nothing of righ-
teousness. They were painfully clean. But inwardly
they stank.[18]

Miller's ethnic self-parody notwithstanding, hard work, self-
discipline, and middle-class respectability did indeed run
strong among German immigrants. Such values were as hal-
lowed in upscale, insulated Bushwick as they were in Yorkville,
a genteel German-American Manhattan stronghold where his
maternal grandparents ultimately had found a home. No one
ever accused Miller himself of having such German virtues. Yet
there was another aspect of his upbringing that Miller would
romanticize more than resent.

Of Miller's three major biographers to date, Jay Martin and
Mary V. Dearborn both emphasize the tension Miller felt between the "Prussian" self-discipline and right living associated
with his mother's side of the family, who came from the north
of Germany and whom he resented for being "Nordic," and
the "Bavarian" appetite for conviviality and dissipation, which
he identified with his father's side of the family, who came
from Southern Germany, below the white-sausage line.[19]
While it was true that Miller's parents seemed to have embodied these distinctions, it was also true, as Dearborn notes, that
both tendencies could be found in both families. The background I wish to trace here may or may not have Bavarian
roots, but it most definitely concerns choosing convivial dissipation over right living, and it most definitely involves siding
with his father rather than his mother.

I am not interested in imputing German qualities to Miller,
nor am I trying to identify what is inherently Germanic about
his writing. What makes the case of Henry Miller provocative
to the student of literary ethnicity is his identification, al-

ternatively burdened and joyous, with a certain milieu: that relatively benign East Side underworld of male "pipe dreamers," who represented the various strands of the New York City polyglot working classes and who were tied to one another by the special friendship generated by their decision to relinquish Alger's ladder. We find this world of the down-and-out ethnic working class depicted in many of the most so-phisticated of American texts of the 1930s, texts authored by writers from the full range of immigrant backgrounds. It is the milieu to which Roth appealed at the end of *Call It Sleep;* it is the milieu out of which O'Neill created his Depression-era master-work, *The Iceman Cometh;* and it is the milieu with which Miller identifies in one of his finest pieces, "The Tailor Shop."

"The Tailor Shop" is a fifty-page autobiographical narrative that Miller thought was important when he wrote it, and that his editors and anthologizers have favored ever since. Miller made "The Tailor Shop" the centerpiece of *Black Spring* (1938), itself the middle volume of the *Tropics* trilogy. Under what was evidently Miller's editorial guidance, New Directions included it in the first American edition of his writing, the anthology *The Cosmological Eye* (1939). More recently, John Calder chose "The Tailor Shop" for the first posthumous British collection, *A Henry Miller Reader,* compiled in 1985 for Picador Classics.

"The Tailor Shop" is divided into three stretches or narrative sections, set vaguely in the years surrounding the First World War and culled from Miller's memories of working for his fa-ther: an account of the workday at the tailor shop, emphasizing the friends Miller Sr. made there; a pastiche of immigrant local color, celebrating the Miller family's German-American fetes but bitterly skeptical of its petit-bourgeois predilections; and a Joycean meditation on the birth of Miller's own artistic con-sciousness, unfolded against the continuing backdrop of sell-ing clothes and dealing with relatives. What begins, then, as the story of Miller's father and his cronies passes through fam-ily melodrama and concludes as an exploration of young Miller's emerging aestheticism. To make sense of Miller's nar-rative structure is to uncover a previously unsuspected agenda: we must consider why Miller begins his portrait of the artist as a young man not in 1909 at City College (where he was dismayed by academic gentility), not during the mid-1920s (when he took a leave of absence from Western Union to write *Clipped Wings*), and not with his friends in Paris (who converted him from naturalism to modernism), but, of all places, in his father's garment shop.

It seems obvious to say that Miller begins "The Tailor Shop" with his father's buddies in order to credit them in some way with his aesthetic development, yet no one has said it. In the little attention that has been given to "The Tailor Shop," critics assume an Emersonian self-making in which Miller breaks into artistic consciousness by breaking out of the tailor shop and domestic entanglements. Martin writes, " 'The Tailor Shop' gave an account of his frustration when he dreamed of being a writer but worked in his father's tailor-shop."[20] Emphasizing Miller's troubled self-distancing from father and family, Kingsley Widmer interprets the formal shifts that mark the three parts of the narrative—from mimesis through parody into surrealist romanticism—as expressive of "the obvious problems of reaching manhood."[21] Widmer does note that Miller stores up "fragments of memory" yet nowhere ponders the relation between the old men who are the primary article of memory and the alternative modernist voice whose birth is being dramatized.

Martin, Widmer, and the others are right, of course, that "The Tailor Shop" is organized, at the most explicit level of plot and meaning, as a narrative of letting go, of discontinuity. But a strong undercurrent within the narrative and, more important, Miller's formal experimentation tell an alternative story of carrying forth, of continuity. In the case of Henry Miller, there is no need for the kind of aggressively revisionist scholarship that penetrates behind the rhetoric of cultural transcendence to identify ancestral influence. Miller has already done that work for us. In "The Tailor Shop," Miller rescues, deploys, and flaunts an aesthetic inherited from his father's circle of friends.

In the first section of "The Tailor Shop," Miller renews his interest in demystifying upward mobility, but he takes a far different tack from the didactic anticapitalism of *Clipped Wings*. Miller looks back at the men's custom tailoring business from the self-justifying vantage point of the mid-1930s (down and out in Paris and loving it) and shows that, before the war at least, the garment industry meant something more than manly discipline and the righteous pursuit of wealth. Like the young Silas Lapham or David Levinsky, men at work were supposed (both in the sense of presumption and of obligation) to pursue advancement ceaselessly and without compromise. But the men of Miller Sr.'s tailor shop seem to have devoted an inordinate amount of energy to making each other feel better about being stuck (as they saw it) in the capitalist rat race.

In the heyday of his father's business, custom tailoring involved customers at close quarters, a clientele wealthy enough to support not only the work force but hangers-on, and such small growth potential that Miller Sr., owner as well as head tailor, might as well spend much of each day on prolonged liquid lunches.[22] "A joint corporation of father and son, with mother holding the boodle," the tailor shop was the equal, in terms of work, of any of literature's petit-bourgeois sweatshops, including the print shop in *Call It Sleep*, the grocery stores in *Bread Givers* and Bernard Malamud's *Assistant*, the railroad clerking room in Puzo's *Fortunate Pilgrim*, or, for that matter, the Western Union messenger office Miller first presented in *Clipped Wings* and reproduced in the first chapter of *Tropic of Capricorn*.[23] In recreating his father's work life, Miller preaches against the dreariness and anxiety of the business only to celebrate how the work routine requires, permits, and instigates therapeutic relations among men. Taking measurements and modeling the end results, breaking for coffee or a drink or lunch, fretting about accounts receivable, even giving sales pitches do not simply make the work palatable. From work-related activity emerges a sense of community that we too easily call "male bonding": multiply centered, often fractured, yet sustained and sustaining.

At work Miller Sr. maintains contact with a social and ethnic cross section of men buying their clothes, making their livings, or simply hanging out in midtown. Customers with inherited wealth (a majority of those still using custom tailors) pay Miller Sr. not so much for clothing as for informal therapy, recurrently inventing or recycling pretexts to visit the shop, where the fitting room provides a masculine intimacy more charged than an analyst's couch. While customers undress, they kvetch and confess. Bearing witness to their aging, Miller Sr.

offers a mild laying on of hands and the promise of clothing crafted to compensate for the decay of their bodies. The "silk-lined duffers" pay him well for such services, yet he squanders a great deal of the profit (Louise Miller never sees much "boodle") by outfitting a different set of men gratis: his cronies at the Hotel Olcott, whom he seeks out daily for mutual solace and entertainment. "I feel sorry for him and for all merchant tailors who have to kiss rich people's asses. If it hadn't been for the Olcott bar across the way and the old sots he picked up there God knows what would have become of the old man. He certainly got no sympathy at home" (80). While wealthy customers tax Miller Sr. with disguised demands for attention, he in turn uses them as a justification for seeking friendships outside the cash nexus, companionship vibrantly masculine and with an air of homoeroticism threatening only to those outside its sphere.

Throughout the narrative, Miller complains about having to service the egos of the well to do, yet, in depicting his father's friendships with the down and out, Miller celebrates a similar kind of care. Consider, for instance, Paul Dexter. A "dreamer" from Indiana, Dexter dooms himself to continual unemployment because he esteems himself a "$10,000-a-year man" and, unhappily, no prospective employer offers him more than $9,000. Miller Sr. indulges Dexter by providing suits supposedly on account, to help Dexter land "this mythical job," but actually as a form of therapy, ministering to the self-loathing attendant upon not working and not being able "to patronize a good tailor." "Once he landed the job everything would be settled in full. There was never any question about that in Paul's mind" (91). Not only does Miller Sr. clothe Dexter beyond his means, but he looks after him, proverbially, as only a mother could. When a despondent Dexter reappears from one of his periodic binges, Miller Sr. cleans him up and repairs his clothing, then addresses his self-respect by talking him into another suit. "The old man would coax him into it, saying to Paul all the while, 'Nothing's too good for you, Paul . . . nothing!'" (93).

Miller describes only one incident of homosexual consummation: one drunken night Miller Sr. takes another one of these hangers-on, Tom Jordan, home to bed. However occasional actual sex is, and however dependent such occasions are on alcohol, the closeness among the men has an integrity of its own. Habitually contained in an entirely male sphere, that closeness does not depend, by and large, for either its romance or its physicality on the kind of triangulation through women that Eve Kosofsky Sedgwick has found so often characterizes male homosociality.[24] Simply put, the intimacy is out of the closet, confessed, and (better yet) inviting: "The men who passed through my father's shop reeked with love" (119). Miller Sr.'s transgression in bedding Tom Jordan was in going home with him, less a confession than a provocation, since it is hard to imagine that Louise Miller does not know she is in competition, at least emotionally.[25] As Miller says of his father and Paul Dexter: "Never have I seen two men look at each other with such a warm glow of admiration. Sometimes they would stand there looking into each other's eyes adoringly until the tears came" (93–94).

The strongest of Miller Sr.'s friendships exemplifies an interdependence traditionally gendered as "feminine" and designated in much of the ground-breaking work in women-centered feminism as the special (if not exclusive) achievement of women. Yet, as critics have shown, there exists within American literature a tradition of rhapsodic evocations of male sexual and spiritual communion.[26] What Frank Lentricchia has written about the seventh section of Wallace Stevens's "Sunday Morning" also applies to the opening section of "The Tailor Shop": "it joins mainline American literary visions of male utopias," visions, that is, of men who come together without women, in implied or explicit sexual indulgence, to make "in community . . . a fundamental poetry."[27] Whereas Stevens envisions utopia prophetically, Miller looks back in elegy, evoking the past to remind the future.

What is truly utopian about Stevens's ring of men in orgy is that their nakedness effaces social difference. Much of the exhilaration of "The Tailor Shop" comes similarly from flirting, in the midst of the marketplace of work, with intercourse across class and ethnic lines: among customers mainly of established American stock, small-scale managers and salesmen (many Jews and Irishmen), wage laborers of the shop and district (above all, Jews), and the ne'er-do-wells who pass through the shop and bar (America's most democratic subculture). Yet Miller's choice of the adjective "reek" to describe the atmosphere of love emanating most powerfully from the ne'er-do-wells is meant as a reminder that they continue to be distinguished by their scents of poverty. Even when they remove their clothing (much of it donated), they bed down in SROs, rotgut on their breath and in need of a hot bath, marked as beyond the pale of social respectability. Whereas Stevens figures the chanting of his men as an alternative form of work, Miller keeps before us the difference between those like his father, who are able to move at will across the boundary of the marketplace, and those who are shut out of the world of work and its entitlements, a difference that no degree of intimacy can vanquish completely.

As resistance to the social construction of masculinity, the intimacy of the tailor shop, more therapeutic than political, evokes a problem that continues to vex theorists of late capitalism: whether or not capitalism erects so efficient an economy of the self that it can use masculinity not only to motivate production but contain opposition. Though Miller is often thought to have placed his work at a poetic remove from social history, "The Tailor Shop" throws provocative light on a still obscure phenomenon of the capitalist workplace and warrants our attention for that insight alone. Miller's portrait of ethnic male bonding, however, is part of a larger project: he experiments formally not so much in order to analyze the masculine binds of the garment industry as to reproduce in prose the oral culture that those binds make possible.

In labeling "The Tailor Shop" a genre piece and deducing a moral, "the pathetic role of sensitivity in our society," Kingsley Widmer recalls the ghost of *Clipped Wings*. In doing so, he provides little clue that "The Tailor Shop," unlike the earlier novel, is aesthetically sophisticated, extravagant in voice, rhythm, structure.[28] The first section of "The Tailor Shop" can be deemed "a series of character sketches" only if one recognizes that Miller not only describes the community of old men, he embodies it *formally*. In sketching his father's customers and cronies, he mimics their voices and their styles of self-presentation; in ordering and interweaving these cameos, he reproduces the nexus and pacing of their daily encounters with one another.

Miller's transformation of the old men's vernacular culture into writing counters their decline, preserving that culture for historical memory and producing a narrative of immense humor, pathos, and beauty—especially when read aloud.

The men Miller Sr. worships are invariably the most seductive talkers. They include Julian Legree, a matinee idol, who speaks "English in the traditional stage sense, warm, soapy, glutinous English which gives to even the most insignificant thought an appearance of importance" (84); Rubin, one of the bushelmen, who is "a dirty little kike but he knew how to sing" (90); Paul Dexter, whose words, after a drinking bout, "rolled off his tongue like liquid velvet" (93); and Baron Carola von Eschenbach, the son of a Frankfurt brewer, who knows "a thousand jokes, some that had never been told before" (99). Not only the men Miller Sr. loves but those he waits upon and struggles with involve him in an unending stream of verbal sport and intrigue. In a long, involved feud between Miller Sr. and the proprietor of the Olcott, the Millers recruit friends to participate in an implicit barter of suits for food and drink, which results, of course, in yet more talk: "Since it was more pleasant to eat in the company of others he would always invite his cronies to lunch with him, saying to all and sundry—'if that bastard Moffatt won't pay for his clothes then we'll eat them' " (87).

Even when Miller pays only brief testament to the verbal sport of these men, he means to preserve that sport, however fleetingly and on a small scale, by adapting his voice to the personality of the speaker being rendered. In describing George Sandusky, the doorman at the Olcott, Miller's quietly sneaky compliments—"he was a gentleman," "a man who knew how to conduct himself at a funeral or a wedding," "no one could bow and scrape like George"—treat Sandusky in the same oily and unctuous manner that "had endeared him to the Olcott guests" (82–83). Alternatively, Miller labels the bartender Patsy O'Dowd "a foul-mouthed bastard of an Irish mick" in direct imitation of the bartender's own cursing ("call[ing] you a goddamned degenerate cocksucking son of a bitch who hadn't enough sense to pull up his fly") (85). Bunchek's incessant talking manifests a disconcerting, ultimately liberating combination of philosophical solemnity and tolerant irony. Miller dramatizes this combination in a burlesque that could be (this is Miller's point) Bunchek's own: "Bunchek was an ardent member of the Zionist party. He believed that the Jews had a happy future ahead of them. But despite it all he could never properly pronounce a word like 'screw.' He always said: 'He *scruled* her' " (90).

Modulating his voice in mimicry of his characters, Miller makes elaborate use of indirect discourse. The description of the linings and trimmings man is masterful:

> There was Ferd Pattee who sold silk linings and trimmings such as skeins of thread, buttons, chest padding, canvas, etc. A great hulk of a man, like a liner that's been battered by a typhoon, and always walking about in a somnambulistic state; so tired he was that he could scarcely move his lips, yet that slight movement of the lips kept everybody about him in stitches. Always muttering to himself—about cheeses particularly. He was passionate about cheeses, about schmierkäse and limburger especially—the moldier the better. In between the cheeses he told stories about Heine and Schubert, or he would ask for a match just as he was about to break wind and hold it under his seat so that we could tell him the color of the flame. He never said good-by or see you tomorrow; he commenced talking where he had left off the day before, as though there had been no interruption of time. No matter whether it was nine in the morning or six in the evening he walked with the same exasperating slow shambling gait, muttering in his vici-kids, his head down, his linings and trimmings under his arm, his breath foul, his nose purple and translucent. Into the thickest traffic he would walk head down, schmierkäse in one pocket and limburger in the other. Stepping out of the elevator he would say in that weary monotonous voice of his that he had some new linings and the cheese was fine last night were you thinking of returning the book he had loaned you and better put up soon if you want more

> goods like to see some dirty pictures please scratch
> my back there a little higher that's it excuse me I'm
> going to fart now have you the time I can't waste all
> day here better tell the old man to put on his hat it's
> time to go for a drink. Still mumbling and grum-
> bling he turns on his big scows and presses the ele-
> vator button while the old man with a straw hat on
> the back of his head is making a slide for the home
> plate from the back of the store, his face lit up with
> love and gratitude and saying: "Well, Ferd, how are
> you this morning? It's good to see you." And Ferd's
> big heavy mask of a face relaxes for a moment into a
> broad amiable grin. Just a second he holds it and
> then, lifting his voice he bellows at the top of his
> lungs—so that even Tom Moffatt across the way can
> hear it—"BETTER PAY UP SOON WHAT THE HELL DO
> YOU THINK I'M SELLING THESE THINGS FOR?" (88–89)

Pattee's persona, that of a man in an endless monologue with
himself, is exactly reproduced through Miller's own narrative
chatter. Miller builds not just his sentences but his paragraph
out of Pattee's self-presentation, by opening with only a hint of
an introduction, breathlessly mimicking Pattee's parataxis
throughout, then closing the paragraph (and sketch) while its
subject is, as it were, still talking. To that extent, in fact, the reconstruction of Pattee serves as a microcosm for the structure
of the narrative as a whole.

In the case of these men who work in and loiter around the
garment shop, the culture of "the vernacular" means patterns
of interaction as well as of speech. To capture the rhythms of
male friendship (and thus to achieve the mimetic effect that
had escaped him in the didactic naturalism of *Clipped Wings*),
Miller introduces his father's cronies as they might be encountered during an average working day. The timing of each man's
appearance, as well as the narrative space Miller allots to each
man, is meant to reproduce the rhythm of these people in his
father's life: incidental or habitual or extravagantly orchestrated, the occasion of love or hate or mutual entertainment.
Seemingly casual digressions introduce incidental figures: "I
used to stand at the window facing the hotel and watch George

Sandusky hoisting the big trunks on to the taxis" (82). More significant personalities—friends, customers, or business associates—warrant a more careful introduction (the red carpet, narratively speaking) and are highly particularized. Several of Miller Sr.'s oldest cronies like Dexter, Tom Moffatt, and the Bendixes are introduced, then reappear later in the narrative; or their traits seem to reappear in almost identical characters; or their presence is alluded to by the repetition of key phrases earlier applied to them. Customers encountered only in the tailor shop are introduced in the tailor shop and left there; following Miller Sr., we trace the steps of other individuals into the bars and back again to the shop, where they might loll the afternoon away in the big plush chairs of the waiting room.

Just as Miller's sentences capture the spirit and mimic the rhythms of the men he is recreating, so his overall structure for the first part of "The Tailor Shop" reproduces the rhythms of contact and intervention among the men. In opening the narrative, for instance, Miller anticipates and complains about one of the most neurotic customers, H. W. Bendix, reproducing stylistically the anticipation and complaints about Bendix that young Miller and his father make to themselves on the way to work each morning:

> The day used to start like this: "As so-and-so for a little something on account, *but don't insult him!*" They were ticklish bastards, all these old farts we catered to. It was enough to drive any man to drink. There we were, just opposite the Olcott, Fifth Avenue tailors even though we weren't on the Avenue . . . .
> Mornings, eight A.M. or thereabouts, a brisk intellectual walk from Delancey Street and the Bowery to just below the Waldorf. No matter how fast I walked old man Bendix was sure to be there ahead of me, raising hell with the cutter because neither of the bosses was on the job. (79)

As readers, we are plunged without warning into a world not our own, marked by the imperfect verb construction "used to" both as tedious and as somehow already finished. Even after several readings of the opening sentence, it is difficult to figure out whether one of the customers ("these old farts") is asking the cutter to ask Miller Sr. for something on account, or whether, say, Miller Sr. is asking Henry to ask one of their suppliers for something on account. What is clear, however, is that the verbal brinkmanship engaging the Millers, their customers, their employees, and their suppliers overflows the workplace and the workday. Miller throws us, just entering his narrative, into the as-yet-unclear mechanics of the tailor shop in order to demonstrate how he, setting out to work each morning still foggy from sleep, finds himself immersed in interactions that predate the morning and indeed seem to have been going for some time—if for twenty-seven years, as Miller claims for the Bendixes at one point, then before he was even born.

In depicting the appearance and disappearance of men like Pattee in his father's life, Miller equivocates between a day in the life of the tailor shop and the life of the tailor shop squeezed into a single day. Using the imperfect tense, unmediated transitions, and repetitions of image and event, he layers beneath a morning-to-night progression the trajectory of the longer term:

> Nearly all the customers were round-shouldered and potbellied, especially the old bastards who had nothing to do all day but run from the shirtmaker to the tailor and from the tailor to the jeweler's and from the jeweler's to the dentist and from the dentist to the druggist. There were so many alterations to be made that by the time the clothes were ready to be worn the season had passed and they had to be put away until next year, and by next year the old bastards had either gained twenty pounds or lost twenty pounds and what with sugar in their urine and water in the blood it was hell to please them even when the clothes did fit. (90–91)

Focusing on the clothing regime that brings his father and his customers together, Miller is able to render the way the days felt phenomenologically, as they pass one after the other, season after season, and, finally, year after year.

It is a tenet of Miller's dissent from modernism to resist those kinds of structuring principles that allow critics to speak of privileged moments, microcosms of the whole, and scenes primal to the writer's literary imagination. Yet here, in the very middle of his Paris trilogy, he relents and produces a narrative in which the dictum of form mapping content retains descriptive force, however much the actual structure is innovative in representing an unprecedented subject. Miller's mandate is to create a narrative that accurately represents the experience of his father's cronies; his gambit is what we might call linguistic reincarnation: to body forth these men through the flesh of prose itself, approaching something like a visceral appreciation of who they were, how they lived, and why they are to be missed.

For all Miller's formal dexterity, at the end of the first section of "The Tailor Shop" we are tempted to pigeonhole the story as a modernist update on local color, a sophisticated yet ultimately mainline instance of what Warner Berthoff identifies as the "single formal genre that is native and peculiar to the American imagination in literature": "the circumstantial elegy . . . the detailed narrative lament for a disappearing, though perhaps only recently and precariously established, order of life."[29] At the close of the first section, Miller recollects how it felt to bury his father's cronies as they died out, one after another, no one to replace them:

> Regularly, every season, there were a few deaths. Sometimes it was a good egg like Paul, or Julian Legree, sometimes a bartender who had picked his nose with a rusty nail—hail and hearty one day, dead the next—but regularly, like the movement of the seasons themselves, the old buzzards dropped off, one by one. *Alors,* nothing to do but draw a red line slantwise down the right-hand side of the ledger and mark 'DEAD.' (97)

Consonant with the feeling of elegy, Miller shifts focus from the old men to himself as a youth, a shift of theme that announces, in lieu of any explicit designation, the break between sections. As Miller remembers striking the old men from the ledger of the tailor shop, he reenacts that gesture thematically by jettisoning the portrayal of the old men from his narrative agenda.

Underscoring this impression is a transition in style as well, as Miller moves from embodying the intercourse of the tailor shop to telling sexual tall tales, an apparent return to pornographic business as usual. Yet it is through sexual hyperbole that Miller moves his most extravagant effort to salvage and redeploy the oral culture of the old men. In the second section of "The Tailor Shop," he brags of heterosexual conquest in a way that recalls the kind of stories the old men used to tell one another. But Miller's strategy of aesthetic recreation goes beyond the content of those stories to deal with their context: he intends not only to tell the same sort of stories the old men told but to reproduce in the relation between his narrator and the bemused reader the community of ethnic male storytelling with its discourse of sexual self-display, knowingly vicious in its misogyny.

The first sexual tall tale is told upon the occasion of the death of Miller Sr.'s favorite, Paul Dexter, and Miller Sr. himself is credited with instigating the event that Miller narrates. "A short time [after Dexter's death] the old man, moved by some strange whim, urged me to call on Paul's wife and offer my condolences." Miller's language here is coy but transparent: Miller Sr. has asked him to seduce Dexter's widow Cora. Miller Sr.'s request that his son perform as a marital surrogate for Dexter is complicated by the fact that the old man's grief for Dexter is itself partly sexual. In the subsequent exercise of passion, Cora is enfolded in a ambiguous series of sexual displacements. These displacements, however, are not carefully delineated; Miller, for instance, *likes* sleeping with women. What commands our attention is less the act of intercourse than the way it is invoked in notorious Miller style:

> She greeted me in a low-cut mourning gown, a beautiful clinging gown of black velvet. It was the first time I had ever had a tête-à-tête with a woman bereft, a woman whose breasts seemed to sob out loud. I didn't know what to say to her, especially about Paul. I stammered and blushed, and when

she asked me to sit beside her on the couch I almost
fell over her in my embarrassment.

Sitting there on the low sofa, the place flooded
with soft lights, her big heaving loins rubbing
against me, the Malaga pounding my temples and
all this crazy talk about Paul and how good he was, I
finally bent over and without saying a word I raised
her dress and slipped it into her. And as I got it into
her and began to work it around she took to
moaning like, a sort of delirious, sorrowful guilt
punctuated with gasps and little shrieks of joy and
anguish, saying over and over again—"I never
thought you would do this . . . I never thought you
would do this!" And when it was all over she ripped
off the velvet dress, the beautiful low-cut mourning
gown, and she put my head down on her and she
told me to kiss it and with her two strong arms
she squeezed me almost in half and moaned and
sobbed. And then she got up and she walked
around the room naked for a while. And then finally she got down on her knees beside the sofa
where I was stretched out and she said in a low tearful voice—"You promise you'll love me always,
won't you? You promise me?" And I said Yes with
one hand working around in her crotch. Yes I said
and I thought to myself what a sap you've been to
wait so long. She was so wet and juicy down there,
and so childlike, so trustful, why anybody could
have come along and had what's what. She was a
pushover. (96)

Miller does indeed meet his father's injunction to take Dexter's
place, not so much by making love to the widow while the
body was still warm as by telling the story twenty years later in
a fashion worthy of Dexter and of the dying men he epitomized.

In following Dexter's representative death with this anecdote, and in shaping it with his representative voice, Miller is
not merely throwing more light back upon the male oral cul-

ture that he has already effectively illuminated. For Miller and the old men to whom he once reported are not the only ones who bear witness to the ravishing of Cora. By presuming that the (male) reader will be seduced by the story of Cora, Miller implicates him in keeping this particular form of camaraderie alive.

Miller is often censured for objectifying women. In *Sexual Politics*, Kate Millett goes beyond the standard argument to accuse him of plotting to preclude women from the discourse of art itself.[30] The anecdote of seducing Cora, because of its sheer inventiveness, suggests that Miller means the ultimate purpose of sleeping with women to be storytelling among men, reproducing misogyny in the play between speech act and reader's response. To participate in the Cora incident, the reader must be willing to assume the persona of an "old man," a fellow bar patron and worker in men's custom tailoring. In effect, Miller is recreating a community of writer and readers that trades in sexual braggadocio and includes women only by a transsexuality of their imagination.

There is no question that Miller depicts women in degrading and hateful ways, prompting biographers to engage in psychological speculation.[31] His misogyny is grotesque enough to disturb almost all readers, men as well as women, but it is also so outrageously self-indulgent that it amuses and even seduces many of us, women as well as men, deflecting the question of whose psyches are being laid bare. At any rate, sexually graphic passages in the *Tropics* are often very funny, in "The Tailor Shop" completely so.

The second of Miller's tall tales, in which he provokes his wife by bringing the penniless Baron Carola von Eschenbach home to live, is brilliantly self-reflexive, satirizing the exclusive energies within old-time sexual narrative even as it reproduces them. This anecdote begins, surprisingly, with Miller's unnamed wife's initiation into the sex talk of extradomestic male precincts. When the baron first sits down to dinner, he regales Miller's wife with tales of trysts and escapades: "puritanical bastard that she was, she never so much as blushed when he told a few of his risqué stories. She thought they were delightful—*so European*" (99). Miller, however, has very little patience for the baron's gesture, which constitutes a slow, hence promising rapprochement between workplace and household, transcending boundaries of ethnicity, class, and, above all, gender. Injecting himself into the conversation, he deploys a piece of private information (supplied by the baron and symbolically associated with male subculture) that is meant to alienate his wife and reestablish the exclusivity of storytelling. "I tried to break the news gently, but how can you be gentle about a subject like syphilis? I didn't call it syphilis at first—I said 'venereal disease.' *Maladie intime, quoi!*" To dispel his wife's romance with the male subculture, Henry invokes the specter of disease, tricking her into identifying the narration of sexual tall tales with actual sexual acts, the reception of such tales with venereal contagion itself:

> But just that little word "venereal" sent a shudder through my wife. She looked at the cup he was holding to his lips and then she looked at me imploringly, as though to say—"how could you ask a man like that to sit at the same table with us?" I saw that it was necessary to bring the matter to a head at once. "The baron is going to stay with us for a while," I said quietly. "He's broke and he needs a place to flop." My word, I never saw a woman's expression change so quickly. "*You!*" she said, "*you* ask *me* to do that? And what about the baby? You want us all to have syphilis, is that it? It's not enough that *he* has it—you want the baby to have it too!" (100)

Young Miller's ruse succeeds because his wife feels threatened by the idea of venereal disease and thus is willing to retreat from her embrace of the baron and his world. It succeeds because Miller the writer creates for Miller the character a wife sufficiently middle class and domestic that she collapses upon the pronouncement of syphilis into what he calls "uterine hysteria."

Miller reflexively lays claim to his narrative as a form of male tell-all that reveals how disgusting and unhealthy the underground experience of men actually is, baiting female readers (signified by the wife) to lose sight of the difference between what men do and how they talk. Where Miller himself is coming from is suggested by what happens to the baron when the young housewife rescinds her solicitous attention and goes into histrionic retreat. Simply put, she emasculates the homeless baron: "after he had gotten all through with his promises, after he had begged her forgiveness a hundred times, after he had knelt down and tried to kiss her hand which she drew away abruptly, he sat down on the toilet seat, in his cutaway and spats, and he began to sob, to sob like a child" (101). The scene not merely solicits but seems to require that the reader affirm a sexist truism: to make one's confession to a woman is to risk humiliation, so keep your secrets among men who, in common failings, understand.

In the anecdote of the baron, Miller depicts the desire of women with class aspirations for the companionship of marginal men as a small ember that, if flamed, spells catastrophe for the men. The baron's encounter with Miller's wife dramatizes a momentary opening and subsequent tightening of the male circle, a give and take that also is reproduced on a structural level. Just as young Miller introduces his wife to the baron, so Miller as narrator introduces her to us: "My wife— one of my first ones—was highly flattered to sit at the table with a baron" (99). From the beginning, Miller refuses to dignify her with a name or even a rank (first wife? second? third?), her appearance in the text being at his command. Representing the potential for a female readership, the character "Henry's young wife" is invited into the narrative, only to undergo ritual sacrifice as the community of male storytellers and male listeners is reestablished.

In the denouement of the episode, Miller uses his wife's response to Eschenbach, which he instigated, as an excuse to ignore her during her second pregnancy, which is itself a further ploy for justifying male exclusivity:

> She used to succumb to fits of melancholy and, lying on the bed with that watermelon staring her in the eye, she would commence to sob fit to break your heart. Maybe I'd be in the other room, stretched out on the couch, with a big, fat book in my hands, and those sobs of hers would make me think of the Baron Carola von Eschenbach, of his

gray spats and the cutaway with braided lapels, and
the deep red rose in his buttonhole. Her sobs were
like music to my ears. . . . Anyway, after she had
worked herself up to a state of collapse, when the
neighbors couldn't stand it any longer and there
were knocks on the door, then her aged mother
could come crawling out of the bedroom and with
tears in her eyes would beg me to go in there and
quiet her a bit. "Oh, leave her be," I'd say, "she'll get
over it." Whereupon, ceasing her sobs for a moment the wife would spring out of bed, wild, blind
with rage, her hair all down and tangled up, her
eyes swollen and bleary, and still hiccoughing and
sobbing she would commence to pound me with
her fists, to lambast me until I became hysterical
with laughter. (102)

Like the protagonist of Charlotte Perkins Gilman's story "The
Yellow Wallpaper," Miller's wife is relegated to an even more
restricted domestic sphere, her bedroom, against which she
cries and screams and hits. It is tempting to see in the wife's
complaint a protest on behalf of women confined to the company of mothers and children, denied access to the male world
of big, fat books. The male storytellers comprehend the bid for
participation in their circle as threatening to their sanctity and
thus dismiss it as self-deluding and misguided.

In Miller's portrait, what women construe as a desire for the
exchange of language and story is in fact "only" covetousness
of male sexuality, in which sexuality is understood with suffi-
cient narrowness that women can be appeased without breaking male ranks to any significant degree. He constructs
protofeminism as a form of whining domestic jealousy, which
allows him to still its challenge according to the old adage
about what's wrong with difficult women. Young Miller brings
his wife to her senses by giving her what she really needs:

Afterwards, when I had quieted her down a bit,
when I realized that she really needed a kind word
or two, I would tumble her on to the bed again and
throw a good fuck into her. Blast me if she wasn't
the finest piece of tail imaginable after those scenes

> of grief and anguish! I never heard a woman moan
> and gibber like she could. "Do *anything* to me!" she
> used to say. "Do what you want!" I could stand her
> on her head and blow into it, I could back-scuttle
> her, I could drag her past the parson's house, as
> they say, any goddamn thing at all—she was sim-
> ply delirious with joy. (102–3)

As Miller "quiets" his wife by transforming her cries of outrage
into moans of fulfilled demand, the text makes an appeal to the
reader's putatively masculine sensibility, an appeal nearly suf-
ficient to drown out the challenge that this representation of
the wife articulates.

Miller acknowledges that the underwriting conceit of the
passage—"Do *anything*. . . . Do what you want!"—is a cliché
not just of pornography but of the long-standing tradition of
male talk upon which pornography depends. In the facetious
remark that concludes the passage and section, Miller reminds
his reader of a founding convention of male interchange: "*And
I hope God take me,* as the good master used to say, *if I am lying in
a single word I say*" (103). In other words, when men talk to each
other about women, the truth lies not in the tale but in its
telling—or so Miller and his circle of projected listeners wish to
believe. In this instance, he would like to believe that it does
not matter whether his wife actually "asked for" and received
anal sex or not. But, of course, it does matter whether he made
love to her under the circumstances and in the manner narrated, whether instead he raped her or has otherwise misrepresented what they did, whether he might have made the
whole story up, start to finish. It matters for all concerned
whether he is "merely" bragging about a ritual of marital renewal so as to supplement intimacy with male comradeship, or
whether, alienated from the circle of mother and child-to-be,
he feels compelled to claim the renewal of marriage in order to
contain—through the conceit of rabid heterosexuality—a different form of Eros, friendship among men, which serves,
among other things, as a substitute for a waning of marital sexuality.

It is at this concluding juncture that we can raise the question of Miller's irony, the elementary distinction between

writer and narrative persona. It should be clear that Miller constantly stages the scene of his own writing, but does that reflexivity translate into critical distance? Ibarguen credits him with demystifying by parodic caricature certain crucial trajectories of modernist representation, including various forms of masculinity. In reproducing the East Side male camaraderie of his father's tailor shop, Miller employs the kind of transparent self-exposure that Ibarguen finds characteristic, a clarity that may be taken, in terms of its sexual politics, as either forthright or foolish. To say that a writer creates a narrator whose strategies of masculine representation invite and channel feminist critique does not mean, however, that the given writer would acquiesce to or even comprehend his (or her) indictment. Think of Hemingway and of Faulkner. In this instance we might suspect, in fact, that Miller knows he has it coming and waits to greet the deserved comeuppance with more gleefully chauvinistic invention, much in the spirit of ethnic men of old.

As a whole, "The Tailor Shop" depicts the emergence of Henry Miller the writer as a form of ethnic renewal. *Black Spring* opens with a testament of ethnic identity: "I am a patriot—of the Fourteenth Ward, Brooklyn, where I was raised. The rest of the United States doesn't exist for me, except as idea, or history, or literature" (3). What has been misleading in the recovery of "the rise of Henry Miller" is that his text of reference is neither Howells's *Silas Lapham* nor Cahan's *David Levinsky,* the prototypes of mainstream and ethnic realism, but rather Joyce's *Portrait of the Artist as a Young Man,* a novel traditionally classified as the testing ground of European modernism but also of interest as an Irish-continental novel of ethnic passage.

A Portrait of the Artist as a Young Man polemicizes on behalf of expatriation with a deafening oracular eloquence: "I go to encounter for the millionth time the reality of experience and to forge in the smithy of my soul the uncreated conscience of my race."[32] For Joyce, the pathway to self-understanding and literary immortality requires an ever greater distancing from the Dublin of his youth, the petit-bourgeois extended family, and the Irish Catholic Church. Like Howells leaving Ohio for the Brahmin circles of Boston or Yezierska making her way from the Lower East Side to Washington Square, Joyce hallows a road from the putatively parochial confines of his youth to an international community of letters, headquartered first in London, then in Paris. Modeling his own "Portrait" after Joyce's, Miller uses the antithesis between ethnic experience and the ascent into artistic consciousness to structure the concluding section of "The Tailor Shop." Dominating the section is a fragmentary, often hallucinogenic evocation of the young artist as a tailor, an apprentice writer ever more troubled by the discrepancy between his world-class literary ambition and the seemingly fruitless tedium of a garment man's daily rounds.

The mood is ready and anxious. The fear is that biography recapitulates history.

> My whole life is stretching out in an unbroken morning. I write from scratch each day. Each day a new world is created, separate and complete, and there I am among the constellations a god so crazy about himself that he does nothing but sing and fashion new worlds. Meanwhile the old universe is going to pieces. The old universe resembles a busheling room in which pants are pressed and stains removed and buttons sewn on. The old universe smells like a wet seam receiving the kiss of a red-hot iron. Endless alterations and repairs, a sleeve lengthened, a collar lowered, a button moved closer, a new seat put in. But never a new suit of clothes, never a creation. There is the morning world, which starts from scratch each day, and the busheling room in which things are endlessly altered and repaired. (115)

As Miller negotiates his way out of the tailor shop into the profession of writing, he equates the demise of custom tailoring with his self-distancing from the business and characterizes both processes as a fall into an alienating modernity: "Night drops like a boom of thunder, deposits me on the floor of the pedestrian highway leading nowhere eventually, but brightly ringed with gleaming spokes along which there is no turning back nor standing still" (113). Illustrated throughout the concluding section, the "pedestrian highway" means, first and foremost, Miller's daily rounds: pounding the streets of New York for his father while aestheticizing his experience of the city.[33]

Attaching more importance to these final pages than to the portrait of the old men preceding it, critics celebrate the birth of authorial vocation in Miller as an abandonment of the familial/familiar world of the tailor shop. Widmer stresses his adolescent leave-taking: "maturity . . . came hard."[34] For Martin, the difficulty is more pragmatic, a matter of how to find the time and energy to write while working in the family business. As reflections on what Miller likely experienced in the late 1910s, these emphases are persuasive, but the anxiety dominating the final section of "The Tailor Shop" reflects not just the period when Miller worked for his father but his long apprenticeship from that time through the entire decade of the 1920s: until his imagination fired his self-confidence in Paris, allowing him to speak of a more entangled, evolutionary relationship between remembering the tailor shop and creating art.

For Miller, the world of garment shop camaraderie was substantively close and structurally identical to a paternal legacy. Since the moment he dropped out of college, Miller had been placed under heavy pressure to step into his father's shoes and continue the Müller-Nieting tradition of tailoring. He had been able to resist the workaday business of tailoring, but this respect for the masculinity of the garment shop put a compelling spin on the familial expectation, which was strengthened by seeing the old men die:

> The men my father loved were weak and lovable.
> They went out, each and every one of them, like
> brilliant stars before the sun. They went out quietly
> and catastrophically. No shred of them remained—
> nothing but the memory of their blaze and glory.
> They flow now inside me like a vast river choked
> with falling stars. (115)

Miller was despondent not only because the old men were dying out, not to be replaced, but also because, dying, each man was instantly forgotten, receiving no memorial and leaving no bequest. Miller felt an obligation to them he alone could fulfill (that "vast river" of their memory), but whether even he could find a way to give lasting testimony to their spirit he did not know.

In the wake of Miller's decision to write, a second, related problem emerged: could the offspring of German-American shop workers and shop managers, an autodidact who had given up his chance for university credentials, who faced the emergence of a social aristocracy in American letters, ever become a major writer? In one of Anzia Yezierska's autobiographical stories, the protagonist ponders her decision to abandon the Lower East Side for Washington Square: "Would her writing ever amount to enough to vindicate the uprooting of her past? What had she, after all, but a stifling, sweatshop experience, a meager, night-school education, and this wild, blind hunger to release the dumbness that choked her?"[35] A greater anxiety runs beneath Miller's complaints about the daily tedium of tailoring, an anxiety that threatened to consume him in the 1920s: the quintessentially ethnic anxiety of "insufficient influence."

In the penultimate paragraph of "The Tailor Shop," Miller meditates on the question of influence, less rawly but no less nakedly than Yezierska:

> Once I thought there were marvelous things in store for me. Thought I could build a world in the air, a castle of pure white spit that would raise me above the tallest building, between the tangible and the intangible, put me in a space like music where everything collapses and perishes but where I would be immune, great, god-like, holiest of the holies. It was *I* who imagined this, I the tailor's son! I who was born from a little acorn on an immense and stalwart tree. In the hollow of each acorn even the faintest tremor of the earth reached me: I was part of the great tree, part of the past, with crest and lineage, with pride, *pride*. And when I fell to earth and was buried there I remembered *who* I was, *where* I came from. Now I am lost, *lost*, do you hear? You don't hear? I'm yowling and screaming—don't you hear me? Switch the lights off! Smash the bulbs! Can you hear me now? (127)

Miller figuratively evokes the "lost generation" only to measure, pointedly, his distance from the ennui of too much education, too much standing, too much privilege. By saying he is lost, Miller wonders whether his German-American ancestors have equipped him sufficiently to make the transition from "the Gentile world that I knew from the ledger" to the community of modernist letters of which he desired to be a part—a Paris filled with expatriate ethnic New Yorkers, or, in Miller's own phrase, "the Jewish world that I am about to know from life" (113).

Throughout the 1920s, Miller had attempted to solve the problems of cultural debt and insufficient influence simultaneously: to convert his past, especially his work experience, into literature through the well-established techniques of naturalism. Faced for over a decade with the evident failure of *Clipped Wings*, Miller came to believe that his obligation to the past was still unfulfilled while he increasingly feared that his descent—"I the tailor's son"—precluded true literary accomplishment.

Where *Clipped Wings* failed, "The Tailor Shop" succeeds. In the final third of the narrative, Miller plants references, often mere recurrences of phrase or imagery, that conjure up the spirits of the old men. In his angst, Miller's narrator seems to take no notice of these ghosts, but they strike the reader as returns of the repressed, shocking reminders of what is already in the text and hence of what the doubting Miller eventually will achieve. Then, in the waning moments of "The Tailor Shop," the narrative voice quiets to Emersonian calm, only to burst open, completing the reversal, into Uriel-like confidence. This ascent into self-assurance must be read as an anticipatory retrospection, in which the aspiring writer represented by the narrative voice of the text catches up with the reader, prefiguring a future that includes the writer's production of the text itself. Having aestheticized the speech community of the old men, Miller is able to claim his father as his muse and his father's cronies as the enabling force of one of his most persuasive texts.

This final reversal of mood is signaled by a pastiche of some famous lines by Walt Whitman, lines that seemed to have been in the back of Miller's mind for years, baiting him. When he settled in Paris in March 1930, Miller brought with him—in addition to several changes of clothing, the drafts of two unpublishable novels, and ten dollars—a copy of *Leaves of Grass*. This is the passage (from *Song of Myself*) that was obsessing him:

> My tongue, every atom of my blood, form'd from this
>   soil, this air,
> Born here of parents born here from parents the
>   same, and their parents the same,
> I, now thirty-seven years old in perfect health begin.

When he wrote home that April, Miller measured himself against Whitman's confidence of genealogy and place, with great and bitter irony: "Jesus, when I think of being thirty-eight, poor, and unknown, I get furious."[36]

And yet, only five years later, as "The Tailor Shop" comes to a close, he is able to mimic the very same lines with good-natured facetiousness:

> Twenty-one I am, white, born and bred in New York, muscular physique, sound intelligence, good breeder, no bad habits, etc., etc. Chalk it up on the board. Selling out at par. Committed no crime, except to be born here.
>
> In the past every member of our family did something with his hands. I'm the first idle son of a bitch with a glib tongue and a bad heart. (126)

While the final section of "The Tailor Shop" attempts to recapture Miller's struggle throughout the 1920s, and thus is dominated by angst, this moment of self-confidence anticipates his achievements of the mid-1930s and alludes to the achievement realized in the first section of the text.

In imitating Whitman's swagger, Miller demonstrates a new appreciation, acknowledging for the first time a resonance between his own ambition and Whitman's achievement, as another Brooklyn boy who could make poetry out of street vernacular and the homosocial spirit of male camaraderie.[37] In a way Yezierska, for instance, never could, Miller here accepts how distant he has become from his blue-collar ethnic heritage, because he intuits that his portrayal of the garment shop has adequately addressed, for the first time in his career, the lingering and linked problems of betrayal and enablement.

With Anaïs Nin at his side, the Miller of the mid-1930s knows that literary expatriation is a far cry from garment-district marginality, whatever the parallels between the Olcott and Parisian cafés. But he also knows that if he has been unwilling to reincarnate the old men professionally, he nonetheless has succeeded in resurrecting them in his text. Eulogized, they take their place in "The Tailor Shop" at the head of a line of masculine aesthetic play, which will pass through Miller, their devotee, to a formidable third generation, including most of the Beats, Thomas Pynchon, Norman Mailer, Erica Jong, and Martin Scorsese.[38] For his own part, Miller need no longer suspect his ancestral credentials. His vernacular past has allowed him not simply to produce autobiography or to reproduce social history but to design and execute a challenge to the academic reception of Eliot, Joyce, and the mythic method.[39]

Miller ends "The Tailor Shop" with a tongue-in-cheek resurrection of the silk-lined duffers, now identified with the narrator himself:

> All right, then! I'm going to dance for you! A merry whirl, brothers, and let her whirl and whirl and whirl! Throw in an extra pair of flannel trousers while you're at it. And don't forget, boys, I dress on the right side. You hear me? Let 'er go! *Always merry and bright!* (128)

The memory Miller invokes in his celebratory conclusion is not so much that of a distant era, when he had to attend to old men unhappy with the cut of their trousers, as a memory of the very recent narrative past: a memory of what the text itself accomplishes. In autobiographical sketches, writers often acknowledge that they have been inspired by nonliterary precursors. Because his text has done the work of recovery, Miller's testament to his father's cronies is less nostalgic and his claim to incarnate them more self-congratulatory. No longer need he employ the verb forms of the imperfect, consigning the old men to a time that once was. Rather, he has brought the boys back to life, merry and bright, dancing with him through narrative in the present tense.

5

Changing the Rituals: Courageous Daughtering and the Mystique of *The Woman Warrior*

> At one time, the ceremonies as they had been performed were enough for the way the world was then. But after the white people came, elements in this world began to shift; and it became necessary to create new ceremonies. I have made changes in the rituals. The people mistrust this greatly, but only this growth keeps the ceremonies strong.
>
> Leslie Marmon Silko, *Ceremony*

Among contemporary immigrant narratives, none has been more lauded, more often anthologized, or more widely taught across the humanities than Maxine Hong Kingston's memoir novel, *The Woman Warrior* (1976). It has been treated to an early canonization.[1] Opposing camps either praised or denounced the alacrity of this reception: many celebrated it as proof that an Asian American can achieve literary greatness by exploring her own culture while others condemned it as proof that Asian Americans continue to pander opportunistically to racist exoticism.

Although critics sufficiently alert to Orientalism do not describe Kingston as exotic, a disconcerting tendency to impute mystery to *The Woman Warrior* has remained.[2] "*The Woman Warrior* was startling because of its freshness," recalls novelist Anne Tyler, "It wasn't a book that called to mind any other."[3] Theoreticians speak of the doubleness of the memoir—a shuttling between two languages, two audiences, and two cultures—in such a way as to sustain the aura of impenetrability that surrounds the book. In "Ethnicity and the Post-Modern Arts of Memory," an essay that is becoming increasingly influential, Michael M. J. Fischer argues that the particular tyranny of the Chinese past that weighs so heavily on Kingston is its inscrutability: "a series of fragments of traditional stories, myths, and customs imposed by parents, but not adequately explained," fragments that must be "made coherent" in order to articulate "what it means to be Chinese-American."[4] More directly still, Reed Way Dasenbrock argues that in negotiating linguistic boundaries Kingston's text purposefully defeats "intelligibility" in order to confront readers with the ineffability of ethnic difference.[5]

It is true that *The Woman Warrior* frustrates generic distinctions among autobiography, novel, folklore, and sociological essay and, as a result, has vexed booksellers, prize committees, and others seeking to slot it under a standard classification. Throughout the book, Kingston cannibalizes and resituates old Chinese fairy tales, Cantonese village legends, and the gossip of her Stockton girlhood. Historical and autobiographical references fade in and out; transitions are not mediated and frequently not even acknowledged; pronouns, tenses, and active and passive voices alternate in idiosyncratic, sometimes hallucinatory ways.

Yet *The Woman Warrior* is neither as innovative in form nor as discomforting in its amalgamations as critics have assumed. Providing a framework for the book, is, of course, the genre of immigrant narrative, which William Boelhower shows has been "highly institutionalized" for almost a century.[6] The way Kingston fuses fact and myth, her multiple voices, the insertion of oral traditions into written narrative—all date, at least, from the rise of modernism. What lifts *The Woman Warrior* above the run-of-the-mill autobiographical novel is not so much its experimentation per se, although it is beautifully written, as the thematic focus of those experiments: a vein of contemporary literary inquiry that has been of ready interest, hence legibility, well beyond Asian America.

Ironically, those who have least welcomed *The Woman Warrior* have been the most insistent about its readability, which they credit, defensively but persuasively, to its feminism. When *The Woman Warrior* was published, a male outcry

radiated out of Los Angeles, San Francisco, and Seattle from
the Combined Asian Resources Project, especially from writer
Jeffery Paul Chan and psychologist Benjamin R. Tong, who
accused Kingston of attempting to "cash in" on a "feminist fad"
and thereby "selling out . . . her own people."[7] In 1991, Penguin published *The Big Aiiieeeee!*, a thick anthology of Chinese-
and Japanese-American writing, from which Kingston (along
with Amy Tan and David Henry Hwang) is deliberately and
pointedly excluded.[8] The editors argue that *The Woman Warrior*
climaxes a sad tradition of Chinese-American collaborationist
autobiography, incarnating "the racist mind" (this is the phrase
they apply to Kingston) of white supremacist America.[9] In the
first essay of this anthology, Frank Chin, an accomplished
playwright and the author of *Donald Duk*, repudiates in particular Kingston's feminist-dreamwork version of the legendary
girl warrior, Fa Mu Lan, which he contends is meant to be "an
inspiration to Chinese American girls to dump the Chinese
race and make for white universality."[10]

Despite the uncompromising terms of Kingston's repudiation, other scholars of Asian ancestry, particularly women and
particularly Chinese Americans, have not shied away either
from identifying with her prose or defending her achievements.[11] In the now-standard introduction to Asian-American
literature, Elaine H. Kim sets aside the question of gender in
The Woman Warrior to insist instead on its Chinese-American
specificity: "*The Woman Warrior* is about women, but it is primarily about the Chinese American's attempt to sort fact from
fantasy in order to come to terms with the paradoxes that
shape her life as a member of a racial minority group in America."[12] In the lead essay of a special issue of *MELUS* on women
writers, Sau-ling Cynthia Wong directly challenges the effort
to discredit Kingston for encouraging stereotypes and mis-
representing tradition: "the last thing one needs for ethnic literature is the requirement that it set forth 'correct' ideas."[13] Yet
nowhere in her summary of the charges does she mention
Kingston's commitment to feminism, which is, after all, itself a
"politically correct" agenda of inquiry that is often at odds with
sensitivity to racism, and nowhere in her exegesis of *The
Woman Warrior* does she identify it as a product of the Berkeley
1970s focused on women's issues.

It is a disturbing by-product of academic fashion—the romanticizing of U.S. ethnicity coupled to the waning of liberal feminist inquiry—that we have so easily lost sight of Kingston's basic agenda. There are exceptions.[14] In *Between Worlds* (1990), Amy Ling insists that *The Woman Warrior* is the most important of Kingston's books, thereby resisting the swing of critical interest toward Kingston's second book, *China Men* (1980), a text much more hospitable to recent concern for deconstructing Eurocentrism.[15] Rather than soft-pedaling Kingston's work as cultural bipartisanship, Ling reminds us of her skepticism: "Kingston . . . is openly and vociferously critical of things Chinese." For Ling, the narrative is a prime example of feminist writing as a form of rebellion, "an act of defiance against the weight of historical and societal injunctions," that is specifically, sharply applicable to women of Chinese ancestry.[16] I agree with Ling that the wellspring of *The Woman Warrior* is the gender consciousness of a Chinese-American woman, and I wish to emphasize, more strongly than she does, the tapping of that wellspring by the mainstream discourse of second-wave feminism.

Kingston assembled the five narratives that make up *The Woman Warrior* from a larger group of short pieces, most of which surface in her second book, *China Men*. She meant this first book to be, in the full 1970s' feminist sense, a women's book. "There is a Chinese word for the female I—which is 'slave,'" quips Kingston, angrily. "Break the women with their own tongues."[17] Her first three chapters are based on stories her mother told her about women in China; the last two depict her female relatives in the United States. The book's recurrent, indeed obsessive, subjects are canonical women's issues: circumscription, madness, and voice.

"I went away to college—Berkeley in the sixties—and I studied, and I marched to change the world, but I did not turn into a boy" (47). Berkeley in Kingston's time was a center of emergent second-wave feminism. Although Kingston acknowledges few influences, surely she was tutored in the critique of patriarchy, generated in the late 1960s and early 1970s by theorists such as Shulamith Firestone, Kate Millett, and Susan Brownmiller. She probably became familiar as well with first efforts to create what Gerda Lerner, Adrienne Rich, Susan

Griffin, and others call "a woman-centered analysis." For
Kingston, encountering such thinkers meant finding someone
outside the Chinese-American community who could illuminate its interiority in ways that those within had not.[18]

In *The Woman Warrior*, Kingston describes what the traditional community looks like when a woman has learned, outside the home, to think otherwise:

> From afar I can believe my family loves me funda-
> mentally. They only say, "When fishing for trea-
> sures in the flood, be careful not to pull in girls,"
> because that is what one says about daughters. But I
> watched such words come out of my own mother's
> and father's mouths; I looked at their ink drawing of
> poor people snagging their neighbors' flotage with
> long flood hooks and pushing the girl babies on
> down the river. And I had to get out of hating range.
> I read in an anthropology book that Chinese say,
> "Girls are necessary too"; I have never heard the
> Chinese I know make this concession. Perhaps it
> was a saying in another village. I refuse to shy my
> way anymore through our Chinatown, which tasks
> me with the old sayings and the stories. (52–53)

Without question, the *donnée* of *The Woman Warrior* is anger at
the oppression of women in Chinese-American culture, and
the ghost that most haunts it is guilt at the alienation from folk
and culture that feminism instigates.

In *Of Woman Born*, published in the same year as *The Woman
Warrior*, Adrienne Rich calls for "courageous mothering": "The
most notable fact that culture imprints on women is the sense
of our limits. The most important thing one woman can do for
another is to illuminate and expand her sense of actual possibilities. . . . To refuse to be a victim: and then go on from
there." Rich assumes a readership of women, by and large
adults, who are angry at their mothers for acquiescing to
domesticity and for teaching their daughters to do the same.
The individual and collective pasts of her audience are assumed to be inherently tragic. "What is it we wish we had, or
could have, as daughters?" She answers her own question primarily in terms of an actual healing of the mother-daughter

bond. "As daughters we need mothers who want their own freedom and ours."[19] For women whose mothers are both alive and receptive, reconciliation opens the door to mutual acceptance, if not approval. For the more embattled, the path to reclaiming one's mother appears to lie elsewhere.

None of Rich's contemporaries may feel a greater need for courageous mothering than the daughter of an immigrant, yet none may receive less explicit traces of past dissent or less explicit encouragement to freedom of choice. It is for this reason that the battle *against* patriarchy but *for* mothers requires what I would call courageous daughtering. This means not only the courage to speak out against one's heritage and clan but the resourcefulness to identify traces of women's dissent in the interstices of tradition and family history. For the embattled, courageous mothering becomes, paradoxically, the daughter's responsibility, the daughter's achievement—not because the mother lacked self-determination but because of the indirectness with which she exercised independence, the foreignness of the arena in which her struggles took place, and the suppression of those struggles in the oral histories. A daughter must learn to identify the ways in which her mother *has* been courageous, even when that rebellion has been carried out in another culture's terms, circuitously and in disguise; even when her mother has never admitted wanderlust or long ago repressed its memory; even when, out of fear and love, her mother has discouraged or has cultivated the appearance of discouraging the expansion of limits for her daughter.

Kingston's agenda in *The Woman Warrior* is not only to explore her experience of Chinese patriarchy but also to experiment, beyond criteria of historical or biographical veracity, with forms of cultural recovery and intergenerational rapprochement, especially challenges to the legacy of female capitulation. If to be the daughter of Chinese immigrants in America is to be burdened with an especially censorious inheritance, as Kingston insists, then it is also to be graced with a potential antidote, what she calls "talking-story." Parents, especially mothers, told their children Confucian and Cantonese village morality tales, using a fantastic idiom. These stories were reproduced and elaborated by successive generations. What we regard today as the postmodernist technique of enabling feminist fantasy is being invented in the mid-1970s, five years be-fore the release of Alice Walker's *Color Purple*. It emerges from the pen of a Chinese-American woman because she inherits not only oppression, as we all do, but also a form of narrative play especially well suited to the subversion-cum-reclamation that courageous daughtering entails.

In *The Woman Warrior*, Kingston establishes the need for fem-inist dissociation and then takes up the task of imaginative re-covery. She searches through the archives of familial memory for traces of antipatriarchal energy—a drive within the culture toward its own undoing—and identifies those traces in the history and myths of her female predecessors. She then talk-stories: magnifying those traces, rewriting the legends, re-shaping that history to legitimate and inspire the project of ex-panding the limits of Chinese-American women's lives. "We have to do more than record myth," she proclaims in an inter-view, "That's just more ancestor worship. The way I keep old Chinese myths alive is by telling them in a new American way."[20] Kingston rejects outright the Chinese community's ef-fort to transplant and preserve an unchanged heritage in the United States. Over the very vocal protests of this community, she propounds a dissenting vision, one in which Chinese women are seen to have already been at work removing the bindings from their feet but not to have found, until now and on this side of the Pacific, allies to their cause and opportunities within their reach. Requiring that the past sanction the pres-ent, Kingston reimagines Chinese-American myth-history with a vengeance.

The gateway into *The Woman Warrior* was and is "No Name Woman." The only part of the book Kingston permitted to be published in advance was this twenty-page narrative, which she gave to *Viva*, an experimental and short-lived women's magazine.[21] When she later arranged the five chapters that make up *The Woman Warrior*, each of which can stand on its own, she placed "No Name Woman" first. In the major an-thologies of American literature developed in the late 1980s and early 1990s, as well as in the *Norton Anthology of Writing by Women*, every selection from Kingston is from *The Woman War-*

rior, and all but one of those selections reprints the first chapter.[22] The canonization of *The Woman Warrior* has proceeded without a major exegesis in large part, it seems to me, because "No Name Woman" does the work of instruction for us.

"No Name Woman" is a primer in feminist revision, containing the agenda of the book in miniature and with directions. In a few paragraphs, Kingston summarizes the story of the suicide of her father's sister as it has been passed along, in confidence, to her. She then interprets the narrative as an object lesson in Cantonese village misogyny, a rendering not without probability, consistent with how she has learned of the suicide as well as with what she knows of Chinese sexuality, womanhood, and village rule. In the second half of the chapter, she revises her interpretation well beyond the probable, transforming her aunt from a rape victim into a romantic rebel, thereby preserving the antipatriarchal drive of the story while giving it a less withering moral. "Unless I see her life branching into mine, she gives me no ancestral help" (8). Encapsulating malady, diagnosis, and prescription, Kingston's order of presentation instructs us in the whys and hows of Chinese-American feminist extravagance.

In 1924, the "no name" aunt was married to a man leaving for America as part of a contingent that included Kingston's father, grandfather, and uncles. Their wives stayed behind, living together and working the family farm. Too many months later, "no name woman" conceived a child. One night, toward the end of her pregnancy, the villagers raided the Hong family farm, slaughtering livestock, mutilating possessions, and smearing blood through the house. "Some of them, probably men and women we knew well, wore white masks" (4). The Hong women stood stiff in shame. That night, the aunt gave birth in the pigsty, alone, then drowned herself and the baby in the family well.

Kingston deduces that her aunt must have been raped, repeatedly, by a man from the village, with whom she would have come in regular contact. "I wonder whether he masked himself when he joined the raid on her family." Perhaps, in fact, "he organized the raid against her" (6, 7). In order to police sexual equilibrium, the village made the victim a scapegoat, humiliated her into suicide and the murder of her firstborn. Rendered nameless, she was stripped of her identity and struck from the scrolls of Hong family history.

For Kingston, the instance of her unnamed aunt brings the crucial issues in Chinese patriarchy to the fore: censure and silence. The aunt was terrified at the demand for sex, but complied, speechless: "she always did as she was told" (6). The villagers never asked her if she was raped; they held her responsible for the repercussions caused by the absence of voice they themselves had inflicted. "The real punishment was not the raid swiftly inflicted by the villagers, but the family's deliberately forgetting. . . . they saw to it she would suffer forever" (16). She was silenced in life, silenced out of life, and silenced after death.

The second half of "No Name Woman" is a fantasy spun on the thread of a hint that the aunt may have had some choice in her fate. "Adultery is extravagance. . . . My aunt could not have been the lone romantic who gave up everything for sex" (6). Yet Kingston imagines that the escape of the men to America provoked her aunt into questioning the injunction to sexual conformity they had left behind for the women to mind:

> The heavy, deep-rooted women were to maintain the past against the flood, safe for returning. But the urge west had fixed upon our family, and so my aunt crossed boundaries not delineated in space.
>
> The work of preservation demands that the feelings playing about in one's guts not be turned into action. . . . But perhaps my aunt, my forerunner, caught in a slow life, let dreams grow and fade and after some months or years went toward what persisted. Fear at the enormities of the forbidden kept her desires delicate, wire and bone. She looked at a man because she liked the way the hair was tucked behind his ears, or she liked the question-mark line of a long torso curving at the shoulder and straight at the hip. (8)

Against the norm of burying one's sexuality, the aunt in this speculation attended to her appearance, stalked a lover, and courted her fate. "She plied her secret comb. And sure enough she cursed the year, the family, the village, and herself." (10)

As the pursuer rather than the pursued, the aunt is transformed into the martyred heroine of an antipatriarchal melodrama: Hester Prynne reconceived as a Chinese peasant. No longer a rapist, the unknown lover becomes beneficiary of the aunt's defiant refusal to reveal him to the village for punishment. The suicide spares the aunt not only the shame of being held in lifelong contempt as an example to others but also spares her the guilt of raising a child without the requisite male descent line. "It was probably a girl; there is some hope of forgiveness for boys" (15). The murder is not so much an act of despair visited upon the innocent as it is an embrace of the child ("mothers who love their children take them along" [15]) and an embrace of the romantic love match in which that child was conceived (a reinvesting of the symbol akin to Hester's embroidering of the letter).

The Hong women's complicity in their own oppression becomes an issue within the story because they allowed themselves to be shamed into not defending the aunt. They "looked straight ahead," and, more important, in the wake of the event, they acquiesced to the erasure of the aunt from official clan memory, closed ranks against her with the villagers and with the men. In this acquiescence, Kingston is most angry at her mother. Brave Orchid revealed the existence of the aunt on the occasion of her daughter's first menses, to assure her that the family's right to her chastity remained inviolable even in the United States and that daughterly impiety would be avenged as in the case of the aunt: " 'Now that you have started to menstruate, what happened to her could happen to you. Don't humiliate us. You wouldn't like to be forgotten as if you had never been born. The villagers are watchful' " (5). It is the ghost of Brave Orchid's ultimatum that haunts Kingston twenty years later and is the implicit target of her revisionism in this first chapter and the two that follow.

Elegantly and nastily, Kingston symbolizes Brave Orchid's effort to socialize her into patriarchy in terms of the dominant metaphors of the chapter: as a transfer from mother to daughter of the habit of silencing other women and of censuring oneself. Three times, including the riveting first paragraph, Brave Orchid is quoted as warning her daughter against repeating the aunt's tale. In each instance, she invokes masculine authority—the name of the father—which she has internalized and now conveys: "'Don't tell anyone you had an aunt. Your father does not want to hear her name. She has never been born'" (15). After the third injunction, Kingston remarks that it has taken her twenty years to figure out how insidious her mother has been. Brave Orchid not only dictated against her sexual self-determination, but conscripted her into the conspiracy that made the history of the aunt unspeakable in the first place: "they want me to participate in her punishment. And I have" (16).

At issue in the aunt's pregnancy, censure, and suicide are questions of women's victimization versus defiance, silence versus speech, the same matters that are at issue when Brave Orchid tells the story to Kingston at the onset of her menses. Signaled in the first paragraph and made explicit on the closing page of "No Name Woman" is Kingston's determination to intercede in the intergenerational cycle of victimization, now at work on this side of the Pacific, by breaking the conspiracy of silence surrounding the aunt. Disseminating the aunt's story in defiance of her mother's expressed wishes allows Kingston to testify not only to the ambiguous history of a single Chinese peasant woman but to a tradition of Hong women, now transported to America, talking-story without the mediation and against the wishes of Hong men.

At the least, Brave Orchid's sharing of her sister-in-law's secret was an initiation into a subculture of women's fear and anger. Whether or not it was meant as something more is a question Kingston means to render moot by the publication of "No Name Woman." Brave Orchid's apparent ultimatum against communal trespass can now be seen to have sown the seeds of its own destruction. Kingston has been willing to betray their mother-daughter confidence, suggesting that beneath their contract of silence lies an unspoken sanction of countercultural voice. The implicit purpose of Kingston's first chapter is to characterize her mother as an unconscious agent of dissent. Brave Orchid's declared intent in revealing the aunt's history places her beyond repudiation among her own generation, yet her revelations are substantive enough to license condemnation of the village and pared down enough to invite inspirational fantasy.

In foregrounding Kingston's revisionist imagination, I risk leaving the impression that "No Name Woman" is too schematic or merely didactic. Yet Kingston means her strategy of rewriting to be, as it is here, textured, playful, and expansive: not an anecdote like her mother's, and not a conceit, but a full-blown talk-story. In introducing the idea of her aunt as a seductress, for instance, Kingston dallies over the aesthetics of the aunt's sexuality, which she would rather have been sophisticated in a traditional way and which she prays was reciprocated: "I hope the man my aunt loved appreciated a smooth brow, that he wasn't just a tits-and-ass man" (9). At the end of the chapter, she explores the aunt's comprehension of the self-devastation her wanderlust has wrought—loverless, a foreign body implanted within now struggling to get out, her family and the villagers aligned against her—via a stunning image of agoraphobia: "The black well of sky and stars went out and out and out forever; her body and her complexity seemed to disappear" (14). In giving voice to the aunt's self-determination, Kingston invents voraciously but with a certain kind of discipline, annexing discrete bits of family lore to create a more nuanced portrait of the wellspring of romantic desire.

"No Name Woman" begins darkly and heavily, with the felt weight of a mysterious, overbearing heritage, but it lightens toward the middle, as if Kingston were registering in her tone the reaffirmation of the past that she means this kind of story-telling to accomplish. I find particularly inspiriting her probing of the aunt's unprecedented self-regard and sexual appetite. By incorporating the strange fact that her aunt returned to live with the Hongs as well as rumors of her grandfather's eccentricity, she is able to temper her portrait of her aunt's heroism with descriptions of less-appealing traits, while at the same time reassigning "credit" for her unconventionality to her family, especially to the men:

> She may have been unusually beloved, the precious only daughter, spoiled and mirror gazing because of the affection the family lavished on her. When her husband left, they welcomed the chance to take her back from the in-laws; she could live like the little daughter for just a while longer. There are stories that my grandfather was different from

other people, "crazy ever since the little Jap bay-
oneted him in the head." He used to put his naked
penis on the dinner table, laughing. And one day he
brought home a baby girl, wrapped up inside his
brown western-style greatcoat. He had traded one
of his sons, probably my father, the youngest, for
her. My grandmother made him trade back. When
he finally got a daughter of his own, he doted on
her. They must have all loved her, except perhaps
my father, the only brother who never went back to
China, having once been traded for a girl. (10–11)

Here Kingston conjectures to the point of crediting her family
with resisting traditional boy love. Yet the concluding note of
this passage leaves open the possibility that her father should
be exempted from this revisionist testimony of girl love among
the men.

Despite the extravagant play, Kingston does not so readily
discount the cost of her revisionist practice as her detractors
claim she does. Transgressing the Chinese-American equivalent of *omertà* is the price she has decided to pay to vanquish
the oppressive onus of the secret. From the point of view of her
family and the immigrant community to which it belongs,
Kingston "exposes" not only her aunt's shamefulness but her
own, revealing publicly that the Hongs have a daughter so un-
mindful of family honor that she tells its secrets to the world.
Her violations accomplished, she awaits the reprobation that
no doubt will ensue when family members reject the book's
"darker sections," as she later reports they do.[23] Because
Kingston is a famous American author who can go wherever
she wishes, the villagers may be relatively powerless to punish
her on earth, but the culture they struggle to uphold, and that
she so offends, is not without more far-reaching resources.

"No Name Woman" ends on the figure of the aunt, who,
because she is not fed by her descendants' worship, wanders
"always hungry, always needing" through the afterlife.
Kingston's revelations, structured to her own desires, are no
solace to the aunt—solace requiring "paper suits and dresses,
spirit money, paper houses, paper automobiles, chicken,
meat, and rice into eternity"—but rather a final brutal insult:

>My aunt haunts me—her ghost drawn to me because now, after fifty years of neglect, I alone devote pages of paper to her, though not origamied into houses and clothes. I do not think she always means me well. I am telling on her, and she was a spite suicide, drowning herself in the drinking water. The Chinese are always very frightened of the drowned one, whose weeping ghost, wet hair hanging and skin bloated, waits silently by the water to pull down a substitute. (16)

The weeping ghost is the embodiment of a partially alien culture that justifiably seeks its revenge upon her, a revenge she experiences not as an assimilated colonial, for whom a ghost is but a cartoon, but as an American-born daughter who is Chinese enough to know what a ghost means in its own idiom. I believe Kingston understands that her feminist license has betrayed even the women it means to champion, who in suffering dishonor plague her in return. To read with Kingston rather than against her is to credit her with being frightened of what she has had to do.

To identify immigrant novels with premigratory aesthetic forms usually involves more than a touch of ethnic romanticism, but Kingston's second chapter, "White Tigers," is a literal exercise in Chinese myth revision. It offers an elaboration of a children's rhyme, "The Ballad of Mu Lan," which continues to be as popular among Chinese Americans as "London Bridge Is Falling Down." "The Ballad of Mu Lan" is a while-you-work as well as a while-you-play song, especially for girls, since its rhythms mimic the shuttling of a loom. Kingston's version is among the latest in a long line of reworkings—storybooks, novels, plays, and movies—a line that has recently passed from the Westernizing pop culture industry of Hong Kong through Kingston to the highbrow revisions of Broadway phenomenon David Henry Hwang.

Once again, Kingston credits her earliest memories of Fa Mu Lan to Brave Orchid:

>At last I saw that I too had been in the presence of great power, my mother talking-story. After I grew

up, I heard the chant of Fa Mu Lan, the girl who took her father's place in battle. Instantly I remembered that as a child I had followed my mother about the house, the two of us singing about how Fa Mu Lan fought gloriously and returned alive from war to settle in the village. I had forgotten this chant that was once mine, given me by my mother, who may not have known its power to remind. She said I would grow up to be a wife and a slave, but she taught me the song of the warrior woman, Fa Mu Lan. (19–20)

Kingston is not yet willing to attribute feminist intentionality to her mother, "who may have not known its power to remind," but certifies the effect: "I would have to grow up a warrior woman" (20).

In "White Tigers," Kingston retells the story of Fa Mu Lan in the first person, changing details and reinflecting the echoes of its traditional moral. She mixes into the inherited narrative conceits taken from "the [kung fu] movies at the Confucius Church" in the 1950s, the Berkeley subculture of the 1960s, and the gender politics of the 1970s. Kingston says that even she cannot distinguish between legend and personal invention, "where the stories left off and the dreams began" (19). Nonetheless, we can follow the tracks of Kingston's desire in terms of the tension between family loyalty and the feminist project.

Fa Mu Lan is a child of Chinese legend. When she is seven years old, she is taken from her parents and brought to the mountains, where a seemingly ageless couple trains her in the martial arts and their accompanying philosophy. After fifteen years of preparation, Fa Mu Lan takes her father's place in battle, disguising herself as a man. She avenges her family, her fellow villagers, and the Chinese peasantry in general. At each stage of her adventure, she is lauded by her family, who express gratitude for her apprenticeship, bless her when she departs for battle, and welcome her home after victory as if she were an eldest son.

Kingston interprets Fa Mu Lan, in unprecedented fashion,

as a protofeminist. Whereas the traditional story emphasizes bleak sacrifice, the abandoning or postponing of conventional desire, she emphasizes a desirable role transcendence, actualizing antitraditional energies. "Chinese executed women who disguised themselves as soldiers or students, no matter how bravely they fought or how high they scored on the examinations" (39). Yet Kingston preserves the traditional emphasis of the chant, which is its lesson in "perfect filality." Kingston's version of Fa Mu Lan signifies not simply boundary crossing, like the nameless aunt, or parental respect, as in the original narrative, but a combination of the two, wherein one may locate a feminist utopianism that is specifically (can one say "classically"?) Chinese.

In choosing to tell the story of the unnamed aunt, what interested Kingston was imagining that the aunt had knowingly risked dishonoring the family in order to pursue the forbidden for herself. Although Mu Lan rides far from home and engages in the activities of men, in the sense dictated by the story's own terms of value, Mu Lan's adventure is less transgressive than the adultery of the aunt. What interests Kingston in "The Ballad of Mu Lan" is that Mu Lan's adventure has always exemplified Confucian piety. Leaving home is imagined as an act not of personal willfullness but of extraordinary filial dedication. What is important about Mu Lan's sacrifice is not that she is subjected to physical danger (although that is true) but that she must suspend the flow of natural girlhood and submit to what is necessary to master a difficult art. Her honor, similarly, is not a matter of individual vainglory but of bringing empire-wide esteem upon family and community and, therefore, of being esteemed by them in return.

Kingston slashes the filiopiety of Mu Lan into the consciousness of her readers by incising it, literally, on the swordswoman's back. The scene is perhaps the most often quoted, and certainly the most controversial, in the book:

> My mother washed my back as if I had left for only a day and were her baby yet. "We are going to carve revenge on your back," my father said. "We'll write out oaths and names."

"Wherever you go, whatever happens to you, people will know our sacrifice," my mother said. "And you'll never forget either." . . .

My father first brushed the words in ink, and they fluttered down my back row after row. Then he began cutting; to make fine lines and points he used thin blades, for the stems, large blades.

My mother caught the blood and wiped the cuts with a cold towel soaked in wine. . . . If not for the fifteen years of training, I would have writhed on the floor: I would have had to be held down. The list of grievances went on and on. If an enemy should flay me, the light would shine through my skin like lace. (34–35)

The traditional Confucian emphasis of the ballad is dazzlingly embodied in a postmodernist conceit of writerly inscription: the female avenger goes to war branded with parental sanction and familial cause.

In *The Big Aiiieeeee!*, Frank Chin argues that the inscriptions "belong" to Yue Fei ("a man whose tomb is now a tourist attraction at West Lake, in Hanzhou city") and have been appropriated by Kingston and incorporated in "White Tigers" in order "to dramatize cruelty to women." According to Chin, Kingston reconfigures Mu Lan "to the specs of the stereotype of the Chinese woman as a pathological white supremacist victimized and trapped in a hideous Chinese civilization."[24] I suppose I may be reading through rose-colored glasses here, but I read Mu Lan's inscriptions as a graphic embodiment of parent-daughter solidarity, a colorful fairy-tale conceit with which the reader (imagining herself a heroine, too) identifies. " 'Thank you, Mother. Thank you, Father,' " I said before leaving. They had carved their names and addresses on me, and I would come back" (37).

I agree with Chin that Kingston's strategy in revising "The Ballad of Mu Lan" is epitomized in those carvings, but I define that strategy differently—to identify and accentuate the sanctioning of protofeminism—and I judge it to be a brilliant stroke, aesthetically, psychologically, and politically. There are, however, certain currents in "White Tigers" reflecting emergent concerns of the 1970s that now sound somewhat contrived, even granting a no-holds-barred definition of the fairy tale. Fighting for the peasantry against the Dark Empire, medieval Chinese style, Kingston's Mu Lan epitomizes a class populism that may or may not be to an individual reader's taste. I like it myself.

Less to my taste is the feminist organicism of the narrative: a combination of cost-free spiritualism, clear-cut politics, and household-workplace arrangements that distract the reader from the basic wish list of the chapter. In a sequence combining the self-loss of Carlos Castenada with the self-realization of Outward Bound, a rabbit jumps into the fire, nicely saving the warrior from having to break her vow to be humane to animals. When staffing her army, she chooses only those sons whose departure will not break any hearts rather than the soldiers with the most potential. Similarly, Kingston's Mu Lan claims, "My army did not rape, only taking food where there was an abundance" (37). In an extended romance, the avenger unites with her husband and bears him a son, yet she continues to fight all the while, until the baby drops: a conceit whose wonderful implausibility and invocation of female fertility are marred by a too neat allusion to the dilemmas of courtship and childcare among second-wave professional women. We learn, for instance, that the couple fight side by side before the son's birth; afterwards, the father returns to the village with the infant boy, to "house-husband" him there.

All in all, however, Kingston's optimistic reformulation of the legend of Mu Lan explodes the opposition between clan loyalty and female self-determination under which she and those like her continue to work. Because the woman warrior becomes a leader of men not in defiance of her clan but, heroically, in its defense and with its blessing, the story can be read as a testament to the possibility of transcending gender hierarchies without being forced to embrace outlaw status. It projects back onto the Chinese past the simultaneous and mutual fulfillment of ambitions still thought irreconcilable. On behalf of ambitious Chinese-American women who are already alienated from their families and culture, "White Tigers" provides the argument that an expanded definition of honorable work is already an honored tradition.

Kingston is interested in more than cultural self-justification, however. Whether or not she has embroidered the details, the fact remains that as children she and her American-born peers played at being swordswomen even as they were being trained in housewifery, disciplined to become "American-feminine," and disparaged for not being boys. And the fact remains that for these women, now adults, memories of play-acting return to chastise and provoke them in unconventional ways: the voice of the past speaks to the present in a countervailing idiom. Kingston's implicit point is not that a woman of Chinese descent can find permission for role exploration in the mythic record if she looks hard enough, but that, whether or not she goes searching for it, the mythic record is already at work within her, mandating some kind of heroics.

In the coda to "White Tigers," Kingston steps back into her adult autobiographical persona to explore what it has meant, as a child born in the United States, to identify and be encouraged to identify with Fa Mu Lan. On the one hand, there are new opportunities, new ways of serving family and making a living and being loved, many of which are not precluded, because not anticipated, by traditional mores, many of which may be attractive even to immigrant parents. On the other hand, Chinese-American culture remains largely patriarchal, and the legend offers little practical guidance for negotiating the change.

"My American life has been such a disappointment," Kingston declares, underscoring how the memory of Mu Lan hurts (45). She has been unable to assimilate the class politics of her family's dispossession by the Communists to the Robin Hood-like antifeudalism of the story. She has been ashamed that she lacks the temperament to battle her family's second dispossession by urban renewal and to fight racism more generally. And she remains convinced that the time for guru spirituality and kung fu discipline has passed. "I don't want to be a medium," she says. "And martial arts are for unsure little boys kicking away under fluorescent lights" (52). Regarding her own education in America, she has never been sure whether her accomplishments in school (all A's) were being applauded as dutiful and heroic or being dismissed as an American transcription of "the outward tendencies" traditionally attributed to females. What she has been sure of is that overt signs of parental approval went only to her brothers, and that throwing tantrums in disgust has earned her the reputation for being the Hongs' resident "bad girl."

In the most withering moment in the coda, Kingston returns to her disingenuous portrayal of Mu Lan as a mother-warrior, this time unpacking the contemporary issues of superwomanhood, freedom within marriage, and "the Cinderella complex":

> Once I get outside the house, what bird might call me; on what horse could I ride away? Marriage and childbirth strengthen the swordswoman, who is not a maid like Joan of Arc. Do the women's work; then do more work, which will becomes ours too. No husband of mine will say, "I could have been a drummer, but I had to think about the wife and kids. You know how it is." Nobody supports me at the expense of his own adventure. Then I get bitter: no one supports me; I am not loved enough to be supported. (48)

What Kingston is saying here is that the kind of feminist utopianism in which office and home are successfully cross-fertilized sets women up for compounded labor and no-win situations.

Because of the domestic/workplace split in the economy, the vision of having it all compels women either to work double duty or to play domestic "dragon lady" to their lovers. Even if a woman does put in double time, she resents not being supported within this society, the most leisured in history. For immigrant daughters, especially the impressively mobile Asian Americans, feminist utopianism may prove to be outright dangerous. "Even now China wraps double binds around my feet," Kingston says (48). When the specter of feminism-cum-filiopiety plays into and reinforces parental expectations, expectations already inflated by the natural rhythms of the immigrant American dream, daughters here in America are faced with having to be "good girls" both in the old ways and in the new.

The first three chapters of *The Woman Warrior* build an increasingly persuasive case for "ancestral help" from Brave Orchid, the original narrator of the three stories Kingston retells (the suicide of the nameless aunt, the legend of girl warrior Fa Mu Lan, and a history of Brave Orchid's own medical training). The bare outlines and contexts of the source narratives suggest an increasingly positive picture of Brave Orchid even without Kingston's intervention. By aggressively recasting her mother's narratives, Kingston steps up Brave Orchid's courage at each level, chapter to chapter. Brave Orchid emerges already an unconscious provocateur in "No Name Woman," then as a self-conscious sponsor of her daughter's feminism, who gives Kingston's project the stamp of clan approval. In "Shaman," in the greatest extravagance of Kingston's fantasy, Brave Orchid herself becomes a leader in feminist revisionism, a medicine woman who "changes the rituals" in order to sponsor the professionalization of other women.

There are moments in *The Woman Warrior* when Kingston paints Brave Orchid as an ethnic stereotype: the immigrant mother who lives vicariously through her daughter. In *Of Woman Born*, Rich discounts the bravery of women who stimulate their daughters' lives without acting to improve their own, hinting darkly that the mother-to-daughter transfusing of ambition can constitute another form of oppression if unaccompanied by personal example.[25] According to Rich, courageous mothering ends only with the strike for self-determination; for Kingston, by extension, courageous daughtering ends only with the demonstration, necessarily revisionist, of a mother's quest for independence. Although she knows Brave Orchid is disappointed with her life in America, Kingston probes beyond the stereotypes of bitterness and the transfer of ambition. Looking back through family history, she finds more than enough signs that Brave Orchid, now reduced to telling stories, once acted on her own behalf.

In the title, "shaman" refers generally to Brave Orchid's brief career in China. After the deaths of her first two children when she was thirty-five, Brave Orchid found herself alone in China. She was receiving a steady supply of funds from her emigrant husband, but she no longer had anyone to spend it on but herself. So she left home and enrolled in the two-year program at the To Keung School of Midwifery. After graduation, she returned to her former village and practiced medicine for several years, until the Communist Revolution. Joining her husband in the United States, she was unable to meet the requirements for certification as an obstetrician and turned instead to raising children and helping to run a family laundry. On at least four occasions, she has taken out her diploma and reminisced within earshot of her eldest daughter:

> "When I stepped out of my sedan chair, the villagers said, 'Ahhh,' at my good shoes and my long gown. I always dressed well when I made calls. Some villagers would bring out their lion and dance ahead of me. You have no idea how much I have fallen coming to America." (76–77)

Out of a few sketchy details and the passion of her mother's recollection, Kingston weaves the single longest narrative in *The Woman Warrior*.

As a midwife, Brave Orchid is regarded as a miracle worker, what the peasants understand a medicine woman to be. "She had gone away ordinary and come back miraculous, like the ancient magicians who came down from the mountains" (76). For Kingston, the real miracle is not the practice of medicine but the fact of her mother practicing it. The author's recreation pays testimony to her mother's courage and power in breaking away from the village, completing her training, and reconstituting herself within a profession among similarly uprooted women. One hundred twelve women began school with Brave Orchid; only thirty-seven were graduated. In Kingston's telling, most of the women drop out of the program not because they could not handle the sciences, though the education is rigorous; rather, most were lost trying to negotiate between domesticity and the professions, another one of those formidable boundaries "not delineated in space."

In *China Men*, Kingston credits her father with the idea of sending his wife to medical school, but in *The Woman Warrior* the decision is her mother's own.[26] Brave Orchid desires her freedom: she takes the first step in abandoning motherhood, the families of her father and her husband, and village life generally. "Not many women got to live out the daydream of women—to have a room, even a section of a room, that only gets messed up when she messes it up herself" (61). Completing the degree means financial independence, community respect, and an identity (not of parents, not of a husband) of her own.

In expanding the limits of her own life, Brave Orchid also expands those of her "daughters," who, in this case, are the other students. Although her diploma says she was twenty-seven at the time of graduation, Kingston says she was actually thirty-seven. Given peasant standards, Brave Orchid is a generation older than her fellow students. Similarly important is her claim that she raised and lost two children before going to medical school. Kingston has never seen proof of older siblings and suspects that her mother is lying to prevent her American-born children from taking for granted their hold over her affections. Whether it is true or not, Kingston's repetition of the claim alerts us to Brave Orchid's role in the medical school. In this rendition, her mother inspires the other students as Rich warrants, provoking them to relinquish the safe oppressions of the past through the example of her own battle won.

The "shaman" of the title refers, more particularly, to Brave Orchid's leadership in the professionalization of the other students. Kingston is interested in the spells her mother learns for curing the ill, but she is much more interested in the spells Brave Orchid improvises for transforming Chinese peasant women into modern doctors. In "Shaman," she devotes fourteen pages to a single ritual of initiation—an exorcism, literally—designed, organized, and conducted by Brave Orchid. I have never read an adequate account of this play within a play, the most prominent ghost story in a work subtitled "Memoirs of a Girlhood Among Ghosts."

In the five years before Brave Orchid arrived at the medical school, a room in the dormitory remained unused for fear of ghosts. One night, Brave Orchid volunteers to sleep in the haunted room to prove that it is not haunted. She falls asleep without incident, reassured by listening to the bedtime chatter of the other students. During the night, after the spirits of the other students drift into dreams, she is visited by an ugly short-haired phantom who seems to feed off her thoughts. She

identifies this phantom as a "Sitting Ghost." Fending off the
ghost by talking to it, she warns it against haunting a medical
school, then recites her lessons aloud until she falls asleep. The
next morning, several of her friends tumble into the room, audience to a terrifying rehearsal of the night's events. Insisting
that the danger has not yet passed, Brave Orchid provokes
them into chanting against the ghost. Later that evening, the
whole school gathers to scrub down the haunted room and
scare the ghost away with the fire of their alcohol burners.
Kingston reports success, resounding in laughter: "When the
smoke cleared, I think my mother said that under the foot of
the bed the students found a piece of wood dripping with
blood. They burned it in one of the pots, and the stench was
like a corpse exhumed for its bones too soon. They laughed at
the smell" (75).

What are we to make of an encounter with a Sitting Ghost by
a thirty-seven-year-old woman preparing to become a doctor?
Yet another indulgence in Asian primitivism? According to
Kingston, successive waves of female medical students have
expressed their fear of abandoning their homes, families, and
places within traditional peasant society through the symbol of
the haunted room: "Even though they had to crowd the other
rooms, none of the young women would sleep in it. Accus-
tomed to nestling with a bedful of siblings and grannies, they
fitted their privacy tighter rather than claim the haunted room
as human territory" (64). On behalf of all the students, Brave
Orchid confronts the loss of "siblings and grannies," then provokes them to do likewise. She performs the ritual functions of
both sacrificial victim and high priestess: as the possessed, she
permits, even forces, the other women to work out their anxieties through her body; as the exorcist, she conducts them
through the procedure.

The exorcism proceeds in three steps. Alone in the haunted
room, Brave Orchid drives the ghost of her past away by con-
vincing herself that she has a new "home," the medical school,
and a new institution of strength, the community of professional women:

> "I'll get fire, Ghost. . . . We have a communal
> kitchen with human-sized jars of oil and cooking

fat. . . . I will make this room so clean, no ghost will
ever visit here again.

"I do not give in," she said. "There is no pain you
can inflict that I cannot endure. You're wrong if you
think I'm afraid of you. You're no mystery to
me. . . . You have no power over a strong woman."
(70)

In the past, Brave Orchid has known her "power" as "a strong
woman" through what she could accomplish in the kitchen,
cooking and cleaning, and in the nursery, telling stories to her
children. Now she turns that knowledge against itself, using
domestic prowess to vanquish her fears of leaving home. The
key strategy in that transition is the pooling of the women's resources, signified by the "communal kitchen."

In the second step of the exorcism, Brave Orchid tests the
formation of community. She recruits several other women,
her closest friends at the school, to complete her personal exorcism:

"Come home, come home, Brave Orchid, who has
fought the ghosts and won. Return to To Keung
School, Kwangtung City, Kwangtung Province.
Your classmates are here waiting for you, scholarly
Brave Orchid. Come home. Come home. Come
back and help us with our lessons. . . . We need
you." (71)

Because chanting in unison affirms the medical school as (and
as a substitute for) home for Brave Orchid, where she is needed
as a colleague, it works to rid her of the invading spirit: "Her
soul returned fully to her and nestled happily inside her skin,
for this moment not travelling in the past where her children
were nor to America to be with my father. She was back among
many people" (72). Brave Orchid's assurances last only "for
this moment," however, because the new community of professional women is still tentative and will remain so until the
other students have vanquished their own anxieties.

In the third step, Brave Orchid rallies the entire school to a
group exorcism: "The story about the ghost's appearance and
the coming ghost chase grew, and students snatched alcohol

and matches from the laboratories" (74). Brave Orchid leads the chanting, which the others echo, affirming the communal "we":

> "I told you, Ghost," my mother chanted, "that we would come after you." "We told you, Ghost, that we would come after you," sang the women. "Daylight has come yellow and red," sang my mother, "and we are winning. Run, Ghost, run from this school. Only good medical people belong here. Go back, dark creature, to your native country. Go home. Go home." "Go home," sang the women. (75)

Kingston shifts between Brave Orchid's representative "I" and the group "we" to signify the dialectic necessary for the formation of community. As each woman overcomes her fears, a new social structure becomes possible; as finding a place within a new social structure seems more and more possible, each woman is able to overcome her fears, trusting in a new kind of "we." The ghost of the past is forced to flee not only Brave Orchid but the souls of the other women and the medical school as a whole.

Kingston summarizes in the language of feminist anthropology: "The students at the To Keung School of Midwifery were new women, scientists who changed the rituals" (75). As the student leader of To Keung, Brave Orchid creates a rite of initiation, deploying ghost stories to usher younger women over the threshold separating the professions from domesticity. Her shamanism is, in effect, a prototype for her daughter's project: turning culture back in upon itself, using the past to redirect the momentum of its legacy, expanding and even violating community to preserve membership in it. In "Shaman," Brave Orchid not only becomes a professional; she prefigures the activity of ethnic-feminist revision necessary for creating a postpatriarchal Chinese-American culture.

In the climactic centerpiece of *The Woman Warrior*, Kingston blurs the distinction between Brave Orchid's storytelling and her own. To remind ourselves that Kingston retains the upper hand in interpreting her mother's medical training is not to reprimand Kingston, who never pretends otherwise. Rather, it is to emphasize her implicit dissent from the self-pitying and ethnocentric mandate of Rich's "courageous mothering." It is to credit her with taking the task of identifying and embracing maternal self-determination into her own hands. And it is to suggest that few immigrant daughters have ever been so courageous, so *shamanistic*, in telling their mothers' stories.

At the beginning of "A Song for a Barbarian Reed Pipe," the long final chapter of *The Woman Warrior*, Kingston compares her style of talking-story to an intricate knot that was outlawed in China when it was discovered that the effort needed to untie it would make one go blind. The implication seems obvious, but I continue not to find Kingston's work, including "A Song for a Barbarian Reed Pipe," that disorienting. As "No Name Woman" is heir to Kate Chopin's *Awakening* and "Shaman" is heir to Virginia Woolf's *Room of One's Own*, so this chapter takes much of its figurative energy and interpretive direction from the tradition of women's writing that centers on the interplay of voice and madness. This tradition goes back at least as far as Emily Dickinson and goes forward to Sylvia Plath; it includes Charlotte Perkins Gilman's "Yellow Wallpaper," too, which since the 1970s has become one of the most ubiquitous short stories in the Americanist curriculum. Despite its digressions and embellishments, its insider jokes and insider provocations, the chapter unravels easily when approached through second-wave feminist hermeneutics.

"A Song for a Barbarian Reed Pipe" is a series of childhood vignettes, thematically filtered and by and large chronologically ordered, in the now well-established enabling vein: the story of a Chinese girl in America, doubly marginal and thus doubly intimidated, isolated and silent, who skirted the edges of madness only to ascend, after great pain, triumphantly into voice. This tale behind the tale is meant not so much to inspire women readers, though it has done just that for some, as to insinuate how and why *The Woman Warrior* came into being. For a feminist revisionist such as Kingston, the ultimate precursor figure is, perhaps inevitably, her (own childhood) self. In "A Song for a Barbarian Reed Pipe," she walks a delicate and dangerous balance between the Western tradition of feminist fictionalized autobiography she emulates and the Chinese-American experience to which she holds herself accountable.

Kingston tells us that when she was born, Brave Orchid sliced the frenum of her infant tongue. This claim, really an ongoing routine between mother and daughter, is the subject of the first vignette recounted in "A Song for a Barbarian Reed Pipe." I think it is the most deliciously insidious moment in the book.

> My mother cut my tongue. She pushed my tongue up and sliced the frenum. Or maybe she snipped it with a pair of nail scissors. I don't remember her doing it, only her telling me about it, but all during childhood I felt sorry for the baby whose mother waited with scissors or knife in hand for it to cry— and then, when its mouth was wide open like a baby bird's, cut . . . .
> "Why did you do that to me, Mother?"
> "I told you."
> "Tell me again."
> "I cut it so that you would not be tongue-tied. Your tongue would be able to move in any language. You'll be able to speak languages that are completely different from one another. You'll be able to pronounce anything. Your frenum looked too tight to do those things, so I cut it."
> "But isn't 'a ready tongue an evil'?"
> "Things are different in this ghost country."
> (163–64)

In this image, biculturalism is necessitated by migration and facilitated (literally or figuratively) by maternal violence. A daughter's passage from Chinese peasantry into middle-class America is understood to be preeminently a matter of voice: of *vocal empowerment*, exercised by and for the *individual*, with or against (finally she can not know) the will of her mother.

Despite hours of childhood spent searching for scars and comparing tongues with other children, Kingston does not know whether her mother is lying, but confirmation is not really the issue. The key to the conceit of the cut frenum is the way it remains unclear about both intent and effect. Kingston asks, does my mother have my best interests at heart? And, even if she does, does she, born of Canton, know what she is doing to me, born of California? This, in the final analysis, is the much darker question. "Sometimes I felt very proud that my mother committed such a powerful act upon me. At other times I was terrified—the first thing my mother did when she saw me was to cut my tongue" (164). As it remains unclear whether cutting the frenum would actually facilitate or incapacitate speech, so it remains unclear whether Brave Orchid told Kingston the story as a child to encourage her voice or to intimidate her into silence.

Although the ambiguity persists, probability tilts in certain directions. The narrative is probably an invention, a didactic lie Brave Orchid made up when Kingston's introspective and isolationist temperament began to emerge. Brave Orchid can be trusted, I think, in her explanatory claims: that she has recognized the difficulty of making one's way among white ghosts (it will involve pain, courage, and cultural gymnastics) and that she wishes to acknowledge to her eldest daughter that daughter's special needs and special promise. In concealing that acknowledgment beneath the disconcerting mark of violence, Brave Orchid does more than betray the Chinese fondness for speaking in puzzles. As she withholds the right of final approval over what Kingston does, she sanctions a motherly lament—that they all would have been better off if she had only gone ahead and taken out the entire tongue.

It should come as no surprise to readers familiar with Kingston, whose wit is often caustic and whose "dumbfoundedness" is characteristically a nasty rhetorical pose, that she was a "problem" child. What may be difficult to believe, given her irreverent verbosity, is that she was once plagued by not enough talk: a dread of speech, at one time causing episodes of withdrawal and self-laceration that bordered on early insanity. "My silence was thickest—total—during the three years that I covered my school paintings with black paint." From kindergarten through second grade, she assembled these finger paintings into what she remembers as a stage curtain: a partition between herself and possibility, Dickinson's "finer House than prose." "I spread them out (so black and full of possibilities) and pretended the curtains were swinging open, flying up, one after another, sunlight underneath, mighty operas" (165). In this metaphor of the raising of a darkly blank curtain, a Cantonese version of Gilman's wallpaper, Kingston evokes those times of her girlhood when she began to intuit female social contradictions and to imagine instead opportunities for self-determination.

Kingston's fearfully imaginative self-isolation had much to do, she tells us, with negotiating the pressures of divergent socializations. At Chinese school, which she attended in the evenings, immigrant children read lessons aloud in the traditional fashion, "everybody reading together." Individual memorization tests were strictly private. But at public school she was forced to read in English before the class, standing alone and exposed, something that for years she simply could not do. Her mind's eye stared at cultural difference in the form of the two scripts she was being required to master:

> I could not understand "I." The Chinese "I" has
> seven strokes, intricacies. How could the American
> "I," assuredly wearing a hat like the Chinese, have
> only three strokes, the middle so straight? . . . "I"
> is a capital and "you" is lower-case. I stared at that
> middle line and waited so long for its black center to
> resolve into tight strokes and dots that I forgot to
> pronounce it. (166–67)

The two different "I"s epitomized two different scripts that in turn embodied two different languages, between which the child, neither Chinese nor American, would have to negotiate her being.

Even as a child, Kingston noticed that her problem was not unique: "The other Chinese girls did not talk either, so I knew the silence had to do with being a Chinese girl" (166). Running counter to the American demand for individuating self-reliance was its sexual marketplace; the emphasis on "feminine" self-abnegation even infiltrated grade school: "Normal Chinese women's voices are strong and bossy. We American-Chinese girls had to whisper to make ourselves American-feminine. Apparently we whispered even more softly than the Americans" (172). If in the United States abusively mixed signals have created young women's diseases like anorexia and bulimia, which seem to single out the bright and ambitious, then the threat of catastrophe looms large for girls of Chinese ancestry who are, by a legacy turned second nature, especially intelligent and especially determined.

Just as Kingston put aside this business of painting in black, a Chinese girl moved into the neighborhood who was similar to her in many ways and with whom she increasingly, obsessively compared herself. This other girl still "would not talk," not even in Chinese school. One day after classes, cornering her in the girls' bathroom, Kingston tortured this doppelgänger—pulling her hair, pinching her cheeks, clapping her nose and ears, and penning her in—in an effort to make her speak:

> "You don't see I'm trying to help you out, do you? Do you want to be like this, dumb (do you know what dumb means?), your whole life? Don't you ever want to be a cheerleader? Or a pompon girl? What are you going to do for a living? Yeah, you're going to have to work because you can't be a housewife. Somebody has to marry you before you can be a housewife. And you, you are a plant. Do you know that? That's all you are if you don't talk. If you don't talk, you can't have a personality. . . . Well, you're not the type that gets dates, let alone gets married. Nobody's going to notice you. And you have to talk for interviews, speak right up in front of the boss. Don't you know that?" (180–81)

By sixth grade, Kingston had learned to speak the language of conventional femininity—cheerleading and dates, pink-collar employment or upscale marriage—but it was at the expense of her own inner being, symbolized by the girl she tortured.

The adolescent Kingston seemed to have intuited two possibilities: to adopt the voice of middle American standards of female ambition or to let those standards intimidate her into silence. Neither possibility was a viable option: either she would go mad from self-censorship or she would go mad from self-isolation. "I thought every house had to have its crazy woman or crazy girl, every village its idiot. Who would be It at our house? Probably me" (189). In fact, having recognized this, the next day she mysteriously took to her bed, with "no pains and no symptoms," and stayed there the following school year. "Instead of starting junior high school, I lived like the Victorian recluses I read about." Eighteen months later, arising from bed at her mother's insistence, she returned to school to find the mute one still mute and the other Asian girls "starting to tape their eyelids" (182).

"The world is sometimes just," quips Kingston (181). To say she brought the eighteen months of illness upon herself might indicate only that she felt she deserved punishment. But it might also suggest that she needed, one way or another, time to herself, for the very reasons that drove her to berate the other girl in the first place. "It was the best year and a half of my life. Nothing happened" (182). If we read according to the dictates of feminist hindsight, which is essentially how the chapter is generated, then we can interpret the self-imposed rest cure as a crucial first step in mounting a youthful challenge to social and parental expectations. Time out gave Kingston an opportunity to absorb into her psyche the lessons that apparently had emerged in the conversation with her double. It was a liminal period in which she could formulate, to herself at least, the need to find "a voice of her own."

As a teenager, Kingston began to see Brave Orchid not as the protofeminist forerunner of "Shaman" but as an enemy within, the household's central spokeswoman for 1950s women's romances. The talk-story of chapter 4, "At the Western Palace," illustrates how dangerous Hollywood-concocted suburban dreams can be. In this tale Brave Orchid plays the deluded heavy who bullies her sister, Moon Orchid, a Chinese "new woman" who has just emigrated from Hong Kong, into demanding a place as "number one wife" in the household of a long-migrated husband, a wealthy Los Angeles doctor. Brave Orchid's idea is for her sister to gain access to Beverly Hills, but this experiment in storming the gates of "the Western Palace," Chinese-style, drives Moon Orchid literally insane. Fearful of Moon's Orchid's fate, Kingston came to fear all signs that Brave Orchid had a similar agenda in mind for her.

Kingston's suspicion of her mother intensified when a young man of Chinese extraction and debatable age was permitted to camp out, day after day, at the family laundry. Because she had been going dateless in high school, like most of the other Chinese girls, Kingston feared that the youth stalking her had received her parents' approval as a prospective mate. "I head the old women talk about how he was stupid but very rich" (197). To her, he was an ogre, "mentally retarded," a "zombie"—all the more so because her parents' toleration of his courtship seemed to convey a message about what was expected, and not expected, of her. "I studied hard, got straight A's, but nobody seemed to see that I was smart and had nothing in common with this monster, this birth defect" (195). When the boy was discovered to possess a collection of girlie magazines, Brave Orchid, rather than finally rallying to her daughter's assistance, expatiated, " 'My goodness, he's not too stupid to want to find out about women' " (197).

Kingston decided that it was speak now or forever hold her peace. The climactic scene of the chapter is her confession to her mother of two hundred items, things that make her feel guilty or angry or confused, beginning with her suspicions of the rich boy. First she tries whispering them, as if Brave Orchid were her priest, but this only earns her her mother's preemptive disdain. Another day she tries shouting, in the Cantonese peasant way. Brave Orchid shouts back, detailing responses to Kingston's most worrisome questions: the prospective suitors were intended for her sister; Chinese understand the importance of college, even for girls; Kingston ought to be ashamed for leading her siblings, less adventurous by nature, astray; and so forth. One way or another, the exchange evidently worked. "The very next day after I talked out the retarded man, the huncher, he disappeared. I never saw him again or heard what became of him. Perhaps I made him up" (205).

Underlying the litany that Kingston revealed that day to her mother is the fundamental issue of daughterly doubt about maternal intent, which returns us to the issue of what Brave Orchid has been up to all along, talking-story:

> "I don't want to listen to any more of your stories; they have no logic. They scramble me up. You lie with stories. You won't tell me a story and then say, 'This is a true story,' or, 'This is just a story.' I can't tell the difference. I don't even know what your real names are. I can't tell what's real and what you make up. Ha! You can't stop me from talking. You

tried to cut off my tongue, but it didn't work." So I
told the hardest ten or twelve things on my list all in
one outburst.

My mother, who is champion talker, was, of
course, shouting at the same time. "I cut it to make
you talk more, not less, you dummy. You're still stupid. You can't listen right. . . . Who said we could
sell you? We can't sell people. Can't you take a joke?
You can't even tell a joke from real life. You're not so
smart. Can't even tell real from false." (202–3)

Missionaries hover over this scene—Kingston tells about the
nuns in the park using hell-and-damnation scare tactics—but
they ultimately are frustrated. What Kingston receives is not
Christian exoneration but maternal back talk, a combination of
explanation and counteraccusation.

In clarifying her positions, Brave Orchid must break Chinese
traditions of keeping directions indirect, of never speaking
self-reflexively except at the distance of another allegorical
story, at once resonant and safe. She is hurt, deeply, to have to
admit, " 'That's what Chinese say. We like to say the opposite' "
(203). Nevertheless, in braving the cultural divide with this
daughter, who despite her manifest gifts insists on thinking in
the flat-footed American way, Brave Orchid reserves to herself, as vexatious Chinese mothers do, the right to chastise and
be contrary, to contradict her daughter and (seem to) contradict herself.

The general issues of upscale marriage versus education that
caused the teenaged Kingston so much anxiety are embodied
in this contentious interchange between mother and daughter:

"I'm never getting married, never!"
"Who'd want to marry you anyway? Noisy. Talking like a duck. Disobedient. Messy. And I know
about college. What makes you think you're the
first one to think about college? I was a doctor. I
went to medical school. I don't see why you have to
be a mathematician. I don't see why you can't be a
doctor like me."
"I can't stand fever and delirium or listening to
people coming out of anesthesia. But I didn't say I

wanted to be a mathematician either. That's what
the ghosts say. I want to be a lumberjack and a
newspaper reporter." Might as well tell her some of
the other items on my list. "I'm going to chop down
trees in the daytime and write about timber at
night."

"I don't see why you need to go to college at all to
become either one of those things. Everybody else
is sending their girls to typing school. 'Learn to type
if you want to be an American girl.' Why don't you
go to typing school? The cousins and village girls
are going to typing school." (202–3)

The key to this scene—why it is Confucian feminist and not
Christian feminist—is that neither Brave Orchid nor Kingston
reprimands herself with a "mea culpa" breast-beating. Each
takes the offensive, epistemologically and emotionally, even
as she clarifies her position: like mother like daughter, and vice
versa.

Kingston's coming into voice in "A Song for a Barbarian
Reed Pipe" is meant to anticipate the writing of *The Woman Warrior* itself. Because of Brave Orchid's combination of elucida-
tion and obstreperousness, this scene, in the final analysis, is
not just another set piece of 1970s feminism but a model for a
new kind of Chinese-American women's writing—a model
taken up by Amy Tan and Gish Jen—in which the kind of rep-
artee that has already begun among mothers and daughters
within Chinese-American homes is reproduced and embel-
lished in written form.

This is not to say that, from the perspective of her mother
and the transitional culture she represents, Kingston is no
longer a problem child. She gives her mother narrative space to
talk back, but she does not ask permission for producing the
narrative in the first place. That jump from arguing in private to arguing in public is a leap of revisionist imagination,
a declaration of mother-daughter continuity, which Brave
Orchid would not necessarily recognize and of which she does
not necessarily approve. Kingston's relatives have often
stopped reading *The Woman Warrior* in anger and disgust, and
for good reason: "'Chinese smeared bad daughters-in-law

with honey and tied them naked on top of ant nests,' my father said. 'A husband may kill a wife who disobeys him. Confucius said that.' Confucius, the rational man" (193). If the Chinese tradition of womanhood was to keep quiet about the forces that oppress, given how little was to be gained and how much was to be lost, the Chinese-American tradition is to speak, to cross the threshold with confessions-cum-accusations. But the sanction for that crossing remains murky, as has been true of many acts of ethnic translation authored by the second generation, only more so here, because Kingston is of Chinese descent and because she is a woman.

At the end of *The Woman Warrior*, Kingston announces one last tale: "Here is a story my mother told me, not when I was young, but recently, when I told her I also am a story-talker. The beginning is hers, the ending, mine" (206). What follows is Kingston's version of the ancient story of Ts'ai Yen.

In 175 A.D., when she was twenty years old, Ts'ai Yen, a poetess of the Han people, was captured by a Southern Hsiung-nu chieftain, made his concubine, and taken far away from her home to live with him. The Han considered the Hsiung-nu, who did not speak Chinese, to be barbarians. Yet Ts'ai Yen discovered among them a form of flute music so compelling ("its sharpness and its cold made her ache") that she taught herself to sing in emulation of it (208). "Ts'ai Yen sang about China and her family there. Her words seemed to be Chinese, but the barbarians understood their sadness and anger" (209). Ts'ai Yen was able to adapt Hsiung-nu flute music to the human voice so that it would powerfully communicate desire, suffering, and protest even across the alienating barriers of language and culture. After twelve years of captivity, she at last was ransomed home, and her compositions, especially "Eighteen Stanzas," were received gratefully into the musical heritage of her people.

This final revisionist tale is an implicit reflection on Kingston as an artist of the diaspora. She transforms the talk-story of Ts'ai Yen into a metanarrative as she attempts to close her postmodern Western novel. Kingston says of Ts'ai Yen's ancient experiment in multiculturalism, "Eighteen Stanzas for a Barbarian Reed Pipe," "It translated well" (209). Although Ts'ai Yen composed songs about China for her foreign audience, Kingston's celebration of the power of translation does not refer, as one might expect, to what those foreigners were able to glean about China from Ts'ai Yen. Rather, the translation that Kingston has in mind works the boundary from "the savage lands" back to the village of the Han, and it has to do with the rendering of the music of the barbarian soul to a Han audience on "their own instruments." Ts'ai Yen's successful translation of Hsiung-nu flute music into Han voice allegorizes Kingston's project of translating the Western feminist imagination into the idioms of Chinese(-American) culture.

In this conclusion Kingston is working up, one last time, an enabling fantasy. "The swordswoman and I are not so dissimilar," she had declared earlier. "May my people understand the resemblance soon so that I can return to them" (53). The final dreamwork of *The Woman Warrior* is Kingston's version of that classic hope of ethnic literature, that the community from which one has come will receive into its care the gift of song that has been won outside its walls and that constitutes, above all, a battle cry for the expansion of human possibility within them.

Conclusion:
Remaking America, Revisited

In late 1988, when I was well along in the writing of this book, I came back from teaching in Switzerland and heard, for the first time, the neologism "multicultural." In the media's account of the scholarly debate over the issues invoked by the term, there seemed to be little but raw polarization, and the poles were hauntingly familiar: art versus sociology, universalism versus parochialism, self-transcendence versus self-interest, "truth, justice, and the American way" versus tribalism and Balkanization. As the right wing tells the story, and not only the right wing, the case for ethnic literature now rests on the complementary convictions that the American canon and those who sponsor it are forces for maintaining the status quo while ethnic literature focuses primarily on challenging oppression and ushering readers into worlds apart, aesthetic and otherwise. In this book, I have taken up the cause of ethnic literature, but the strategies I have deployed and the discoveries I have made push well beyond the reductiveness of the multiculturalism debate.

Immigrant offspring do not inherit access to mainstream arts and letters. This point is not just a complaint about nativist prejudice; it is a fact about what ethnic writers really want: first and foremost, to *participate,* however much dissenting and with however great a difference, in the national community of letters. Even before pen goes to paper, the aspiring writer has been through a fight, but the fight has been directed not so much against the cultural monopoly of the mainstream as against the cultural hermeticism of the ethnic group. Puzo, Yezierska, Roth, Miller, Kingston: each became enamored of the Word in English, and each battled family, community, and tradition to remake his or her life through it.

The first paradox of the ethnic writing I have analyzed is that it uses mainstream literary devices to perform acts of sociological discovery vis-à-vis particular ethnic groups, to identify forms of cultural persistence (whether in the basic outline of the historical record or running deeper than language and social contact) that challenge the linear narrative of assimilation, whether from family to business, orthodoxy to secularism, or dutiful daughterhood to traitorous feminism. Each of the five writers I have investigated criticizes America, as charged; but the America they criticize is in each instance less the one their immigrant ancestors found upon arrival than the one their fellow ethnics are currently in the process of remaking.

To insist that writers coming from the outside have embraced mainstream literary strategies is to verify what the media and the self-proclaimed academic right think they already know: that there are elements in established American, European, and Western culture worthy of pursuit by those who do not come by it naturally or easily. Yet to establish the desirability of national and Western letters is to uncover only one-half of a reciprocal process. It is the other half, the prodigious de facto influence of ethnic tributaries on mainstream U.S. culture, that professed monoculturalists especially need to hear.

In each instance I have investigated, writers have reached readers outside their ethnic groups, always intriguing scholars and in key instances capturing the public at large. With sales well over one million, Roth's *Call It Sleep* is not only the most Jewish novel ever produced by an American (as Alfred Kazin claimed once again in 1991), it is also the most sustained analysis of childhood responsibility for the Oedipal cycle we have, regardless of language.[1] Approaching half that number of readers in one-fourth the time, Kingston's *Woman Warrior* not only reclaims strains of female self-determination for the growing community of Asian-American intellectuals, it provides paradigms for readers of other groups to wage battles at home, and for writers of other groups—Alice Walker, Mary Gordon, Helen Barolini, perhaps Sandra Cisneros or Gloria Anzaldúa, as well as Joy Kogawa, Amy Tan, and David Henry Hwang—to do so, like Kingston, before a literary public. Puzo's *Godfather* is not only among the more powerful explosions of the ideology of American individualism ever scripted; it is the best-known and arguably the most influential work of creativity by an American after the Second World War. In short, readers both here and abroad have found in the American ethnic imagination forms of beauty and affect, courage and wisdom applicable to their own lives.

To challenge the reductive oppositions of the multiculturalism debate is to underscore, then, not only the artfulness of what we have already taken as ethnic but the ethnicity of what we have, in this century, already taken as art. I am speaking now not only of the seductive and incorporating power of the literature on which I have focused—marked and marketed as Jewish, Italian American, Chinese American, and so forth—but also of the work in various genres and media produced by putatively "dehyphenated" immigrant offspring, works that do indeed speak to audiences of many origins and nationalities (Aaron's "universal Republic"), yet are able to do so not because they are "transcendent" in idiom but because they speak in ways that are emphatically, irredeemably ethnic.

As I see it, the double curse of the newcomer to American arts and letters (to prove to the ancestors that one has not assimilated, to prove to the world at large that one's people have what it takes) has affected even those who did not choose to produce autobiographical commentaries on ethnic passage and those who may not have recognized that they have internalized that double curse. The narratives I discuss in this book are only the tip of an iceberg—by which I mean the clichéd images of proportion and visibility. Increasingly throughout this century, the reciprocity between national literature and ethnic experience, for those descended from Europe, has become less a matter of what national culture can do for ethnicity than a matter of what ethnicity can do for national culture.

The task of examining underappreciated forms of ethnic persistence within mainstream culture begins with identifying coteries of artists who share descent lines, descent lines that emerge—if only upon occasion, larger loyalties and agendas notwithstanding—in telltale forms of self-reflexivity. A more expansive registering of ethnicity than I have wanted to do here would consider, for instance, the influence of Irish and Anglican Catholicism in the making of high modernism (James Joyce in prose, T. S. Eliot in poetry, Eugene O'Neill in drama) and of Russian Judaism both in its dissemination (Lionel Trilling, Philip Rahv, and the New York intellectuals) and in its midcentury existentialist reincarnation (Delmore Schwartz, Saul Bellow, Bernard Malamud, and others). On the populist side of the ledger, one also would want to uncover the contributions of Russian Jewish producers and directors, Irish Catholic writers and actors, and Italian Catholic designers and technicians, in the development of the film industry and later in television (where these roles become mixed). I am fascinated, too, by the presence of ethnics in the contemporary music industry, not only Frank Sinatra and Bob Dylan but also the Roman Catholic icons of anthem rock and stadium pop (including Bruce Springsteen, Madonna, Jerry Garcia, and U2). Closing the high literature/popular culture circle, it should come as no surprise that immigrant offspring are also the writers who have given us our most incisive commentary on postmodern spectacle culture: from Theodore Dreiser and Nathanael West through the polyethnic Beats (Allen Ginsberg, Jack Kerouac, Tom Dooley, Diane DiPrima) to writers of our own time, such as Norman Mailer, John Gregory Dunne, and Don DeLillo.[2]

By highlighting the contributions white ethnicity has made to mainstream America, I mean to remind those made anxious by multiculturalism that the country has been through such a revolution before. Henry Pratt Fairchild, a Yale graduate and later a professor at New York University, once warned of the latest arrivals from Eastern and Southern Europe: "America was brought to this continent, brought by the Pilgrim Fathers in the Mayflower. . . . The typical immigrant of the present does not really live in America at all, but, from the point of view of nationality, in Italy, Poland, Czech-Slovakia, or some other foreign culture."[3] In 1926, when Fairchild published these words in *The Melting-Pot Mistake*, more than twenty-five million newcomers had planted roots in the United States over the past half-century. Despite the heinously biased immigration restriction laws, which Fairchild had helped to pass, it was, from the point of view of the Anglo-Puritanism Fairchild claimed to represent, very much too late. By 1926, even the most cautious immigrants of the great migration had spawned hopes that their children, unlike themselves, would be "genuine Americans." Even the most Americanized of those children were busy making lives for themselves that reflected, if only covertly, the blood knowledge of the past.

Listening to the clamor of fear and distrust regarding the emergence of Americans of color, including frighteningly reminiscent efforts to shut down immigration from certain parts of the world, I take solace in the millions of "new new immigrants," many of them technically refugees, who have already settled in the United States: immigrants from Mexico and the Caribbean, from Iran and Ukraine, from India and Pakistan, as well as from China, Japan, Korea, and Vietnam.[4] When I see their offspring in my classrooms, clench-jawed to earn the pride of both their foreign-born parents and their American-born teachers, I imagine what it must have felt like at City College in the 1920s, or at Harvard in the 1950s, and I rejoice. In the street poetry of my *paesan*, Yogi Berra, a professional baseball player and manager, one of many who left the indelible mark of Italian peasantry on the most American of pastimes, "it's déjà vu all over again."

Notes

Introduction

1. Leslie Fiedler, *Waiting for the End* (New York: Stein and Day, 1964), 74. It has become the practice of the Modern Language Association never to use hyphens in ethnic group designations, the agenda being to dispel the lingering stigma of the "half-breed," the misnomer of binationalism, and the imputation that Americans can be divided into those who are 100 percent and those who are not. I have chosen to follow the long-standing practice of hyphenating standard ethnic group compounds (with the exception of Native American and its synonyms) when these compounds are used as adjectives: Italian-American literature, African-American experience, etc. I use the adjectival hyphen because I am old-fashioned in matters of the word and cautious in matters of ethnicity. Also, the grammatical hint is easier on the eyes. For an illumination of the issue, both in general and with regard to those of Italian ancestry, see Anthony Julian Tamburri, *To Hyphenate or Not to Hyphenate* (Montreal: Guernica, 1991).

2. Irving Howe, *World of Our Fathers* (New York: Simon and Schuster, 1976), 585.

3. Daniel Aaron, "The Hyphenate Writer and American Letters," Smith *Alumnae Quarterly*, July 1964, 215. In Aaron's examples, those writers "behind the minority barricade" are mainly realists of an earlier generation while aspirants to the "larger United States" are postwar modernists. Aaron writes from deeply held belief. His aesthetic assumptions are those of his time, although his cultural politics are by no means wholly conservative. He relegates Abraham Cahan, Mike Gold, James T. Farrell, and Richard Wright to the sociological past, but he asserts as a given what is not everywhere given: the literary election of Jewish contemporaries Saul Bellow and Bernard Malamud. He also advocates the candidacy of African Americans Ralph Ellison and James Baldwin, as he supports Ellison in the famous Howe-Ellison debates. Aaron distinguishes between the situations facing black and

white minority writers by suggesting that the black writer, on the one hand, is prevented by racism from the full dehyphenation proffered to the descendants of Europeans but, on the other hand, is in the position (by dint of a special marginality once accorded to "the renegade Jew") to "disclose to that white majority truths about itself that this white majority has heretofore refused to entertain" (ibid., 215). See also Howe, "Black Boys and Native Sons," *A World More Attractive* (New York: Horizon, 1963), 98–122, and Ralph Ellison, "The World and the Jug," *Shadow and Act* (New York: Random House, 1972), 107–43.

4. See Wayne Charles Miller, "Introduction," *A Gathering of Ghetto Writers: Irish, Italian, Jewish, Black, and Puerto Rican* (New York: New York University Press, 1972), 1–71, and Katharine D. Newman, "Introduction," *Ethnic American Short Stories* (New York: Washington Square Press, 1975), 13–23.

5. Helen Barolini, "Introduction," *The Dream Book: An Anthology of Writings by Italian American Women*, ed. Barolini (New York: Schocken, 1985), 3–56; Jules Chametzky, *Our Decentralized Literature: Cultural Mediations in Selected Jewish and Southern Writers* (Amherst: University of Massachusetts Press, 1986); Allen Guttmann, *The Jewish Writer in America: Assimilation and the Crisis of Identity* (New York: Oxford University Press, 1971); Charles Fanning, "Introduction," *The Exiles of Erin: Nineteenth-Century Irish-American Fiction*, ed. Fanning (South Bend, Ind.: University of Notre Dame Press, 1967), 1–17; Elaine H. Kim, *Asian American Literature: An Introduction to the Writings and Their Social Context* (Philadelphia: Temple University Press, 1982); Dorothy Burton Skårdal, *The Divided Heart: Scandinavian Immigrant Experience through Literary Sources* (Lincoln: University of Nebraska Press, 1974).

6. Many if not the majority of classic immigrant novels are outright hostile to inherited traditions or to their dominant development in North America—for example, Abraham Cahan's *Rise of David Levinsky* (1917), O. E. Rolvaag's *Giants in the Earth* (1927), James T. Farrell's Lonigan trilogy, Mordecai Richler's *Apprenticeship of Duddy Kravitz* (1957), Philip Roth's *Goodbye, Columbus* (1959), Mario Puzo's *Fortunate Pilgrim* (1964), and Piri Thomas's *Down These Mean Streets* (1967). For all the winsomeness and nostalgia commonly credited to dialect stories, many remind us that the tight-knit communities of the immigrants were insular and restrictive, and that the self-determination we value often meant abandoning them. Immigrant communalism becomes attractive primarily when the immigrant community is no longer a force to be reckoned with and therefore can be invoked as a model for establishing interdependence among middle-class individuals, couples, and nuclear families. Some of the blunter protest novels, dismissed as

"mere" indictments of xenophobia and economic exploitation, shed significant light on how the pain of poverty and discrimination registered on individuals working out of particular cultural perspectives, why they and their communities responded as they did, and which responses produced the kinds of self-replicating cycles that tempted outsiders to blame the victim.

7. Bruce Novoa, *Chicano Authors: Inquiry by Interview* (Austin: University of Texas Press, 1980); *Irish-American Fiction: Essays in Criticism*, ed. Daniel J. Casey and Robert E. Rhodes (New York: AMS, 1979); Abraham Chapman, "Introduction," *Jewish-American Literature: An Anthology of Fiction, Poetry, Autobiography, and Criticism*, ed. Chapman (New York: New American Library, 1974); Rose Basile Green, *The Italian-American Novel: A Document of the Interaction of Two Cultures* (Rutherford, N.J.: Fairleigh Dickinson University Press, 1974).

8. William Boelhower, *Through a Glass Darkly: Ethnic Semiosis in American Literature* (New York: Oxford University Press, 1987), with a forward by Werner Sollors; Mary V. Dearborn, *Pocahontas's Daughters: Gender and Ethnicity in American Culture* (New York: Oxford University Press, 1986); Sollors, *Beyond Ethnicity: Consent and Descent in American Culture* (New York: Oxford University Press, 1986); and *The Invention of Ethnicity*, ed. Sollors (New York: Oxford University Press, 1989). This last collection includes a salient introduction by Sollors, essays by Dearborn and Boelhower, and an earlier version of chapter 1 of this book, "Blood in the Marketplace," which I wrote with the encouragement of Sollors and Jean-Christophe Agnew. Dearborn first drafted *Pocahontas's Daughters* as a Ph.D. dissertation (Columbia University) under Sollors's directorship. Boelhower first published *Through a Glass Darkly* in Italy (Venice: Edizioni Helvetia, 1984), where Sollors "discovered" it and sponsored its publication in the United States.

Sollors and Boelhower have had fascinating and telling cross-Atlantic, intercultural careers: a German expatriate, Sollors wrote *Beyond Ethnicity* after first publishing a book on Amiri Baraka and taking positions at Columbia and then Harvard University; an American expatriate, Boelhower wrote *Through a Glass Darkly* after first writing a book on Italian-American autobiography and taking a position at the University of Venice. The work of these scholars reflects in large measure knowing firsthand what distinguishes the emigré in the United States or the American abroad, and hence what Americans—regardless of class, ethnicity, or region—have in common, protest and romance to the contrary.

9. Falling on the chronological cusp between the "new ethnicity" and "beyond ethnicity" studies, Marcus Klein's *Foreigners: The Making of American Literature, 1900–1940* (Chicago: University of Chicago

Press, 1981) is a very important book (noted, but not noted enough) that combines established methods of myth-and-symbol synthesis with ground-breaking sensitivity to class, race, and ethnicity. While Klein focuses primarily on varieties of 1930s naturalism and their roots in the 1920s, his study also deserves attention for its introductory analysis of high modernist Western Civ. erudition as a myth of ancestry. Klein argues that the offspring of the American mercantile old-family elite, Eliot and Pound especially, feared they would be culturally dispossessed by the foreigners in their midst.

10. Most immigrant writers attended college, studied traditional forms of literature, and took courses in professional writing, often at prominent institutions. Many became faculty members themselves. Much ethnic writing was instigated or encouraged by professors, sociologists, and editors, among them such central figures as William Dean Howells, Brander Matthews, John Dewey, Austin Warren, and Norman Foerster. Well before the Depression, mainstream presses including Houghton Mifflin, Macmillan, Harper, and Boni and Liveright were among the leaders in publishing ethnic works. Such imprimaturs of reception as the Pulitzer Prize for Biography, Book-of-the-Month-Club selection, Modern Library editions, movie contracts, and writing fellowships frequently went to ethnic writers before World War II and routinely thereafter. Edward J. O'Brien's *50 Best American Short Stories 1915–1939* (Boston: Houghton Mifflin, 1939), for instance, combined stories by Sherwood Anderson, Ernest Hemingway, Willa Cather, William Faulkner, and F. Scott Fitzgerald with selections from James T. Farrell, Pietro DiDonato, William Saroyan, Konrad Bercovici, and Benjamin Rosenblat. See Thomas J. Ferraro, "Ethnicity and the Literary Marketplace," in *The Columbia History of the American Novel*, ed. Emory Elliott (New York: Columbia University Press, 1991), 380–406.

11. Promising avenues for further investigation include the intersections between immigrant and nonimmigrant minority literatures. I am intrigued by the way African-American mobility novels inflect the up-from-the-ghetto genre with the accents of the slave narrative. Sollors has pointed out correspondences between Cahan's *Yekl* (1896) and Charles Chesnutt's "Wife of His Youth" (1899) as well as between James Weldon Johnson's *Autobiography of an Ex-Colored Man* (1912) and Cahan's *Rise of David Levinsky* (Sollors, *Beyond Ethnicity*, 149–73). More is at issue in these intersections than even Sollors has addressed. For instance, as pseudo-autobiographies of self-betrayal in which "the self" is understood in cultural terms, both *David Levinsky* and *Ex-Colored Man* insinuate, beneath ethnic and class mobility, a homosocial "passing" into heterosexuality. There differences emerge once again, since Cahan unveils the homoeroticism (and misogyny) of Tal-

mudic scholarship whereas Johnson implicates black homosociality in socioeconomic disenfranchisement (anticipating Baldwin, Toni Morrison, and Gloria Naylor). Noteworthy as well in the African-American tradition is the episodic novel of unfulfilled "pilgrimage," in which protagonists keep "moving on" as they confront, recurrently, the overt and hidden injuries of racism in America: *The Autobiography of an Ex-Colored Man* is a forerunner of the genre; Nella Larsen's *Quicksand* (1928) and Zora Neale Hurston's *Their Eyes Were Watching God* (1938), its prototype; Ralph Ellison's *Invisible Man* (1952) and Morrison's *Tar Baby* (1981), its consummation.

12. Michael Awkward, "Negotiations of Power: White Critics, Black Texts, and the Self-Referential Impulse," *American Literary History* 2 (Winter 1990): 581–606; Lawrence J. Oliver, "Deconstruction or Affirmative Action: The Literary-Political Debate over the 'Ethnic Question,'" *American Literary History* 3 (Winter 1991): 792–808; Renato Rosaldo, "Others of Invention: Ethnicity and Its Discontents," *Voice Literary Supplement*, Feb. 1990, 27–29; Ramón Saldívar, *Chicano Narrative: The Dialectics of Difference* (Madison: University of Wisconsin Press, 1990); Curtis C. Smith, "Werner Sollors's *Beyond Ethnicity* and Afro-American Literature," *MELUS* 14 (Summer 1987): 65–72; and Alan Wald, "Theorizing Cultural Difference: A Critique of the 'Ethnicity School,'" *MELUS* 14 (Summer 1987): 21–34.

13. Since beginning his work on multicultural literature, Sollors has been aware of the risk of bracketing social and political oppression; he has also distinguished between the communal form and the particularized content of ethnic representation. These are heuristic devices that take us only so far. In a more recent essay, he reconstructs the individual grounds of dissent offered by Zora Neale Hurston and Hannah Arendt to the *Brown v. Board of Education* desegregation decision, both of which have been the object of scholarly censorship and both of which demonstrate the dangers of projecting contemporary political debate back onto the past. Sollors, "Literature and Ethnicity," in *The Harvard Encyclopedia of American Ethnic Groups*, ed. Stephan Thernstrom et al. (Cambridge, Mass.: Harvard University Press, 1980), 853; *Beyond Ethnicity,* 36–39, 54–56; and "Of Mules and Mares in a Land of Difference: or, Quadrupeds All?" *American Quarterly* 42 (June 1990): 167–90.

14. Herbert J. Gans, "Ethnicity, Acculturation, and Assimilation," forward to Neil Sandberg, *Ethnic Identity and Assimilation* (New York: Praeger, 1974), vii–xiii; Howe, "The Limits of Ethnicity," *New Republic*, 25 June 1977, 17–19; Gunnar Myrdal, *The Center Magazine*, July–Aug. 1974, 26–30; and Stephen Steinberg, *The Ethnic Myth: Race, Ethnicity, and Class in America* (New York: Atheneum, 1981).

15. Sollors's own deepest interest is in what sociologists call "ethnogenesis," the emergence of ethnic consciousness from alternative forms of personal and group affiliation, which he sees as a primary form of Americanization. He finds a crucial instance of this process being illustrated in a writer's embrace of ethnicity: the writer takes on a public identity and gains access to the community of letters, paradoxically, by claiming and publicizing ethnic marginality. With this favored example, Sollors warns against overestimating the "authenticity" of the writer, which for him is a challenge to the invocation of insider authority by ethnically identified critics. My own work begins with attending to writerly self-transformation, but my interest lies in writers whose alien origins are beyond dispute and whose writing recovers forms of cultural persistence other than the maintenance or reclaiming of a hyphenated consciousness. See Sollors, "Literature and Ethnicity," 663, and *Beyond Ethnicity*, 11–13.

16. We have already begun to receive comparative analyses of immigrant writing by peoples of color based on the common ground of oppression by Euro-American imperialism, including internal colonization in the United States. My suspicion, for which my analysis of Kingston is a single small indication, is that the use of well-established up-from-the-ghetto conventions in this literature has necessarily been underestimated, and that unrecognized currents within certain texts will emerge when those texts are seen in the light of earlier or contemporaneous European-descended immigrant writing. I have in mind, first and foremost, the work of Kingston and other Asian North Americans (Gish Jen calls her book *Typical American*), but also work produced by the Chicanos of the 1970s (Ernesto Galarzo, Rudolfo Anaya, Ron Arias), by certain Carribean writers (Edward Rivera, Judith Ortiz Cofer, the first books of Paule Marshall and Oscar Hijuelos), and by such representatives of migration from "the Orient" as Phillip Lopate and Bharati Muckherjee. The two strategies of analysis would intersect, for instance, in interpreting Joy Kogawa's *Obasan*: Naomi's need to speak up against Canadian anti-Japanese policies forces her to violate Japanese norms of femininity, an assimilationist desecration of the internal self that she likens at one point to an abortion.

17. It is a fear perhaps compounded by the brilliance with which Boelhower (in addition to Sollors) has diagrammed the structural basis of the traditional immigrant narrative. See Boelhower, "The Immigrant Novel as Genre," *MELUS* 8 (Spring 1981): 3–13, and "The Making of Ethnic Autobiography in the United States, 1880–1911," in *L'Immigration européenne aux États-Unis (1880–1910)*, ed. Jean Cazemajou (Bordeaux: Presses Universitaires de Bordeaux, 1986), 157–68.

18. Mario Puzo, "The Italians, American Style," *The Godfather Papers and Other Confessions* (New York: Fawcett, 1972), 182.

Chapter One

1. Puzo may have received inspiration or encouragement for his emphasis on the familial aspect of the Mafia either from Joseph Valachi, whose Senate hearings were in 1963 and whose testimony appeared in Peter Maas's *The Valachi Papers* (New York: G. P. Putnam, 1968), or from Luigi Barzini, *The Italians* (New York: Bantam, 1965), 284. Maas's publisher is also Puzo's; Don Vito's leading competitor is named Barzini.

2. John G. Cawelti, *Adventure, Mystery, Romance: Formula Stories as Art and Popular Culture,* (Chicago: University of Chicago Press, 1976), 78. See also E. J. Hobsbawn, "Robin Hoodo: A Review of Mario Puzo's *The Sicilian,*" *New York Review of Books,* 14 Feb. 1985, 12–17; Fredric Jameson, "Reification and Utopia in Mass Culture," *Social Text* 1 (Winter 1979): 130–48; John Sutherland, *Bestsellers: Popular Fiction of the 1970s* (London: Routledge & Kegan Paul, 1981), ch. 3; and John Paul Russo, "The Hidden Godfather: Plentitude and Absence in Francis Ford Coppola's *Godfather I* and *II*" in *Support and Struggle: Proceedings of the 17th Annual Conference of the American Italian Historical Association,* ed. Joseph L. Tropea et al. (New York: American Italian Historical Association, 1986), 255–81.

3. Jameson, "Reification and Utopia," 146.

4. Puzo's own scattered comments on the social realities behind *The Godfather* reveal little. In an interview, he emphasizes that the novel was not meant to be realistic, but romantic: "To me *The Godfather* isn't an exposé; it's a romantic novel" (quoted in Tom Buckley, "The Mafia Tries a New Tune," *Harper's Magazine,* Aug. 1971, 54). In *The Godfather Papers,* Puzo claims to have written the novel "entirely from research," then testifies that actual mafiosi found his fictional depictions very true to life (Puzo, *The Godfather Papers and Other Confessions* [New York: Fawcett, 1972], 35).

5. Puzo's autobiographical novel, *The Fortunate Pilgrim* (New York: Atheneum, 1964), seems on its surface to exemplify the long-standing tradition of interpreting Italian-American familialism as a barrier to mobility. One reviewer wrote: "The writer renders with fidelity the life-style of an Italian-American community in which Old Country values of propriety, order, and obedience to established authority collide with New World ambition, initiative, and disdain for tradition" (Sheldon Grebstein, "Mama Remembered the Old Country," *Saturday Review,* 23 Jan. 1965, 44). Yet the novel harbors a countervailing analysis, demonstrating how the Puzo family used traditional values to in-

sure a steadily progressive mobility, culminating in Mario's freedom to become a writer.

6. Herbert J. Gans, *Urban Villagers: Group and Class in the Life of Italian-Americans* (New York: Free Press, 1962); Virginia Yans-McLaughlin, *Family and Community: Italian Immigrants in Buffalo, 1880–1930* (Ithaca, N.Y.: Cornell University Press, 1977); Thomas Kessner, *The Golden Door: Italian and Jewish Immigrant Mobility in New York City, 1880–1915* (New York: Oxford University Press, 1977); Thomas Sowell, *Ethnic America* (New York: Basic, 1981).

Most Italian immigrants to the United States came from the Mezzogiorno, the regions of Italy south and east of Naples, including Sicily. The traditional view of Italian-American ethnicity is extrapolated from several very well known mid- to late twentieth-century studies of southern Italy: Phyllis H. Williams, *South Italian Folkways in Europe and America: A Handbook for Social Workers, Visiting Nurses, Schoolteachers, and Physicians* (New Haven, Conn.: Yale University Press, 1938); Carlo Levi, *Christ Stopped at Eboli*, trans. Frances Frenaye (New York: Farrar, Straus & Giroux, 1947); Edward Banfield, *Moral Basis of a Backwater Society* (New York: Free Press, 1958); and Ann Cornelisen, *Women of the Shadows* (New York: Dell, 1976). These texts prompted American-born social workers like Leonard Covello and scholars such as Gans, Sowell, Kessner, Yans-McLaughlin, and Rudolph Vecoli to adopt a variant on the "culture of poverty" argument for blue-collar Italian Americans, although Cornelisen, for one, warns against approaches based on "residual vestiges of peasant mentality" (*Women of the Shadows*, 220).

For an overview of traditional scholarship on Italian Americans, including an analysis of its limitations, see Micaela di Leonardo, *The Varieties of Ethnic Experience: Kinship, Class, and Gender among California Italian-Americans* (Ithaca, N.Y.: Cornell University Press, 1984), 17–25, 96–108.

7. Leonard Covello, "The Influence of Southern Italian Family Mores upon the School Situation in America," in *The Italians: Social Backgrounds of an American Group*, ed. Francesco Cordasco and Eugene Bucchioni (Clifton, N.J.: Kelley, 1974), 516.

8. Francis A. J. Ianni with Elizabeth Reuss-Ianni, *A Family Business: Kinship and Social Control in Organized Crime* (New York: Russell Sage Foundation, 1972), 55. The desire to place the Mafia along an Old World/New World continuum resurfaces in the work of historian Humbert S. Nelli, who adopts the opposite position from Ianni. Nelli concedes the "group unity" and "cooperative effort" of Italian-American mobs, but he stresses the individualism and "American way of life" of the gang leaders. See Humbert S. Nelli, *The Business of*

Crime: Italians and Syndicate Crime in the United States (Chicago: University of Chicago Press, 1976), 255–57.

Scholars of the Southern Italian Mafia also insist on the evolving interdependence of familial and/or fraternal organization and capitalist enterprise. The Italian Mafia is thought to have been restructured in recent years in imitation of the Italian-American Mafia. See Pino Arlacchi, *Mafia Business: The Mafia Ethic and the Spirit of Capitalism,* trans. Martin Ryle (New York: Schocken, 1986); Anton Blok, *The Mafia of a Sicilian Village 1860–1960: A Study of Violent Peasant Entrepreneurs* (New York: Harper and Row, 1975); and E. J. Hobsbawn, *Primitive Rebels: Studies in Archaic Forms of Social Movement in the 19th and 20th Centuries,* 2d ed. (New York: Praeger, 1963), ch. 3.

9. For a review of recent theoretical work on ethnicity in the social sciences, see Werner Sollors, "Theory of American Ethnicity, or: ? S ETHNIC?/TI AND AMERICAN/TI, DE OR UNITED (W) STATES S S1 AND THEOR?" *American Quarterly* 33 (Bibliography 1981), 257–83. On the function of domesticity within capitalism, see Eli Zaretsky, *Capitalism, the Family, and Personal Life* (New York: Harper and Row, 1976).

10. Abner Cohen, *Two-Dimensional Man: An Essay on the Anthropology of Power and Symbolism in Complex Society* (Berkeley and Los Angeles: University of California Press, 1974), 99. See also Cohen, "Introduction," *Urban Ethnicity* (London: Tavistock, 1974), ix–xxiv.

11. Rose Basile Green, *The Italian-American Novel: A Document of the Interaction of Two Cultures* (Rutherford, N.J.: Fairleigh Dickinson University Press, 1974), 355, 357, 364. See also Robert Viscusi, "De Vulgari Eloquentia: An Approach to the Language of Italian American Fiction," *Yale Italian Studies* 1 (Winter 1981): 21–38.

12. Puzo, *The Godfather* (New York: G. P. Putnam, 1969), 216; hereafter cited parenthetically in the text.

13. Cohen, "Introduction," *Urban Ethnicity,* xvii.

14. Peter Dobkin Hall, "Marital Selection and Business in Massachusetts Merchant Families, 1700–1900," in *The American Family in Social-Historical Perspective,* 2d ed., ed. Michael Gordon (New York: St. Martin's Press, 1978), 101–14. See also Ivan H. Light, *Ethnic Enterprise in America: Business and Welfare among Chinese, Japanese, and Blacks* (Berkeley and Los Angeles: University of California Press, 1972); John Bodnar, Roger Simon, and Michael P. Weber, *Lives of Their Own: Blacks, Italians, and Poles in Pittsburgh, 1900–1960* (Urbana: University of Illinois Press, 1982); and Thomas Sowell, *Race and Economics* (New York: David McKay, 1975).

15. Ianni, *A Family Business,* 157.

16. See ibid., 64–65, 92, 116–18.

17. Cawelti, *Adventure, Mystery, Romance,* 52–53. In a review of the first *Godfather* film for *Commentary,* William S. Pechter was perhaps the first critic to emphasize that while the icon of the "Godfather" meant Don Vito Corleone, the narrative belonged to Michael. See Pechter, "Keeping Up with the Corleones," *Commentary* 54 (July 1972): 89.

18. In 1984, Claude Brown reported that "godfather" ranked among the most popular handles, or nicknames, of black inner-city America ("Manchild in Harlem," *New York Times Magazine,* 16 Sept. 1984, 38). It is also a wonderful fact, without being a coincidence, that Puzo's major project after the screenplays for the two *Godfather* films screenplays was scripting *Superman: The Movie* and *Superman II.* For what is the story of Superman if not a metanarrative of immigration about a refugee whose power derives from his dislocation, whose secret identity is hidden under disabling Anglo-conformity as Clark Kent, but whose true promise is revealed in his fight "for truth, justice, and the American way"? And who, conversely, is Don Corleone if not the latest in a continuing series of ethnic supermen? For a discussion of Superman imagery in the context of American ethnicity, see Sollors, *Beyond Ethnicity,* ch. 3.

19. "The Making of *The Godfather,*" *Time* 13 Mar. 1972, 61. John Sutherland reports that by 1980 *The Godfather*'s publishers were claiming worldwide sales of fifteen million copies. The epithet Sutherland gives the novel, "the bestseller of bestsellers," echoes nicely the Sicilian phrase for the boss of bosses, *capo di tutti capi.* Sutherland, *Bestsellers,* 38, 46.

20. For a review of Mafia literature from 1969 to 1975, see Dwight C. Smith, Jr., "Sons of the Godfather: 'Mafia' in Contemporary Fiction," *Italian Americana* 2 (Spring 1976): 191–207. A shorter bibliography appears in Cawelti, *Adventure, Mystery, Romance,* 304 n.

21. Jameson, "Reification and Utopia," 146–47; Cawelti, *Adventure, Mystery, and Romance,* 78.

22. Well into the 1970s, even after the rise of the new ethnicity, it was conventional to attribute Italian Americans' poor performance in the professions, the arts, the American Catholic Church, politics, and big business to the tenacity of familial values and Southern Italian culture. In the last few years, however, the conspicuous rise of Italian Americans has encouraged reversal of the age-old formula. For instance, see Stephen S. Hall, "Italian-Americans: Coming into Their Own," *New York Times Magazine,* 15 May 1983, 29.

23. It is intriguing how Puzo's usage of ethnicity within his career as a writer parallels, broadly speaking, the use of ethnicity depicted in his novels. Puzo began his career, in the now venerable fashion of aspiring American literati, with a novelistic account of his years as an

expatriate (in postwar Germany), *The Dark Arena* (1955). Only subsequently did he specialize in ethnic narrative and become known as a specifically Italian-American writer. With *The Fortunate Pilgrim* (1964), Puzo was able to promote himself as an earnest realist, little known but "serious," as if Italian-American writers toiled honestly on the margins of the American literary community just as their characters worked on the margins of the American economy. With *The Godfather* (1969) and its offspring, Puzo launched himself on a career both as a popular novelist and a Hollywood screenwriter, exploiting ethnic materials for power and profit, as if in sync with the exploitation of family and ethnicity by his Mafia characters.

24. Jameson, "Reification and Utopia," 145.

25. Pauline Kael, "Fathers and Sons," *New Yorker*, 23 Dec. 1974, 64.

26. Quoted in William S. Pechter, "*Godfather II*," *Commentary*, Mar. 1975, 79.

27. Kael, "Fathers and Sons," 64.

28. Jameson, "Reification and Utopia," 147.

29. Isaac Rosenfeld, "David Levinsky: The Jew as American Millionaire," in *Jewish-American Literature: An Antholoy*, ed. Abraham Chapman (New York: New American Library, 1974), 619

30. Pechter, "*Godfather II*," 79.

31. Stanley Kaufmann, "On Films," *New Republic*, 1 Apr. 1972, 26.

32. Pechter, "*Godfather II*," 80. Pechter was also the only critic to recognize the retrospective romanticization of *Godfather II*.

33. I have chosen *Prizzi's Honor* because I greatly admire both the novel and the film. It is impressive that neither the writer nor the director is an Italian American, and I take it as a tribute to Puzo and Coppola that Condon and Huston have been so successfully stimulated by Italian-American creativity. Among other significant achievements in portraying Italian Americans by those not of Italian extraction are Arthur Miller's *View from the Bridge*, the most significant play ever written about Italian Americans, and Norman Jewisohn's *Moonstruck*, which is not only wonderful schlock but evocative as well of the operatic qualities of Italian Americans.

34. Richard Condon, *Prizzi's Honor* (New York: Coward, McCann & Geoghegan, 1982), 11–12; hereafter abbreviated parenthetically in the text.

35. Puzo uses the term *consigliori* throughout *The Godfather*, which may be dialect; Condon spells it *consiglieri* in the Tuscan fashion. Condon's spelling seems to be more common.

36. Don Corrado, Angelo Partanna, and Vincent Partanna are all widowers. (It is exceedingly strange, in a world in which men kill men, that these three have outlived their womenfolk.) Eduardo takes

mistresses but does not marry. And Charley, who lost his mother as a child, is a bachelor pressing fifty. These men "mother" each other, incorporating the female realm into the male, the personal into the professional. Appropriately enough, the one significant Prizzi female, Maerose (the only Prizzi who cooks better than Charley) is an outcast. Exiled, Maerose spends the course of the novel conniving to be forgiven for her sins and readmitted to the family.

37. Condon, *Prizzi's Honor* (New York: Bantam, 1986), [iii].

Chapter Two

1. William Lyon Phelps, "How the Other Half Lives," *Literary Digest International Book Review* 2 (Dec. 1923): 21 An influential literary journalist as well as an academic, Phelps was a popularizer of Yeats and Yezierska's most sustained supporter.

2. O'Brien was the editor of the *Best Short Stories* annual from its inception in 1915 until the early 1940s. In the early years, he catalogued every short story in America's forty most popular magazines and journals (over a thousand stories a year), ranking them with one, two, or three asterisks of distinction (or none at all). In 1920, he chose Yezierska's "Fat of the Land" as the best story of the year and ranked her first collection, *Hungry Hearts*, among the top ten American books of the year. See *The Best Short Stories of 1920*, ed. O'Brien (Boston: Small, Maynard, 1920).

3. Edythe H. Brown, "A Hungry Heart," *Bookman* 58 (Sept. 1923–Feb. 1924): 270; Carol B. Schoen, *Anzia Yezierska* (Boston: G. K. Hall, 1982), 35, 49–50, 74–77.

4. Alter Brody, "Yiddish in American Fiction," *American Mercury* 7 (Jan. 1926): 205–7; Samson Raphaelson, "True Yiddish Flavor," *New York Herald Tribune*, 25 Oct. 1925, 7; Yosef Gaer, "Her One Virtue," *Menorah Journal* 12 (Feb. 1926): 105–8; and Johan J. Smertenko, "From the Ghetto Depths," *Saturday Review of Literature*, 10 Oct. 1925, 192. Although Yezierska published her fourth novel in 1932, Albert Halper indicated that she was by then a relic of the past, one of the "headliners in the good old days" who had "sunk from sight because she found no new themes to replace her old ones" (Halper, "Notes on Jewish-American Fiction," *Menorah Journal* 20 [Apr. 1932]: 65).

5. Irving Howe, *World of Our Fathers* (New York: Simon and Schuster, 1976), 269.

6. In addition to unpublished dissertations of the late 1960s and early 1970s, renewed interest in Yezierska began with a critical discussion in Allen Guttmann, *The Jewish Writer in America: Assimilation and the Crisis of Identity* (New York: Oxford University Press, 1971), 33–35; with the reprinting of *Hungry Hearts* by a library specialty press as well

as two important sketches in Wayne Charles Miller, *A Gathering of Ghetto Writers: Irish, Italian, Jewish, Black, and Puerto Rican* (New York: New York University Press, 1972); and with Jo Ann Boydston's surprising discovery of John Dewey's love poems about Yezierska, recounted in her introduction to *The Poems of John Dewey*, ed. Boydston (Carbondale: Southern Illinois University Press, 1977), ix–lxvii.

7. Mary P. Ryan, "The Breadgivers: Immigrants and Reformers: 1865–1920," *Womanhood in America: From Colonial Times to the Present* (New York: New Viewpoints, 1979), 118.

8. Alice Kessler-Harris, Introduction to Anzia Yezierska, *Bread Givers* (New York: Persea, 1976), xvi. Through Persea Press, Kessler-Harris has brought *Bread Givers*, *Hungry Hearts* (a 1920 story collection), and *Red Ribbon on a White Horse* (the 1950 autobiography) back into print. She has also edited *The Open Cage* (an anthology of stories and sketches), written two critical introductions, and involved Yezierska's daughter, Louise Levitas Henriksen, in the recovery of her mother's works.

9. Funk and Wagnalls advertisement, *Literary Digest International Book Review* 2 (Nov. 1923): 96.

10. Yezierska, "The Immigrant Speaks," *Good Housekeeping*, June 1920, 20–21; "An Immigrant among the Editors," *Literary Digest International Book Review* 1 (Mar. 1923): 1, 6, 67; "The Struggles of an Immigrant Author," *Literary Digest International Book Review* 1 (Sept. 1923): 17–21; and "Mostly about Myself," *Children of Loneliness: Stories of Immigrant Life in America* (New York: Funk and Wagnalls, 1923), 9–31.

11. At birth in Russia, she was called Anzia by parents who went by the name Yezierska, but, upon immigration, Yezierska's eldest brother renamed the family Mayer and gave Anzia a new first name, Hattie, by which she was known until she published her first story at age thirty-five. Hattie Mayer's choice of "Anzia Yezierska" as a nom de plume was a self-dramatization of her emergence as a writer, akin to Samuel Clemens's invention of "Mark Twain." She may have understood her nom de plume as a recovery of her European birthright, but "Yezierska" also functioned as a marketing technique for underscoring her foreignness. Whereas Irwin Granich became Mike Gold and Nathan Weinstein became Nathanael West, Mayer became "Yezierska," an exotic name liable to be misspelled (which it was) and mispronounced (which it must have been).

12. After the waning of their apparently unconsummated affair, Yezierska wrote a review of Dewey's *Democracy and Education*, in which she criticized him for an elitism of language and sentiment ("Prophets of Democracy," *Bookman* 52 [Feb. 1921]: 496–99). The most important accounts of Dewey in Yezierska's fiction are "To The Stars,"

Children of Loneliness, 77–98, and *All I Could Never Be* (New York: Brewer, Warner, and Putnam, 1932).

13. See Mary V. Dearborn, *Love in the Promised Land: The Story of Anzia Yezierska and John Dewey* (New York: Free Press, 1988), and Louise Levitas Henricksen, *Anzia Yezierska: A Writer's Life* (New Brunswick, N.J.: Rutgers University Press, 1988).

14. Yezierska, *Bread Givers: A Struggle between a Father of the Old World and a Daughter of the New*, ed. Kessler-Harris (New York: Persea, 1976), 1–2; hereafter cited parenthetically in the text.

15. In portraying the desperation of Smolinsky's later years, Yezierska perhaps anticipated her own experience and certainly the magazine stories she was to publish in her seventies and eighties, which treated "older Jews without money." Yezierska, *The Open Cage: An Anzia Yezierska Collection*, ed. Kessler-Harris (New York: Persea, 1979), 211–51.

16. I owe my understanding of realism to the community of teachers and students associated with the Program in American Studies at Yale University, who made the Gilded Age "incorporation of America" a primary focus during my years there. See Jean-Christophe Agnew, "The Consuming Vision of Henry James," in *The Culture of Consumption: Critical Essays in American History, 1880–1980*, ed. Richard Wightman Fox and T. J. Jackson Lears (New York: Pantheon, 1983), 65–100; Richard Brodhead, *The School of Hawthorne* (New York: Oxford University Press, 1986); Michael Denning, *Mechanic Accents: Dime Novels and Working-Class Culture in America* (New York: Verso, 1987); Amy Kaplan, *The Social Construction of American Realism* (Chicago: University of Chicago Press, 1988); Alan Trachtenberg, *The Incorporation of America: Culture and Society in the Gilded Age* (New York: Hill and Wang, 1982); and Christopher P. Wilson, *The Labor of Words: Literary Professionalism in the Progressive Era* (Athens: University of Georgia Press, 1985).

17. Deborah Dash Moore, *At Home in America: Second Generation New York Jews* (New York: Columbia University Press, 1981).

18. Howe, *World of Our Fathers*, 269.

19. In a trenchant critique of an earlier draft of this chapter, Laura Wexler pointed out to me that Yezierska effaces the violent dispossession of European Jewry. When Mrs. Smolinsky explains to her daughters the family's fall in class status, she remembers how their father had squandered much of their inheritance in religious absorption. Yet the elliptical nature of her testimony suggests that she is not telling the whole story: "'Maybe Solomon got himself rich first and then sang his Songs, but your father wanted to sing first and then attend to business. He was a smart salesman, only to sell things for less than

they cost. . . . And when everything was gone from us, then our only hope was to come to America' " (34). Mrs. Smolinsky says "was gone from us," but we need to hear "was taken from us." We need to inquire, with Wexler, into the dangers of the immigrant's will to forget and the second generation's ignorance of what really happened.

20. Dearborn, "The Making of an American Ethnic," in *The Invention of Ethnicity,* ed. Werner Sollors (New York: Oxford University Press,

21. Rachel Bowlby, *Just Looking: Consumer Culture in Dreiser, Gissing, and Zola* (New York: Methuen, 1985), 4.

22. Philip Fisher, *Hard Facts: Setting and Form in the American Novel* (New York: Oxford University Press, 1987), 157–62.

23. Schoen, *Anzia Yezierska,* 64–65, and Kessler-Harris, introduction to *Bread Givers,* xvii.

24. Mary Antin, *The Promised Land* (Boston: Houghton Mifflin, 1969), 64.

Chapter Three

1. Irving Howe, *A Margin of Hope: An Intellectual Autobiography* (New York: Harcourt Brace Jovanovich, 1982), 151.

2. Lionel Trilling, "Of Sophistication," *Menorah Journal* 14 (Jan. 1928): 108; "Burning Doorbells," *Menorah Journal* 15 (Nov. 1928): 483–86; and "Genuine Writing," *Menorah Journal* 19 (Oct. 1930): 88–92.

3. Joseph Wolf, "Portrait of the Artist as a Child," *Partisan Review* 2 (Apr.–May 1935): 95.

4. Delmore Schwartz, *In Dreams Begin Responsibilities* (Norwalk, Conn.: New Directions, 1938); Daniel Fuchs, *Summer in Williamsburg* (New York: Vanguard, 1934); Meyer Levin, *The Old Bunch* (New York: Simon and Schuster, 1937); Charles Reznikoff, *By the Waters of Manhattan* (New York: Charles Boni, 1930).

5. Trilling, "Genuine Writing," 88. For a similar judgment, see Albert Halper, "Notes on Jewish-American Fiction," *Menorah Journal* 20 (Apr. 1932): 61–69.

6. Wolf, "Portrait of the Artist," 96.

7. For early praise, see Horace Gregory, "East Side World," *The Nation,* 27 Feb. 1935, 255, and John Cournos, "Truth and Fiction," *Menorah Journal* 24 (Winter 1936): 150–59. For the rediscovery, see "The Most Neglected Books of the Past 25 Years," *American Scholar* 25 (Autumn 1956): 472–504; Leslie A. Fiedler, "The Jew in the American Novel" (1957), reprinted in *To the Gentiles* (New York: Stein and Day, 1972), 96–97; Fiedler, "Henry Roth's Neglected Masterpiece" (1960), reprinted in *A Fiedler Reader* (New York: Stein and Day, 1977), 211–19;

and Howe, "Life Never Let Up," *New York Times Book Review,* 25 Oct. 1964, 1, 61–62.

8. Cleanth Brooks, R. W. B. Lewis, and Robert Penn Warren, *American Literature: The Makers and the Making,* 2 vols. (New York: St. Martin's Press, 1973), 2:2395.

9. Trilling, "Genuine Writing," 92.

10. Howe, *World of Our Fathers,* (New York: Simon and Schuster, 1976), 589.

11. Fiedler, "The Jew in the American Novel," 96. For a recent testimonial, underscoring solidarity across gender lines, see Judith Ruderman, "Call It Wonderful: An Account of One Woman's Love Affair with the 'Other' Roth," *North Dakota Quarterly* 56 (Summer 1988): 95–100.

12. *American Literature: A Prentice-Hall Anthology,* ed. Emory Elliott et al. (New York: Prentice-Hall, 1991), vol. 2; *The Heath Anthology of American Literature,* ed. Paul Lauter et al. (New York: D. C. Heath, 1990, vol. 2; *Heritage of American Literature,* ed. James E. Miller, Jr. (New York: Harcourt Brace Jovanovich, 1991), vol. 2; and *The Harper American Literature,* ed. Donald McQuade et al. (New York: Harper and Row, 1987). There are also no selections from Roth in *The American Tradition in Literature,* ed. George Perkins et al. 7th ed., 2 vols. (New York: Random House, 1990), and *The Norton Anthology of American Literature,* ed. Nina Baym et al. 3d ed., 2 vols. (New York: Norton, 1989).

13. *Columbia Literary History of the United States,* ed. Elliott (New York: Columbia University Press, 1988), esp. 745–46, 576–77, 755, 860.

14. Quoted in David Bronsen, "An Interview with Henry Roth," *Partisan Review* 36 (1969): 270.

15. Wai-chee Dimock, "Slippery Connections," *American Literary History* 2 (Spring 1990): 131–43.

16. Robert Stepto, "1910–1945: Afro-American Literature," *Columbia Literary History of the United States,* 785–99.

17. Fiedler, "Partisan Review: Phoenix or Dodo?" *To the Gentiles,* 44.

18. Howe, *A Margin of Hope,* 137.

19. Daniel Aaron, "The Hyphenate Writer and American Letters," Smith *Alumnae Quarterly,* July 1964, 215.

20. Randolph Bourne described such communities of letters as "transnational," writing from the perspective of the long established: "It is not uncommon for the eager Anglo-Saxon who comes to a vivid American university to-day to find his true friends not among his own race but among the acclimatized German or Austrian, the acclimatized Jew, the acclimatized Scandinavian or Italian. There he finds the cosmopolitan note" (Bourne, "Trans-National America," *War and the Intellectuals: Essays by Randolph S. Bourne 1915–1919,* ed. Carl Resek [New York: Harper & Row, 1964], 118).

21. Quoted in Bonnie Lyons, "An Interview with Henry Roth," *Henry Roth: The Man and His Work* (New York: Cooper Square, 1976), 161.

22. Quoted in Bronsen, "An Interview with Henry Roth," 270.

23. Quoted in Lyons, "An Interview with Henry Roth," 168.

24. Fiedler, "Henry Roth's Neglected Masterpiece," 216.

25. Quoted in Lyons, "An Interview with Henry Roth," 168.

26. The phrases are chapter titles in Lyons, *Henry Roth*, 39, 56.

27. Mario Puzo, "Choosing a Dream: Italians in Hell's Kitchen," *The Godfather Papers and Other Confessions* (New York: Fawcett, 1972), 29.

28. Fiedler, "Henry Roth's Neglected Masterpiece," 215.

29. See Abraham Cahan, *Yekl and The Imported Bridegroom and Other Stories of the New York Ghetto* (New York: Dover, 1970), 33–38.

30. Henry Roth, *Call It Sleep* (New York: Avon, 1964), 11; hereafter cited parenthetically in the text.

31. Eugene O'Neill, *The Great God Brown; The Fountain; The Moon of the Carribees; and Other Plays* (New York: Random House, 1926).

32. Lyons, "An Interview with Henry Roth," 160.

33. Marcus Klein, *Foreigners: The Making of American Literature, 1900–1940* (Chicago: University of Chicago Press, 1981), 196.

34. For a study that synthesizes the new social history on immigration, with substantial references, see John Bodnar, *The Transplanted: A History of Immigrants in Urban America* (Bloomington: Indiana University Press, 1985).

35. Raymond Williams, *The Politics of Modernism: Against the New Conformists*, ed. Tony Pinkney (London: Verso, 1989), 45, 34. Williams speaks out of a long tradition, which began in Roth's time, of conceptualizing the modern condition as that of urban migration. For instance, see Robert E. Park, "Human Migration and the Marginal Man," *American Journal of Sociology* 33 (May 1928): 881–93; Everett V. Stonequist, *The Marginal Man: A Study in Personality and Cultural Conflict* (New York: Russell and Russell, 1937); and Georg Simmel, *The Sociology of Georg Simmel*, trans. and ed. Kurt H. Wolff (New York: Free Press, 1950), 402–9.

36. Williams, *The Politics of Modernism*, 45.

37. Guttmann, *The Jewish Writer in America: Assimilation and the Crisis of Identity* (New York: Oxford University Press, 1971), 54.

38. Klein, *Foreigners*, 196.

39. Quoted in Lyons, "An Interview with Henry Roth," 170, 167.

40. Werner Sollors, "Melting Pots," *Beyond Ethnicity: Consent and Descent in American Culture* (New York: Oxford University Press, 1986), 66–101.

41. Williams, *The Politics of Modernism*, 34.

42. Quoted in Lyons, "An Interview with Henry Roth," 170.

43. Fiedler, "Roth's Neglected Masterpiece," 219.

Chapter Four

1. The following make no mention of Miller: Wayne Charles Miller et al., *A Comprehensive Bibliography for the Study of American Minorities* (New York: New York University Press, 1976); Babette F. Inglehart and Anthony R. Mangione, *The Image of Pluralism in American Literature: An Annotated Bibliography on the American Experience of European Ethnic Groups* (New York: American Jewish Committee, 1974); Arthur R. Schultz, *German-American Relations and German Culture in America: A Subject Bibliography* (Millwood, N.Y.: Kraus, 1984); Michael Karesztesi and Gary R. Cocozzoli, *German-American History and Life: A Guide to Information Sources* (Detroit: Gale, 1980); and Henry A. Pochmann and Arthur R. Shultz, *Bibliography of German Culture in America to 1940* (Madison: University of Wisconsin Press, 1953).

2. Editor Philip Butcher includes an excerpt from *Tropic of Capricorn* in a section on "King Prejudice" in *The Ethnic Image in Modern American Literature: 1900–1950,* 2 vols. (Washington, D.C.: Howard University Press, 1984), 2:328–33.

3. See *The Future of American Modernism: Ethnic Writing Between the Wars,* ed. William Boelhower (Amsterdam: Amerika Instituut, 1990).

4. Alfred Kazin places Miller among a cohort of a dozen writers who came out of "the slums, farms and factories" and furnished American writing with "the banked-up experience of the plebes" (Kazin, *Starting Out in the Thirties* [New York: Vintage, 1980], 12–13). Marcus Klein cites him as one among "widely disparate examples" of the thesis that the real "aesthetic" of proletarian literature was not so much a doctrinaire critique of capitalism as the "sustaining even joyous" vitality of America's "lower depths" (Klein, *Foreigners: The Making of American Literature, 1900–1940* [Chicago: University of Chicago Press, 1981], 130–31).

5. Malcolm Cowley, *Exile's Return: A Literary Odyssey of the 1920's* (New York: Viking, 1951), ch. 7. For an overview of Miller's reputation for being apolitical, see Edward Mitchell, "Introduction," *Henry Miller: Three Decades of Criticism* (New York: New York University Press, 1971), xiv. Although Mitchell cites Edmund Wilson as dissenting from the majority view, Wilson, along with Cowley and their followers, was, of course, partly responsible for the long-standing equation between going abroad and social insensitivity that has been used to characterize Miller. See Wilson, *Axel's Castle: A Study in the Imaginative Literature of 1870–1930* (New York: Scribner's, 1931), ch. 8.

6. Wilson, "The Twilight of the Expatriates," *A Literary Chronicle: 1920–1950* (Gardon City, N.Y.: Doubleday, n.d.), 212.

7. Richard Pells identifies the following instances of apolitical self-involvement: "Malcolm Cowley's *Exile Return,* Louis Adamic's *My*

America, Michael Gold's *Jews Without Money*, Joseph Freeman's *An American Testament*, Woody Guthrie's *Bound for Glory*, Edward Dahlberg's *Bottom Dogs*, Jack Conroy's *The Disinherited*, James Farrell's *Studs Lonigan* trilogy, Henry Roth's *Call It Sleep*, Nelson Algren's *Somebody in Boots*, Henry Miller's *Tropic of Cancer*, William Saroyan's short stories, all the novels of Thomas Wolfe" (Pells, *Radical Visions and American Dreams: Culture and Social Thought in the Depression Years* [New York: Harper Torchbook, 1974], 202).

Pells's writers are either ethnics or alternatively marginalized, hence "hyphenated," as "working-class" or "rural" Americans. If these works look inward, it is not to celebrate "personal identity" or even (like Emerson) to express epistemological uncertainty but to represent the impossibility of asserting an integral self-identity given the divisive energies (Sicilian/Anglo-American, Jewish/Protestant, working-class/middle-class, etc.) at work in the United States. These texts may not be "revolutionary politics" in a doctrinaire sense, but their treatments of the "divided self" are far more socially engaged than Pells credits.

8. Wendy Steiner, "The Diversity of American Fiction, 1910–1945," in *Columbia Literary History of the United States*, ed. Emory Elliott (New York: Columbia University Press, 1988), 845–72.

9. Raoul R. Ibarguen, "Narrative Detours: Henry Miller and Rise of New Critical Modernism" (Ph.D. diss., Yale University, 1989), 8, 5.

10. In *Clipped Wings*, Miller sketched the biographies of a dozen men whom he had supervised at Western Union. With grinding repetition, he explained how each man, talented and ambitious, had struggled only to be frustrated, time and again, by the nativist/racist, anti-individualist apparatus of corporate capitalism. In other words, during the 1920s, Miller was an ethnic proletarian writer in the traditional sense. Jay Martin, *Always Merry and Bright: The Life of Henry Miller* (Santa Barbara, Calif.: Capra, 1978), 70–75; Ibarguen, "Narrative Detours," 104.

11. Although Miller correctly judged *Clipped Wings* a failure and never tried to publish it, he frequently cannibalized it. During the mid-1920s, he published one excerpt (depicting the prejudices facing a Columbia Ph.D. candidate from India) as a cover essay in W. E. B. DuBois's *The Crisis*. He also submitted some material to *The Menorah Journal*, whose editors received it warmly. They offered him assignments on the Houston Street burlesque and Second Avenue cafés, but never found room for what Miller gave them. The most significant reappearance of *Clipped Wings* material is in the first chapter of *Tropic of Capricorn*, where Miller retells the story of the messengers from his own point of view, as their boss, ending with a diatribe against preju-

dice, imperialism, and the Alger myth, arguably but not certainly eugenicist. Valentine Nieting [Henry Valentine Miller], "Black and White," *The Crisis* 28 (May 1924): 1, 16–17; Mary V. Dearborn, *The Happiest Man Alive: A Biography of Henry Miller* (New York: Simon and Schuster, 1991), 71–72, 91–93.

12. Miller's greatest influence and the correspondent of the "Hamlet" volumes, Michael Fraenkel, had emigrated from Russia to the Lower East Side as an infant, coming to Europe, like Miller, only as an adult. Walter Lowensfels was of German Jewish extraction. William Saroyan was learning to mine his Armenian-American boyhood for modernist narrative. Both in origins and sensibility, Miller's initial intellectual circle in Paris was arguably more ethnic than that of, say, Henry Roth back in New York. Anticipating the later testimony of writers such as William Barrett or Jerre Mangione, Miller wrote: "I too would become a Jew." Miller, *Tropic of Cancer* (New York: Grove Press, 1961), 3.

13. Miller, *The Cosmological Eye* (New York: New Directions, 1938), 107–34, 151–96.

14. Steiner, "The Diversity of American Fiction," 869–70.

15. Miller's paternal grandfather, Heinrich Müller, was born in Minden, Hanover while his maternal grandmother, Barbara Kropf, came from nearby Bavaria; Miller's maternal grandparents, Valentin Nieting and Emilie Insel, both were born in Prussia, in Stessfield Stessen and in Neagleburg, respectively.

16. Robert Ferguson, *Henry Miller: A Life* (New York: Norton, 1991), 3.

17. Dearborn, *The Happiest Man Alive*, 19–54; Ferguson, *Henry Miller*, 2–16; and Martin, *Always Merry and Bright*, 3–20.

18. Miller, *Tropic of Capricorn* (New York: Grove, 1961), 11.

19. Dearborn, *The Happiest Man Alive*, 20–22, 31–32; Martin, *Always Merry and Bright*, 3–11. Ferguson, the third biographer, sharply situates the Millers within immigrant history, the evolution of Brooklyn as an immigrant enclave, and the German presence within the garment trades, but he shies away from ethnic stereotyping, suggesting that Miller, always a mythologizer and often self-contradictory, was especially unreliable when it came to questions of heritage and upbringing. On the first page of his biography he quotes Miller as saying, "I am a mixture of Mongol, Chinese, Tibetan, and Jewish bloods" (Ferguson, *Henry Miller*, 1).

20. Martin, *Always Merry and Bright*, 294.

21. Kingsley Widmer, *Henry Miller* (New York: Twayne, 1963), 48.

22. Miller Sr. shared quarters with five other "boss tailors," each of whom kept his own customer list but used the same pool of journey-

man tailors. Paradoxically, boss tailors often made less money than their workaholic subcontractors. In the case of Miller Sr.'s shop, only one boss, a German by the name of Metz, was affluent. Ferguson, *Henry Miller*, 30.

23. Miller, *Black Spring* (New York: Grove Press, 1963), 79; hereafter cited parenthetically in the text.

24. Eve Kosofsky Sedgwick, *Between Men: English Literature and Male Homosocial Desire* (New York: Columbia University Press, 1985).

25. The rage of Miller's mother reflects more than sexual jealousy or moral outrage. Whether taken literally or not, "making love" to men at work has meant no making money for or spending time on the wife and kids at home. "All [mother] knew how to do was to groan and complain all day," writes Miller (80), but given the evidence, it seems that she may be justified. In pursuing friendships rather than cash, Miller Sr. violates the contractual spirit of his marriage to a woman who is both acquisitive and socially ambitious.

26. *Out of Bounds: Male Writers and Gender(ed) Criticism*, ed. Laura Claridge and Elizabeth Langland (Amherst: University of Massachusetts Press, 1990); Frank Lentricchia, *Ariel and the Police* (Madison: University of Wisconsin Press, 1988), 136–96; David Leverenz, *Manhood and the American Renaissance* (Ithaca, N.Y.: Cornell University Press, 1989); Michael Moon, "'The Gentle Boy from the Dangerous Classes': Pederasty, Domesticity, and Capitalism in Horatio Alger," *Representations* 19 (Summer 1987): 87–110; and a special issue of *The South Atlantic Quarterly*, reprinted as *Displacing Homophobia*, ed. Ron Butters, John Clum, and Moon (Durham, N.C.: Duke University Press, 1990).

27. Lentricchia, *Ariel and the Police*, 157–58.

28. Widmer, *Henry Miller*, 47.

29. Warner Berthoff, *The Ferment of Realism: American Literature, 1884–1919* (New York: Free Press, 1965), 29.

30. Kate Millett, *Sexual Politics* (London: Virago, 1979), 303.

31. Dearborn has been the most active of Miller's psychobiographers, arguing for and speculating on such matters as his mother's withholding of affection, a childhood experiment in buggery with another boy, a later predilection for making love to prostitutes in the presence of male friends, and an anti-Semitism that underlay his intimacy with Jews. In his introduction, Ferguson admits that Miller's massive paper trail seems to "cry out" for psychological interpretation, but he deprecates "too heavy a reliance on a rigidly methodological approach" (Ferguson, *Henry Miller*, xiv).

32. James Joyce, *A Portrait of the Artist as a Young Man* (New York: Viking, 1968), 252–53.

33. Miller's evocation of a "pedestrian highway leading nowhere

eventually," to which he "awakens" each day, clearly evokes the mood and figurative strategy that opens Emerson's "Experience." Emerson regards perception as that which makes the "real" of the quotidian inaccessible. In contrast, Miller finds his quotidian all too real, that is, he finds walking the streets of Manhattan to work and for work threatening a specifically aesthetic consciousness and a specifically literary ambition. See Ralph Waldo Emerson, "Experience," *Selections from Ralph Waldo Emerson*, ed. Stephen E. Whicher (Boston: Houghton Mifflin, 1947), 254–55.

34. Widmer, *Henry Miller*, 48.

35. Anzia Yezierska, "My Own People," *Hungry Hearts and Other Stories* (Boston: Houghton Mifflin, 1920), 228.

36. I am quoting here from section 1 of *Song of Myself* as presented in the 1891–92 edition of *Leaves of Grass*. Walt Whitman, *Walt Whitman: Complete Poetry and Prose* (New York: Library of America, 1982), 188; Miller, letter dated 1 Apr. 1930, quoted in Martin, *Always Merry and Bright*, 180–81.

37. On Whitman's importance to ethnic writers, see Sollors, *Beyond Ethnicity*, 256–58.

38. The Beats' debt to Miller is well known. Pynchon's breakthrough story, "Entropy," is headed by a quote from *Tropic of Cancer*. In the preface to *Henry Miller* (vii), Ferguson comments that his biography and that of Mary Dearborn will be joined by third centenary volume from novelist Jong, a confessed Miller aficionada and coiner of the Milleresque phrase "the zipless fuck." In Scorsese's black comedy *After Hours*, the conversation that initiates the nightmarish pursuit through Greenwich Village revolves around *Tropic of Cancer*, which the woman to be pursued is reading (not implausibly). The film can be construed as an effort to translate Miller's narrative rhythms to the screen, both to embody and to respond to the urban wasteland.

39. During those first few months in Paris, Miller began reading the modernists obsessively because the community of expatriates whom he trusted urged him to do so. Ibarguen argues that Miller not only felt comfortable in the company of these particular expatriates but felt, for perhaps the first time, the power of his Brooklyn vernacular vis-à-vis the "art speech" of university-trained partisans of modernism. Though he was himself capable of sweeping aesthetic discriminations, he had suspected throughout the 1920s that the banner of aesthetic quality Americans had carried overseas was an effort to shore up a specifically social aristocracy, an agenda he found doubly objectionable: on democratic principle and because it seemed to preclude, in particular, such Brooklyn boys as himself. Modernist in taste and East Side in background, Fraenkel and his crowd provoked Miller

to read Eliot and Joyce carefully, insisting that the modernist debate about form and style would speak to him. Taking evident pleasure in his "street smarts," these mentors of modernism convinced him that he would have something to say in response to the modernists. "Write as you talk," Fraenkel urged, "write as you live." Ibarguen, "Narrative Detours," 110; Michael Fraenkel, *The Genesis of the Tropic of Cancer* (Berkeley: Bern Porter, 1946), 12.

Chapter Five

1. *The Woman Warrior* sells steadily, 450,000 copies to date. One chapter or another appears in all four of the major anthologies of U.S. literature published in the late 1980s and early 1990s (Harper, D. C. Heath, Prentice-Hall, and Harcourt Brace Jovanovich) as well as in *The Norton Anthology of Writing by Women in English*. Critical essays on Kingston feature prominently in recent issues of such arbiter journals as *PMLA*, *Signs*, and *American Literary History*. At U.S. colleges and universities, the book is taught in courses ranging from freshman composition to liberal studies to critical theory, and from the Asian-American experience to women's writing to world autobiography to the postmodern novel. In Europe, where the British firm Picador distributes a beautiful softcover edition, it is one of the few contemporary American works that has found an audience. Kingston has accepted speaking engagements as far east as Hong Kong and Beijing. See Reed Way Dasenbrock, "Intelligibility and Meaningfulness in Multicultural Literature in English," *PMLA* 102 (Jan. 1987): 10–19; Leslie W. Rabine, "No Lost Paradise: Social Gender and Symbolic Gender in the Writings of Maxine Hong Kingston," *Signs: Journal of Women in Culture and Society* 12 (Spring 1987): 471–92; and David Leiwei Li, "China Men: Maxine Hong Kingston and the American Canon," *American Literary History* 2 (Fall 1990): 482–502.

2. The writers and critics who first promoted *The Woman Warrior* overemphasized the foreignness of its setting and the exoticness of its themes. In their commentaries, adverbs denoting absolutism policed the boundaries of a cultural and aesthetic hinterland: "inscrutably foreign," "another place entirely," and "a stubbornly, utterly foreign sensibility." Kay Boyle, dust jacket of Kingston, *The Woman Warrior* (New York: Knopf, [1982 printing]); Jane Kramer, "A Review of *The Woman Warrior*," *New York Times Book Review*, 7 Nov. 1976, 1, 18–20; *The Norton Anthology of Literature by Women: The Tradition in English*, ed. Sandra M. Gilbert and Susan Gubar (New York: Norton, 1985), 2337.

Kingston ultimately would complain about being stereotyped as "the exotic, inscrutable, mysterious oriental," citing a half-dozen reviews, all from newspapers. But she does not mention the way the book was marketed, which, it seems to me, must be held partly responsible for its reception, especially at the level of the daily press. Kingston, "Cultural Mis-readings by American Reviewers," *Asian and Western Writers in Dialogue: New Cultural Identities* (London: Macmillan, 1982), 55–65.

3. Anne Tyler, "A Review of *China Men*," *New Republic*, 21 June 1980, 34.

4. Michael M. J. Fischer, "Ethnicity and the Post-Modern Arts of Memory," in *Writing Culture: The Poetics and Politics of Ethnography*, ed. James Clifford and George E. Marcus (Berkeley and Los Angeles: University of California Press, 1986), 194–233.

5. Dasenbrock, "Intelligibility and Meaningfulness," 14.

6. William Q. Boelhower, "The Immigrant Novel as Genre," *MELUS* 8 (Spring 1981): 3–13.

7. Elaine H. Kim, *Asian American Literature: An Introduction to the Writings and Their Social Context* (Philadelphia: Temple University Press, 1982), 198. For an account of the politicization of Chinese Americans in the wake of the Civil Rights and Black Power movements, see Stan Steiner, *Fusang: The Chinese who Built America* (New York: Harper and Row, 1979), ch. 16.

8. Kingston, Tan, and Hwang have found success, critical and middlebrow popular, that is unprecedented for Asian-American writers. Their work has been interdependent at times, and they have expressed mutual respect. For instance, Tan's breathtaking first novel, *The Joy Luck Club* (1989), which focuses on four pairs of mothers and daughters, is deeply indebted to *The Woman Warrior*. A collection of Hwang's early plays, *F.O.B. and Other Plays* (New York: New American Library, 1990), contains a brief appreciative forward by Kingston (vii–ix).

9. Although Kingston is criticized at great length, the single most vicious criticism, published above the signature of the four editors, all of whom are male, is directed at Hwang: "It is an article of white liberal American faith that Chinese men, at their best, are effeminate closet queens like Charlie Chan and, at their worst, are homosexual menaces like Fu Manchu. No wonder David Henry Hwang's derivative *M. Butterfly* won the Tony for best new play of 1988. The good Chinese man, at his best, is the fulfillment of white male homosexual fantasy, literally kissing white ass. Now Hwang and the stereotype are inextricably one" (Jeffery Paul Chan, Frank Chin, Lawson Fusao Inada, and Shawn Wong, "Introduction," *The Big Aiiieeeee! An Anthology of Chinese American and Japanese American Literature*, ed. Chan et al. [New York: Penguin, 1991], xiii). In addition to revealing the anxieties and resentments fueling editorial practice, these comments make it painfully clear that intellectual united fronts, often naively presumed,

in fact may be difficult to come by, both within individual ethnic groups and among representatives of diversely marginal groups.

10. Frank Chin, "Come All Ye Asian American Writers of the Real and the Fake," in *The Big Aiiieeeee!*, 26, 27. Chin's recent fiction has been much praised. I recommend as well the plays with which he started: Chin, *The Chickencoop Chinaman and The Year of the Dragon* (Seattle: University of Washington Press, 1981). The rivalry between Chin and Kingston can be followed in their fiction, because each of them has portrayed the other in barely disguised form, in both instances with much sarcastic wit, and in Kingston's novel-length portrayal of Chin (whom she calls Wittman Ah Sing) with a marked degree of appreciation as well. Chin, "Unmanly Warrior," *The Chinaman Pacific & Frisco R.R. Co.* (Minneapolis: Coffee House Press, 1989), i–v; Kingston, *Tripmaster Monkey: His Fake Book* (New York: Alfred A. Knopf, 1989).

11. Patricia Lin Blinde, "The Icicle in the Desert: Perspective and Form in the Works of Two Chinese-American Writers," *MELUS* 6 (Fall 1979): 51–71; Blinde, "A Review of *China Men*," *Amerasia* 8 (1981): 139–43; Chen Lok Chua, "Two Chinese Versions of the American Dream: The Golden Mountain in Lin Yutang and Maxine Hong Kingston," *MELUS* 8 (Winter 1981): 61–70; Louise Liew, "Ghost Stories," *Bridge* 5 (Apr. 1977): 47–48; and Suzi Wong, "A Review of *The Woman Warrior*," *Amerasia* 4 (1977): 165.

12. Kim, *Asian American Literature*, 199.

13. Sau-ling Cynthia Wong, "Necessity and Extravagance in Maxine Hong Kingston's *The Woman Warrior*: Art and Ethnic Experience," *MELUS* 15 (Spring 1988): 25.

14. Diane Johnson, "Ghosts," *New York Review of Books*, 3 Feb. 1977, 19–20, 29; Mary Gordon, "Mythic History," *New York Review of Books* 15 June 1980, 1, 24–25.

15. The explicit model for *China Men*, Kingston's second book, is William Carlos Williams's *In The American Grain*. "I feel I have continued that book," says Kingston (Timothy Pfaff, "A Talk with Mrs. Kingston," *New York Times Book Review*, 15 June 1980, 25). As postmodernist texts working in chronological tandem, *In The American Grain* and *China Men* repudiate, respectively, the Puritanism of official U.S. culture prior to 1850 and the Eurocentrism grafted onto it thereafter. Williams restores to the record the suppressed histories of Native Americans and European Catholics whereas Kingston recovers the later accomplishments and tribulations of male Chinese immigrants: as pickers in the cane fields of Hawaii and demolition experts on the transcontinental railroad in the nineteenth century, then as laundrymen and restauranteurs humiliated by the exclusion laws and bereft of Chinese women in the twentieth century.

16. Amy Ling, *Between Worlds: Women Writers of Chinese Ancestry* (New York: Pergamon, 1990), 1–20, 119–57.

17. Kingston, *The Woman Warrior* (New York: Alfred A. Knopf, 1976), 47; hereafter cited parenthetically in the text.

18. For a discussion of the feminist encounter with the problem of ancestry, see Hester Eisenstein, *Contemporary Feminist Thought* (Boston: G. K. Hall, 1983), pt. 2. For an insightful debate on the issue, see "Feminist Discourse, Moral Values, and the Law—A Conversation," *Buffalo Law Review* 34 (1985): 11–87, a symposium featuring Ellen C. DuBois, Mary C. Dunlap, Carol J. Gilligan, Catharine A. MacKinnon, and Carrie J. Menkel-Meadow.

19. Adrienne Rich, "Motherhood and Daughterhood," *Of Woman Born: Motherhood as Experience and Institution* (New York: Norton, 1976), 246, 247.

20. Quoted in Pfaff, "A Talk with Mrs. Kingston," 26.

21. Kingston, "The Death of a Precious Only Daughter," *Viva*, Jan. 1975, 75ff. Curtis Publications promoted *Viva* as "an international magazine for women."

22. "No Name Woman" is included in vol. 2 of *American Literature: A Prentice-Hall Anthology*, ed. Emory Elliott et al. (New York: Prentice-Hall, 1991); *The Harper American Literature*, ed. Donald McQuade et al. (New York: Harper and Row, 1987); and vol. 2 of *Heritage of American Literature*, ed. James E. Miller, Jr. (New York: Harcourt Brace Jovanovich, 1991). "White Tigers" is included in vol. 2 of *The Heath Anthology of American Literature*, ed. Paul Lauter et al. (New York: D. C. Heath, 1990).

23. Pfaff, "Whispers of a Literary Explorer" *Horizon*, July 1980, 63.

24. Chin, "Come All Ye Asian American Writers," 3.

25. Rich, "Motherhood and Daughterhood," 247.

26. In *China Men*, Kingston's father sends Brave Orchid to medical school to prepare her for the West: "I will bring you to America on one condition, and that is, you get a Western education. . . . Don't go to a school for classical literature. Go to a scientific school run by white people" (Kingston, *China Men* [New York: Ballantine, 1980], 65). Which account is the more accurate? Hard to tell. In the earlier book, she is crediting her mother with making the first move to independence; in the latter, she is crediting her father with the family's Westernizing impulse. Either one might be the "stretcher."

Conclusion

1. *"Call It Sleep* is the most profound novel of Jewish life that I have ever read by an American" begins Kazin in "The Art of *Call It Sleep*," *New York Review of Books*, 10 Oct. 1991, 15–18.

2. See George Lipsitz, *Time Passages: Collective Memory and American Popular Culture* (Minneapolis: University of Minnesota Press, 1990); Donald Weber, "Repression and Memory in Early Ethnic Television," unpub. paper presented at ASA/CAAS joint meeting, Nov. 1989; and James T. Fisher, *The Catholic Counterculture in America, 1933–1962* (Chapel Hill: University of North Carolina Press, 1989). These works, as well as several recent works on the New York intellectuals, exemplify the expansion of focus in ethnic criticism.

3. Henry Pratt Fairchild, "A Metaphor Gone Wrong: An Excerpt from *The Melting-Pot Mistake*," *The American Mind: Selections from the Literature of the United States*, ed. Harry R. Warfel, Ralph H. Gabriel, and Stanley T. Williams (New York: American Book Company, 1937), 1062–63.

4. On immigration restriction, see Lawrence Auster, *The Path to National Suicide: An Essay on Immigration and Multiculturalism* (Monterey, Va.: American Immigration Control Foundation, 1990). Similar implications, less forthrightly expressed, emerge from Arthur M. Schlesinger, *The Disuniting of America: Reflections on a Multicultural Society* (Knoxville, Tenn.: Whittle Direct Books, 1991), and Richard Brookhiser, *The Way of the Wasp: How It Made America, and How It Can Save It, So to Speak* (New York: Free Press, 1991).

Index

Granich, Irwin (pseud. Mike Gold), 209n.11. *See also* Gold, Mike
Great God Brown, The (O'Neill), 88, 92–94, 97–98
Green, Rose Basile, 22
Griffin, Susan, 157
Guttmann, Allen, 4, 112, 209n.6

Hall, Peter Dobkin, 24
Halper, Albert, 208n.4
Handlin, Oscar, 95
Hazard of New Fortunes, A (Howells), 38
Heart of the Dragon (Cimino), 34
Henricksen, Louise Levitas, 56
Hijuelos, Oscar, 202n.16
Hobsbawn, Eric, 19
Howe, Irving, 2, 8, 14, 54, 87, 88–89, 91, 197n.3
Howells, William Dean, 9, 38, 58, 200n.10; *A Hazard of New Fortunes*, 38; *The Rise of Silas Lapham*, 61
Hungry Hearts (Yezierska), 208nn.2, 6
Hurston, Zora Neale, 201nn.11, 13
Huston, John, 39, 207n.33
Hwang, David Henry, 156, 192; *FOB and Other Plays*, 220n.8; *M. Butterfly*, 220n.9

Iacocca, Lee, 36
Ianni, Francis A. J., 20–21, 25, 43
Ibarguen, Raoul R., 124–25, 147, 218n.39
Iceman Cometh, The (O'Neill), 128
In the American Grain (Williams), 221n.15
Ionesco, Eugène, 112, 116

James, Henry, 16; *The Golden Bowl*, 85
Jameson, Fredric, 19, 35, 37–40
Jen, Gish, 188; *Typical American*, 202n.16
Jewisohn, Norman, 207n.33
Jews Without Money (Gold), 58, 214–15n.7

Johnson, James Weldon, 200–201n.11
Jong, Erica, 153, 218n.38
Joyce, James, 14, 90, 92–94, 116, 118, 194; *A Portrait of the Artist as a Young Man*, 88, 100, 113, 147–48; *Ulysses*, 92–93, 113

Kael, Pauline, 39–40
Kaufmann, Stanley, 42
Kazin, Alfred, 14, 88, 123, 192, 214n.4, 222n.1
Kerouac, Jack, 194
Kessler-Harris, Alice, 54, 67, 209n.8
Kessner, Thomas, 20, 204n.6
Kim, Elaine H., 4, 156
Kingston, Maxine Hong, 11–12, 16, 154–90, 219–22nn; *China Men*, 157, 175, 221n.15, 222n.26; *Tripmaster Monkey: His Fake Book*, 221n.10; *Woman Warrior, The*, 154–90, 192, 219–22nn
Klein, Marcus, 106, 113, 123, 199n.9, 214n.4
Kogawa, Joy, 192; *Obasan*, 202n.16

Larsen, Nella, 201n.11
Lasch, Christopher, 38
Leaves of Grass (Whitman), 152
Lentricchia, Frank, 132
Lerner, Gerda, 157
Levi, Carlo, 204n.6
Levin, Meyer, 58, 87
Lewis, Richard W. B., 88
Lewisohn, Ludwig, 68
Ling, Amy, 157
Lopate, Phillip, 202n.16
Lowensfels, Walter, 216n.12
Lyons, Bonnie, 93

Madonna, 194
Mafia Princess (Giancana), 34
Maggie: A Girl of the Streets (S. Crane), 125
Mailer, Norman, 153, 194
Malamud, Bernard, 130, 194, 197n.3